THE TRIAL OF

Bukharin

HISTORIC TRIALS SERIES

Editor : J. P. Kenyon, Professor of History

University of Hull

THE TRIAL OF

Bukharin

GEORGE KATKOV

FELLOW OF ST ANTONY'S COLLEGE

OXFORD

'A complicated network of decorative
deceit in words and action is a highly essential
characteristic of fascist régimes of all stamps and hues'

From the last article in *Izvestiya* appearing
over Bukharin's signature

𝔰𝔡

STEIN AND DAY

NEW YORK

Copyright © George Katkov, 1969
Library of Congress Catalog Card No. 73-87951
All rights reserved

Printed in Great Britain

Stein and Day/*Publishers*/7 East 48 Street, New York, N.Y. 10017

SBN 8128-1245-X

CONTENTS

THE ILLUSTRATIONS

ACKNOWLEDGMENT

I wish to acknowledge the generous and selfless help of Dr Michael Futrell of the University of British Columbia, who greatly assisted in the extensive revision of an earlier manuscript from which this book has resulted. I am also grateful to Mrs Valerie Jensen for all her help in checking the final text and helping with the proofs.   G.K.

The author and publishers would like to thank the following for permission to reproduce the illustrations which appear in this book:

The Radio Times Hulton Picture Library, for Plates 1, 2, 3, 6; United Press International Ltd, for Plates 4, 5, 7, 9, 14, 15; The Hoover Institution on War, Revolution and Peace, for Plates 8, 10, 11, 12, 13.

PREFACE

Great trials which remain as landmarks in the historical development of mankind have rarely been occasions of which blindfold Justice can be proud. More often than not they have been cases when legality was violated and procedural order corrupted. In some cases the prestige of the judiciary and its reputed impartiality have been made to serve a political purpose alien to the legal order. But even where corruption and sub-servience to political power defiled judicial proceedings, especially in capital cases, the very fact that the court elevated dubious evidence to the status of factual proof and that politicians claimed the dignity of legal procedure for their intrigues points to the unimpaired prestige of the judiciary as the supreme guarantee of legality in society. The ceremonial of impartiality was to be preserved, so that none could dismiss this travesty of the law as Alice dismissed the trial at the end of Lewis Carroll's story.[1]

Marxism, and the Marxist theory of legality and law, changed all this radically and for the first time. Law, being, like the state, only a superstructure in the organisation of human society, was interpreted as one of the instruments of the class struggle, an instrument which in the hands of the property-owning classes served to maintain their privileges but which in the hands of a proletarian dictatorship (in the period of transition to socialism and Communism) was to be a revolutionary weapon to bring about the desired historical changes.

Not merely legislation itself, but its practical application in court was to serve the militant purpose of the Party. It would be self-contradictory, un-Marxist and counter-revolutionary for a Marxist to object to the use of legal procedures for political ends. When Marxist theory became the basis of Soviet ideology, the concept of revolutionary and later socialist legality superseded the weak sproutings of a legal order* which had emerged in the last decades of Russian pre-revolutionary political evolution. Originally the weapon of legal coercion 'in defence of society' was used exclusively against class enemies, that is against those sections of the population which were disinclined to cooperate in the transition to socialism. Gradually, however, when divergencies arose inside the Party and threatened to impede the progress on which the oligarchy, and later Stalin as autocratic ruler, had decided, the sword of the revolution was turned upon the deviationists. Bukharin's trial is the most remarkable of such cases of legal coercion. It throws light on the structure of Soviet society as a whole, on the power of corporate make-believe which was never stronger since the time people stopped identifying themselves with animals as tribal totems. It uncovers the concealed forces that operate in a political group such as the CPSU (Communist Party of the Soviet Union) to ensure that its members comply with the written and unwritten laws and usages of the clan, often at the risk of their lives. It reveals (and this is probably the most humanly moving element in the story) the reluctant submission to these laws of an outstanding and scintillating personality like Bukharin—a submission which in his case did not save him from destruction.

We shall first try to give an impression of Bukharin the man, beginning with his early life. We shall of course be unable to pursue the study of his character beyond the point (in 1917) where his private life, like that of other members of the Russian Com-

---

*Guarantees that political and economic reality would conform with the existing legislation outgrew the purely declamatory phase of the first half of the nineteenth century only after 1864, when the court statutes were introduced. Unfortunately the principles of this legislation were later obfuscated by the introduction of local exceptions to it, and by a strengthening of the legal functions of the administration and bureaucracy.

munist oligarchy, was screened off from impartial observers, to be replaced by a projected image fashioned in accordance with Party requirements. Instead we shall depict the political scene of the twenties in which he was to play a prominent part first as a staunch defender of Stalin's general Party line against its critics and later as an oppositionist himself. This in turn will bring us to the profound conflict which led him, in the nine years between 1929 and 1938, from being a trusted supporter of the supreme ruler and the 'favourite son of the Party', into the dock, accused of being a plotter, counter-revolutionary, traitor, spy, wrecker and assassin.

PART I

The road to the courtroom

1. Bukharin: the formative years

'Only snakes slough their skins
so that the soul may age and live.
We, alas, are not like snakes;
we change our souls, not our skins.'
N. Gumilev[1]

Who would recognise in the ageing man in the dock fighting his last battle with State Prosecutor Vyshinsky the little bookworm who had read almost the whole of Molière at twelve, and fought battles with the street urchins of the Moscow suburb where his family was living? It was then that he became a dedicated rebel. His rebellion took an anti-religious form. A chance reading of Vladimir Solovyev's *Lectures on the Antichrist* led him to the study of the Apocalypse, and to the teenage daydreaming in which he identified himself with the Antichrist. There was however one difficulty: Bukharin's mother was 'a rather intelligent woman and an exceptionally honest, diligent and loving mother'. The mother of the Antichrist was the Great Whore of Babylon. Still the young Bukharin would not renounce his fantastic ambition, and subjected his mother to an embarrassing interrogation in an attempt to uncover a lapse from virtue in her younger days. Daydreaming, backstreet battles, occasional storming of heaven and continuous Micawberism in his family caused by his father's addiction to alcohol did not prevent young Bukharin from being top pupil at school. It needed the awakening of political passions, which came to him very early, to detach him from scholastic pursuits and childish pusillanimity. From the age of fifteen or sixteen he took an active part in various student circles, the scene of protracted quarrels between Russian agrarian socialists (the Socialist Revolutionaries) and the importers of Marxist ideas. This awakened in him a lifelong interest in economic studies, and led him into the camp of revolutionary Marxism. At seventeen, together with his friend Ilya Ehrenburg, he was already organising a strike in a wallpaper factory.

Bukharin set 1906 as the year in which he officially joined the Bolshevik Party and became a professional revolutionary propagandist, organiser and agitator. It was a difficult time for the Bolsheviks; the failure of the 1905 Revolution had discredited the idea of an early armed rising of the proletariat with the object of seizing power, and the industrial workers—an infinitesimal minority of the population in Russia—tended to follow those who promised to lead them along the path of gradual economic betterment through trade unionism and economic strikes. As a member of the Moscow Bolshevik Party organisation, Bukharin was engaged in twin conspiratorial struggles, the one against the Tsarist régime and the security organs protecting it, the other against those whom the Bolsheviks called 'liquidators', i.e. socialists who insisted that direct revolutionary action to seize state power should be temporarily abandoned in favour of economic strikes and a struggle for political freedoms. As a Bolshevik organiser Bukharin was assigned the task of joining legal workers' organisations and awakening their members to the betrayal of the working class by the liquidators. This activity on two fronts left him no time for study in the Department of Economics of the Law Faculty at Moscow University, where he was nominally an undergraduate. The University, he said, merely provided opportunities to organise conspiratorial meetings and disrupt the seminars of respectable liberal professors by heckling.

During his stay at Moscow University Bukharin came into contact with many prominent Bolsheviks who were to play a fateful part in his life and death. With one, N. Osinsky (i.e. Valerian Obolensky) he met repeatedly in the course of his varied career. He spent some time with him in police detention in 1911, when they became intimate friends. He also met the Yakovlevs, brother and sister; the sister, Varvara, was to become, like Osinsky, one of the main witnesses for the prosecution at Bukharin's trial in 1938. The activities of these people, for which they were persecuted by the Tsarist security police, did not consist in direct subversion of the state but rather in propaganda and the indoctrination in Marxist ideology of intellectuals and workers. Direct revolutionary action was impossible at this time of 'the triumph of reaction' inside Russia. Those who wanted such action had to prepare it abroad.

Bukharin's exciting life in Moscow was interrupted by his arrest, at the end of 1910, for belonging to the Moscow Bolshevik organisation, which was then broken up by the secret police. For this first political offence he received a relatively mild sentence of banishment to the Onega region. He seems to have had no difficulty in escaping from there and going abroad.

He settled for a time in Hanover, living modestly and even poorly in workers' households, studying economics, especially agrarian questions, in libraries. His first personal encounter with Lenin dates from 1912. 'Of course his influence on me was enormous,' recalls Bukharin, without further explanation, in his autobiography. Lenin seems to have harnessed Bukharin for regular contributions to the Petersburg *Pravda* and the magazine *Prosveshcheniye*.

Bukharin's pupil and biographer, D. P. Maretsky, writes as follows about this period: 'Maintaining uninterrupted contact, in writing and personally, with Lenin, Bukharin participates intimately in the work of the Duma group of Bolsheviks (the preparation of speeches, reports and so on), at the same time working in Russian social-democratic circles in Vienna and carrying on the struggle against the Mensheviks and Trotskyites.'[2]

In the course of this work Bukharin had his first conflict with Lenin. The head of the Duma Bolshevik group, Malinovsky, had been suspect to many of his Party colleagues since 1911, and Bukharin could not have failed to warn Lenin against him. But Malinovsky was then Lenin's trump card in all his enterprises in Russia. Lenin considered him greatly superior in intelligence and organisational ability to all his other

B

lieutenants. He believed Malinovsky was the victim of Menshevik slander, and supported his action in splitting the social-
democratic group in the Duma, numbering thirteen men, into
two factions—six Bolsheviks and seven Mensheviks. In so
doing he unwittingly fell into line with the head of the
security department of the Ministry of the Interior, S. Beletsky,
who was controlling Malinovsky's machinations on behalf of
the Tsarist government. Even after Malinovsky's sudden
resignation from the Duma, and his flight from Russia under
the threat of exposure in May 1914, Lenin, whilst conceding
that his behaviour was hysterical and irresponsible, dismissed
as stupid and base all the charges of treachery and provocation
brought against him.[3]

After a later quarrel with Bukharin in 1916, Lenin
described him in a letter to Shlyapnikov as a 'studious
economist' but 'gullible [when it comes] to gossip' and
'devilishly unstable in politics'. The term 'gullible' we should
probably read as an allusion to the conflict over Malinovsky.

The Malinovsky affair has still not been fully clarified, but
it is obvious that Bukharin strongly disagreed with Lenin's
protection of a man who was certainly, in his view, a police
agent. His expression of an independent opinion on a practical
question may well have irritated Lenin, and might explain the
latter's intolerant attitude in subsequent theoretical disputes
with him.

In the winter of 1911-12 Bukharin moved to Vienna, where
he attended the lectures of the celebrated Austrian economists
Böhm-Bawerk and Wieser. His criticism of the Austrian School
and its theory of values is contained in his major theoretical
work, *The Political Economy of the Rentier. The Theory of
Value and Profit of the Austrian School* (Moscow, 1919).
His contributions to the legal Bolshevik press in Russia were
characterised by aggressive polemics against established non-
Marxist economists; typical was his review of P. B. Struve's
major work *Economy and Price* entitled 'The Hocus-Pocus
of Mr Struve' (published in *Prosveshcheniye,* 1912). The

polemics against non-Marxist economists went hand in hand with permanent fencing with fellow-Marxists who deviated from the Bolshevik Party line.

On the eve of the declaration of war in 1914 Bukharin was arrested near Vienna and imprisoned in Melk. Like Lenin he was set free on the insistence of Austrian social democrats, and deported over the Swiss frontier.

The early years of the First World War were marked by ceaseless splintering in the socialist camp, particularly in Russian émigré circles. Apart from the great division between defensists and defeatists, conflicts emerged among the latter which finally proved irreconcilable; this is recorded in the proceedings of the Zimmerwald, the Kienthal and the abortive Stockholm Conferences.

In Switzerland Bukharin renewed contact with Lenin, while joining a small but influential circle of Bolsheviks known as the Baugy group. This consisted of Georgy Pyatakov and his girl friend Evgeniya Bosh, her sister E. Rozmirovich, the latter's friend Krylenko and a few others. The group planned to publish a magazine of their own, which would have an editorial board independent from that of the central organ of the party, *Sotsial-Demokrat*. Lenin disliked the idea intensely but had to give in, and even contribute to the first number of the Baugy group's publication *Kommunist*. He did not want to let a group with possibly independent means (Pyatakov's family was wealthy) escape his control.[4]

As usual in such party squabbles it is hard to decide what was at the root of them—organisational or ideological differences. Lenin complained that *Kommunist* was being published at a time when the central organ of the Party was short of money, and Zinoviev and Pyatakov and Bosh wanted to print in it 'everything they pleased while we [i.e. the Central Committee] bear the responsibility for it'.[5] In the summer of 1915 Lenin managed to weaken the Baugy group by despatching Rozmirovich and Krylenko to Moscow—the only serious attempt on his part to use emissaries during the war. Both were arrested almost immediately on arrival in Moscow, where the Bolshevik organisation was thoroughly penetrated and closely supervised by the secret police under the command of P. Martynov, an able gendarmerie officer. Bosh, Pyatakov and Bukharin for their part left for Stockholm via France and England, arriving in Sweden in the autumn of 1915.[6]

Lenin explains his vacillating attitude towards the publication of *Kommunist* in a letter to Shlyapnikov dated March 1916:

> *Kommunist* was a temporary bloc for the attainment of a definite aim. This aim has been attained: the magazine came out, the *rapprochement* (it was possible at that time, *before* Zimmerwald) was attained. Now it is necessary to go along a different road, to go onwards.
>
> *Kommunist* has become harmful. It must be discontinued and replaced by a different name: *Sbornik Sotsial-Demokrata* (under the editorship of the editorial board of *Sotsial-Demokrat*).[7]

This letter to Shlyapnikov makes it clear that Lenin's position had changed since he yielded to Pyatakov's and Bukharin's demands to publish a magazine jointly with them. 'With "the three" (Yurii + Evg. Bosh + Nik. Iv.) we had to make temporary concessions, since at that time it was impossible otherwise to publish the magazine (now it can be done).' In other words Lenin did not have the wherewithal to publish his own magazine in 1915, and so agreed on a joint editorship; now, in 1916, he had found some source of finance for his own magazine, and therefore he was going to shut the others up.

As always these rather sordid considerations were only hinted at, and then only in private correspondence with a trusted friend like Shlyapnikov. For the Party rank and file and his opponents, ideological and doctrinal reasons had to be advanced to justify the rift. Lenin did this by condemning Bukharin's views on the development of imperialist states and the correct socialist attitude towards demands for national self-determination. Bukharin's views were both radical and leftist; what humanity needed was a social revolution which would only be delayed by the atomising process of self-determination. Reproducing a well-known pattern of Marxist argument Bukharin suggested that the concentration of economic power in imperialist systems would facilitate large-scale social transformations.

One might expect from the general trend of his radicalism that Lenin too would have thought in this way. But this was by no means the case. He firmly defended the principle of national self-determination, and attacked imperialism as a form of super-capitalism which had to be destroyed together with capitalism and could not possibly be considered a short cut to social revolution. The polemics between Bukharin and Lenin are extremely confused and bear little relation to the political realities of the time. They are also unpleasant to read because of the shrilly aggressive tone Lenin adopted and his extreme impatience with any socialist who refused to accept the principle of national self-determination. Everyone who disagreed with him on this important question was muddle-headed, vacillating, 'rolling into the swamp'. Bukharin's patience with Lenin went far, but even he felt that his tolerance was being stretched to the limit. Before leaving for the United States, in October 1916, he wrote to Lenin: 'At any rate I ask you one thing: if you will polemicise, etc., preserve such a tone as not to force a split. It would be very painful to me, painful beyond my strength, if joint work, even in the future, should become impossible. I have the greatest respect for you, and look upon you as my revolutionary teacher, and love you.'[8]

It is clear that Bukharin's attitude was that of a consistent Marxist developing the same pattern of ideas as the founders of the doctrine had done, while Lenin was using ideological sophistry to introduce into the theory of traditional radical Marxism concepts basically alien to it. Why did he do it? The question has often been asked before, and some have looked for an answer in Krupskaya's personal account of Lenin's state of mind. Krupskaya wrote: 'Never, I think, was Vladimir Ilyich in a more irreconcilable mood than in the last months of 1916 and the early months of 1917. He was profoundly convinced that the revolution was approaching.' Krupskaya may be right about the exceptionally 'irreconcilable' mood of her consort at the time, but she is certainly wrong in explaining it as the result of his conviction that the revolution was imminent. It was at the beginning of 1917 that Lenin said in so many words that people of his generation might not live to see the revolution. However, there may be a grain of truth in Krupskaya's remarks. Lenin was well aware of the forces at work for revolutionising Russia, a matter of prime concern to him. From his contacts with Parvus (Helphand), from the propaganda to Russian prisoners-of-war organised by the Germans and assisted by Lenin's friends and acolytes, he knew of the two main principles which, although perhaps irreconcilable in theory, were, in combination, the only hope of revolutionising Russia in practice. These were the exacerbation of industrial unrest under the strain of war conditions and the disruption caused by separatist propaganda in the non-assimilated parts of the multi-national empire.[9] Lenin might well have told Bukharin that if he wanted to see a revolution in Russia in his lifetime he should cease to speculate along traditional Marxist lines about general pre-conditions for the transition to socialism, and rather assist the disruptive forces already at work within the country. But Lenin knew that there are certain things that can be done but not talked about, and he replaced the straightforward argument by a complicated theory which was both inconsistent and unconvincing even to such an apt and sympathetic pupil as Bukharin. Soon after the latter's departure for America their discussion was overtaken by events and remained unfinished. To the rank and file of the Party Bukharin emerged from this discussion as an unworldly and doctrinaire theoretician. This did not contradict

Lenin's own verdict on him—'the favourite son of the party' (*lyubimets partii*).

The quarrels concerning imperialism and self-determination caused a certain degree of estrangement between Lenin and Bukharin, who was not initiated into Lenin's conspiratorial war-time activities as was Fuerstenberg-Ganetsky. When Bukharin left for Scandinavia the opportunity arose for him to join the Institute for the Study of the Economic Consequences of the World War in Copenhagen. This institute was founded and run by Helphand-Parvus, and employed a number of Russian émigré social democrats, mainly Mensheviks. Lenin strongly advised against Bukharin's participation in the Helphand enterprise. At the same time, Lenin was well informed of the close cooperation existing between another of his friends, Fuersten-berg-Ganetsky, and Parvus, and in no way disapproved of it. It is clear from Lenin's attitude on this occasion that he viewed Bukharin as a somewhat childish character who could easily fall under bad influences, whereas he trusted Ganetsky's adroitness and cynicism, which he exploited in his indirect contacts with Parvus and the German authorities. Bukharin, however, on reaching Stockholm, tried to initiate an anti-war propaganda campaign of his own, and was helped to smuggle pamphlets into Russia by some Scandinavian socialists. He soon began to suspect that one of those most deeply involved in the printing and despatch of these pamphlets was probably working for the Germans. This was the now well-known Estonian and former Bolshevik, Alexander Keskuela, who in 1915-16 was living in Stockholm and actively furthering German efforts to bring about a revolution in Russia. Bukharin made a great fuss, without however succeeding in exposing the whole German game in Scandinavia, and got himself into difficulties resulting in his arrest and expulsion from Sweden.[10]

After a short stay in Oslo he proceeded, using the cover name of Movsha Dolgolevsky, via Copenhagen to New York. There he took over the editorship of an existing Russian social-democratic paper, *Novy Mir*. He was soon joined by Trotsky.

It is typical that this period of collaboration with Trotsky should have been suppressed in the later authorised biographies of Bukharin. In his autobiography Bukharin himself mentions only his editorship of *Novy Mir* and the fact that he participated in the formation of 'the left wing of the socialist movement'. His pupil Maretsky claims Bukharin maintained contact with Lenin and carried on a struggle against the views then held by Trotsky. The contact could not have been very intimate, because Bukharin continued to publish in *Novy Mir* fragments of his work on the theory of the imperialist state which Lenin had refused to publish. On the other hand Trotsky reports that Bukharin was one of the first people to meet him when he arrived in New York on 13 January 1917; they worked together editing *Novy Mir*. 'The ever-increasing attachment of Bukharin to myself,' wrote Trotsky, 'dates from the time of our common work in New York. This attachment went on increasing until 1923, when it changed into its direct opposite.'[11] Trotsky's arrival in New York infuriated and incensed Lenin. In a letter dated 19 February 1917 to Inessa Armand he heaped abuse on 'the scoundrel' Trotsky, and expressed fears that Bukharin might fall under some undesirable influence.[12] It may have been this fear which caused him to revise his unfavourable judgment of Bukharin's article, rejected by him in 1916. He now expressed his willingness to publish it in *Sbornik Sotsial-Demokrata* No. 4 (the issue never appeared) together with his own corrections of Bukharin's 'minor mistakes' and his condemnation of the 'tremendous lying' and 'debasement of Marxism' by Kautsky.

The tensions and squabbles which had been racking the self-centred little world of the Bolshevik underground in emigration disappeared like smoke at the unexpected news of the fall of Tsarism and the establishment of a democratic order in Russia. It is remarkable how the routes which Lenin, Trotsky and Bukharin chose for their return to Russia reflect and symbolise their respective personalities. Lenin made his fateful journey in the so-called 'sealed coach' through Germany.

There is no reason to believe that this was the only way open to him; many a revolutionary had found other routes from Switzerland to Petrograd. The journey through Germany gave Lenin an aura that marked him out in the eyes of his highly-placed German supporters as the man who would pursue a defeatist policy in Russia to the end. They felt entitled to ask the German government for maximum backing for him and his followers, since this would get Russia out of the war and provide the only chance for Germany to avoid a crushing defeat.

Trotsky chose to cross the Atlantic; he embarked in New York in a flurry of bouquets and speeches, travelling with his wife and children like a prominent journalist returning to his country after a distinguished exile. He was detained in Halifax, Nova Scotia, by the British authorities for almost a month, which he spent in a prisoner-of-war camp 'in an uninterrupted meeting' preaching the gospel of the Russian revolution to German prisoners and telling them about Lenin, Liebknecht, the fall of the Second International and American war intervention. He was freed at the instance of the very provisional government whose overthrow was the main purpose of his journey to Russia.

Bukharin, finally, chose the long leisurely route across the United States, the Pacific, Japan and the Transsiberian to Moscow. He too had his adventures, being detained by some Menshevik local authority in the Urals industrial centre of Chelyabinsk for spreading Bolshevik propaganda in the army. A few months later all three men figured prominently in the ranks of the new ideological oligarchy, and the dissensions of 1916 seemed forgotten.

To follow Bukharin's career after his return to Russia in 1917 is to trace the history of Soviet Russia from the seizure of power until his trial. All this period of his life is reflected in the distorting mirror of the trial itself, and we shall have to go through it point by point, analysing the indictment and Vyshinsky's elaboration of it as well as Bukharin's reactions.

We shall see that behind his detached manner in the court-room, his macabre witticisms and apparent resignation, Bukharin maintained to the end a certain dignity, and in a sense defeated Vyshinsky's attempt (abetted by many of the co-defendants) to blacken and distort his role in the history of Soviet Russia and of the world Communist movement. This firmness, or stubbornness, displayed at a time of supreme ordeal must have surprised not only Vyshinsky but also many of those who regarded Bukharin as a brilliant but unreliable character. We have seen Lenin referring to him (in 1916) as 'devilishly unstable in politics'. An even more devastating description of him was given by Trotsky in 1930:

> The character of this man is such that he always needs to lean on somebody, to be at somebody's side, to stick to someone. At such times, Bukharin is simply a medium through whom somebody else speaks and acts; but you should never lose sight of the medium; for if you do he will, without noticing it himself, fall under a totally opposed influence, just as people fall under a car. He will then begin to abuse his former idol with the same unrestrained enthusiasm with which he exalted it. I never took Bukharin too seriously, and left him to himself, which was tantamount to leaving him to others. After Lenin's death he became the medium first of Zinoviev, then of Stalin; now, whilst these lines are being written Bukharin is going through a new crisis, and new influences of which I know nothing are acting on him.[13]

There is certainly an element of truth in this malicious vignette. We must however remember that both Lenin and Trotsky attached much greater importance to doctrinal stability than did the voraciously inquisitive and self-critical Bukharin. He had joined the revolutionary movement because his normal attitude to life was that of a rebel; but he would never turn rebellion into a doctrine, whether Marxist or otherwise. He claimed and was granted a certain licence in his opinions on questions then still marginal to Communist doctrine, such as literature, 'proletarian culture', technocracy and the like. He always opposed, and was allowed to oppose, the institutionalisation of the Party structure and the bureaucratisation of the Soviet government apparatus, although his attacks on these, vehement and biting as usual, evoked official suspicion. It was usual for Party members to insist on intra-Party democracy and attack bureaucracy—up to the moment when they were appointed to some important post in the Party apparatus or the machinery of the state. Bukharin was a notable exception to this rule. He never aspired to any high office in which he could exercise administrative power. He never headed any of the great satrapies like the Party organisations of Moscow or Leningrad. He was never a People's Commissar, i.e. a minister with departmental duties. His two main posts, as head of the Third International and editor of *Pravda*, he managed to cut to his own pattern, acting by means of persuasion and agitation instead of administering and ordering others about. This was certainly one of the reasons for his discomfiture in the Comintern. At the 6th Congress in 1928 he was still presiding over debates on problems of international Communism while a clever intrigue being simultaneously mounted by Stalin in the Congress lobbies isolated him from his supporters.

In assessing Trotsky's claim that Bukharin simply acted as a medium for others we have to remember that those others wooed him strenuously. With his extensive knowledge, his natural talents, his charm, his total lack of a vulgar appetite for domination, he was a most valuable ally for anyone who wanted to launch a campaign but had not the necessary intellectual subtlety and powers of expression. Bukharin would gladly lend a hand in such a venture, even exaggerating his devotion to the cause he was momentarily serving, though always making the inner reservation that he would drop it if it went too far. This explains why Kamenev, to whose downfall

Bukharin had contributed more than anyone else at the 15th Party Conference and the 15th Congress, had no qualms about discussing with him the political situation resulting from the defeat of the Left opposition. No, Bukharin was not merely the medium of those whom he helped; in helping them he often made them the carriers of his own ideas. The last and perhaps the most spectacular achievement of this kind was his own trial. Vyshinsky and the NKVD agencies which had been preparing the trial were sure every defendant had been broken in and would perform in court according to plan. They may have guessed that Bukharin would prove the exception, and relied on the fact that his isolation would speak against him and reinforce the indictment. But Bukharin broke out of his isolation. Even from the dock he managed to give a lead to Rykov and gradually to instil in him a certain dignity, a certain spirit of resistance to the debasing tactics of the public prosecutor.

Among those who exploited Bukharin's intellectual and debating powers to further their political ends and defeat their adversaries was Stalin; and in this instance it was certainly not Bukharin that was guilty of waywardness but Stalin, who, having defeated the Left opposition, suddenly adopted their programme, or one very similar to it. It was then that he dropped Bukharin, or perhaps that Bukharin refused to follow him and serve as his 'medium' any longer.

Bukharin himself seems to have believed that Stalin's implacable hatred of him was motivated by something like personal jealousy of one intellectually better-equipped and ideologically cleaner than himself. During an interview with Theodore and Lydia Dan in Paris in the spring of 1936 he is reported to have said:[14]

> You just said that you do not know him [Stalin] well; but we do know him ... He even *suffers* from the fact of being unable to persuade everybody including himself that he is greater than everybody, and this suffering of his is probably

the most human trait in his character, perhaps the only
human trait, because his compulsive vindictiveness towards
everybody for this suffering of his, towards everybody and
especially towards those who are in some respects higher and
better than he, is already an inhuman and devilish feature.
If anybody speaks better than him, his fate is sealed, he will
not be left alive, because such a man is a constant reminder to
him that he is not the first, not the best; if anybody writes
better, so much the worse for him, because he, Stalin, and
only he should be the first Russian writer. Well, for Marx
there is no danger any more from Stalin, except that Marx
will be made out to the Russian worker as a minor figure
compared with the great Stalin ... No, no, Fyodor Ilyich
[Dan], this is a small, vicious man, no, not a man but a devil.

'Never shall I forget,' comments Lydia Dan, 'Bukharin's expression at that moment, when his usually good-natured features
were completely distorted by fear and anger.'

Supposing Stalin himself had been forced to stand trial and
been confronted by the prosecution with Bukharin's charge,
what would he have replied? He would certainly have told the
interrogator that Bukharin's explanation was puerile; it was
not Bukharin's capacity to think straighter and express himself
better that led the vindictive Stalin to demand the moral and
physical annihilation of the erstwhile 'favourite son of the
Party'. His motives were far more complicated than that. He
had sought Bukharin's help in confounding the Left opposition
and the Trotskyites. In giving it, Bukharin attacked the left-
wing programme, and elaborated certain principles for the
transition to socialism which would lessen the sacrifices
demanded of his generation of Russians, especially the peasants.
Stalin more than anyone was aware of the potential popularity
of these ideas, having used them to good effect against his left-
wing opponents. But his own programme, like that of the
Left, required of the people (particularly the peasants) supreme
sacrifices and exertions. Having, therefore, temporarily feigned

agreement with Bukharin in order to defeat the Left, Stalin felt impelled to round on him, to denounce his ideas as politically aberrant, to destroy his reputation and blight his latent popularity. The fact that Bukharin did not himself grasp the attraction his ideas held for the people, and did not appeal to the people directly, deserved (Stalin considered) not merely hatred but contempt.[15]

We do not mean to imply that Bukharin was the author of an alternative programme. Stalin's own programme, or the 'general Party line', was not merely an enunciation of the principles governing the transition to socialism. It was a complete system for the enforcement of Stalin's will. The organisation of the Party apparatus, including the Party and Stalin's personal secretariat, the Five-Year Plans, the hierarchy of appointments, the functioning of the security organs, the trials themselves—all these formed part and parcel of it. Its theory as set forth in his speeches and in various editions of his book, *Problems of Leninism*, was conditioned as much by the success or failure of its practical workings as by his vision of the future. Bukharin, for his part, never had an opportunity to put his 'theories' into practice;* he controlled no apparatus, he influenced no appointments; all he could do was argue with Stalin in the rarefied atmosphere of the Politburo or the Central Committee. And this is how Bukharin himself wanted

---

*Bukharin used his great talent to the full in the articles he wrote as editor-in-chief of *Pravda* (up to 1929) and later of *Izvestiya* (1934–37). He also made notable speeches at the 17th Party Congress and the First Congress of Soviet Writers (1934). But in a society like Stalin's Russia the published views of a single individual can make far less impact on political life than they would in an open society. Voters cannot be influenced; officials cannot be moved to urge policy changes on their superiors in consequence of what they have read or heard; teaching establishments are not free to disseminate the theories of an individual without the prior approval of the state. Bukharin's articles and speeches are therefore in a totally different category from Stalin's, which were at one and the same time expressions of individual opinion and obligatory directives backed by the full weight and power of the state.

things to be. He forgot that politics means not just evolving theories as to possible courses of political action but putting them to the test of life. His systematic, and disastrous, abstention from *practical* politics finally proved his downfall. It enabled Vyshinsky and Stalin to convince the Party rank and file, and even foreign observers, that as Bukharin had made no open attempt to realise his ideas in practice, he must have been operating by means of underhand intrigues—intrigues Vyshinsky tried to represent as the great conspiracy of the 'Bloc of Rights and Trotskyites'.

2. Opposition and conformism

The place of the
show trials in the history of the USSR

Both the prosecution and the principal defendants at the Bukharin trial, officially known as 'The Case of the Anti-Soviet Bloc of Rights and Trotskyites', proclaimed it to be the last of the Moscow show trials. The staging of such forensic performances was by then a matter of routine, and held no surprises. However, at one point it looked as if the established procedure was going to be upset when one of the accused, Krestinsky, pleaded 'not guilty'. But this promise of a head-on conflict between the prosecution and a defendant lasted only one day of the ten-day hearing. Krestinsky changed his plea, and the debate reverted to the familiar practice in which defendants vied with the prosecution in heaping accusations on their own heads.

All commentators on the trial agree that it was only an episode, albeit an important one, in a vast historical crisis of which the other public and secret trials of the thirties, involving countless victims, were further manifestations. According to the official version, the Bukharin trial dealt with only one of the numerous conspiracies aiming at the 'overthrow of Soviet power' and the subversion of the Communist Party's noble efforts to lead the peoples of the Soviet Union forward to the millennium of Communism. This particular conspiracy, of the 'Bloc of Rights and Trotskyites', was intertwined with all the other conspiracies which—so the prosecution maintained—had been brokeen up through the vigilance of the Soviet security organs in the preceding years; those of the 'Zinoviev-Kamenev bloc', liquidated in August 1936, and of the parallel 'Trotskyite Centre', exposed at the Pyatakov trial in February 1937, and the 'military plot' of Tukhachevsky and others supposedly liquidated at a secret trial in June 1937.

This spate of conspiracies, however, was in itself only a symptom of a profound malaise, a much deeper conflict, namely, to quote the prosecution, the exacerbation of the basic class struggle, the inevitable prelude to the advent of Communism and the establishment of a classless society. In all the show trials the prosecution went out of its way to prove that these conspiracies were not merely the result of the defendants' personal ambitions, lust for power and resentment at thwarted political aspirations but were a direct consequence of the war waged by the enemies of the working class of the USSR, where the building of socialism is guaranteed by the dictatorship of the proletariat. The prosecution alleged that degenerate ex-revolutionaries had become turncoats and tools of the class enemy, establishing a liaison with Mensheviks and Socialist Revolutionaries, i.e. socialist, or as the prosecution would have it, pseudo-socialist parties which had opposed the Communist Soviet régime from its inception. They had, it was further alleged, entered into agreements with foreign powers, themselves instruments of the class struggle forming the so-called 'capitalist encirclement'. Finally the prosecution set out to expose the accused as conscious or unconscious agents of the surviving remnants of liquidated classes, in particular of the wealthier peasantry (the kulaks).

In putting a few individuals in the dock and arraigning them before the nation and the world the prosecution sought not merely to justify the 'measures of social defence' it proposed to apply to them, but to advance a comprehensive explanation of the intense political struggle which Stalin believed to be in progress in the Soviet Union. Such a struggle justified, in his view, the enforcement of similar or even harsher measures against thousands, nay millions, of other kindred enemies of the régime.

These ideas on the purpose and significance of the trial were developed by the state procurator, Vyshinsky, in his speeches for the prosecution. What was striking in the behaviour of

c

the principal defendants, Bukharin and Rykov, was their apparent acceptance of Vyshinsky's charge that they were degenerate revolutionaries, social turncoats who had defected to the class enemy. Yet at the same time as they admitted the counter-revolutionary nature of their actions they often denied the specific charges preferred by the prosecution, such as clandestine negotiations with foreign powers, espionage, and preparations for the violent overthrow of the régime.

'Independent observers' and analysts—even those not taken in by Vyshinsky's sleight of hand—agree with him that the significance of the trial far transcended the question of whether or not the counts in the indictment could be proved, and that the trial was only an episode in a large-scale political struggle. They recognise that this and the other show trials were only one of the methods whereby Stalin sought to secure once and for all his authority and autocratic power, by silencing or eliminating all critics, whether actual or potential. The trials, like the NKVD police campaign known as the *Yezhovshchina* which ran parallel with them, the tightening of ideological controls in the arts and sciences and the exacerbation of the 'class struggle', all formed part of an overall plan. And the plan was to provide compelling evidence of the existence of a powerful conspiracy both outside and inside the USSR bent on sabotaging, frustrating and finally nullifying Stalin's efforts to bring Communism to the peoples of the Soviet Union.

This explains why with a few minor exceptions none of the defendants at the three show trials were fully rehabilitated during the de-Stalinisation campaign. True, some of them were acquitted of all blame on the provincial level, and became like those local saints of the Middle Ages who were venerated in distant provinces but never beatified according to the solemn rites of the Curia. At a public meeting in Tashkent in 1957, for instance, the Uzbek leader and co-defendant of Bukharin, Ikramov, was absolved of all blame and was declared to have suffered innocently, but this was not mentioned at the time in the central press. The charge of espionage and conniving with the enemies of the Soviet Union which played such an important part in the trials has been dropped from official publications in the post-Stalin era, and even the odious label of 'enemy of the people' is no longer attached to the names of the accused. And yet their sentences have not been quashed in spite of the embarrassment they might have caused, and probably still do cause, to those who claim to have outlived and overcome the cruelties of the Stalin régime. Appeals by relatives of the defendants for their public rehabilitation have been heard with sympathy by the highest authorities, but have still not resulted in action. All this seems to confirm that by and large Vyshinsky's macabre backdrop is still important to the maintenance of the present political system, even though the particular drama played out against it in the thirties will (so it is hoped) pass into oblivion. To insist on the rehabilitation of those who were accused in the show trials is regarded as a dangerous attempt to interfere with the established outlook on politics which provides the mainstay of ideological conformism; for should the capital accusations against their honour and integrity as politicians and human beings prove slanderous and untrue then all the props supporting Vyshinsky's scaffolding might collapse, and the whole surrealistic spectacle of the struggle between the powers of darkness and the powers of light led by Stalin might disintegrate before the eyes of the average Soviet citizen just as it has already done in the minds of the best representatives of the contemporary Soviet intelligentsia.

In our exposition and analysis of what happened during Bukharin's trial we shall therefore try to bring out the true relationship between the accusations of personal shortcomings and specific crimes (e.g. acts of sabotage or treasonable contacts with foreign powers) brought against the twenty-one defendants and the particular features of the political system (e.g. intensive industrialisation or wholesale collectivisation of agriculture) to which they offered an alternative. For the most important among the defendants were politicians, Marxist politicians at that, and the vindication of their honour as individual human beings should be inseparable from the vindication, up to a point, of their political creed and public actions. Not that we would go so far as to claim that they were theoretically right, and that even if they were, their theories could be translated into practice; we claim only that they were sincere and justified in trying to act on beliefs which ran counter to the measures imposed by the dogmatic, un-self-critical and unyielding mentality of Stalin on their country and on the party to which they belonged.

The status of 'oppositionist'

The history of the origins, growth and triumph of Communist autocracy is to a large extent the story of the suppression of all opposition movements arising within the Communist Party.[1] Before 1917 Lenin's paranoid intolerance of deviations which he feared would impair the efficient functioning of the Party was relatively harmless, since those whom he denounced and proscribed were able not merely to survive under the protection of a bourgeois society but even to continue their political activities without, and against, Lenin. To charges that they were betraying the cause of the working class, that they failed to understand Marxist theories of the dynamic of the class struggle, or the relevance of dialectics to everyday politics, Lenin's opponents could reply in kind; and as the political scene shifted such insults were easily forgotten or temporarily laid aside, old friendships were renewed and fresh coalitions emerged between former adversaries, all brothers in Marx.

The seizure of state power in October 1917 changed all that. The decision to rise in arms in Petrograd and overthrow Kerensky's provisional government had been opposed by a group of leading veteran Bolsheviks, headed by Kamenev and Zinoviev, who had in the past maintained close personal contacts with Lenin. They were outnumbered and outvoted in the Central Committee. Ultimately, after the event, they accepted the October Revolution as an accomplished fact, but insisted that the Bolsheviks should share with the other so-called socialist parties the immense task of organising the new socialist state.[2] The negotiations for the formation of a multi-party socialist government were conducted by Kamenev with Lenin's approval which, however, was entirely disingenuous and given merely to gain time. When these negotiations broke down, through Lenin's intransigence, a group of People's Commissars and of members of the Bolshevik Central Committee, backed by Zinoviev and Kamenev, tried to pressurise Lenin by handing in a declaration refusing to serve in a purely Bolshevik government, which they foresaw would have to rely on terror to maintain itself. The rebels' resignation from the Central Committee and the Council of People's Commissars was accepted and they were threatened with expulsion from the Party. In an ultimatum addressed to them by a majority of the Central Committee and dated 6 November 1917, and in a declaration of the Central Committee drawn up by Lenin, it was suggested that the rebel Bolsheviks should pursue their aims outside the Communist Party organisation. But only the next Congress of Soviets or the present Soviet Executive Committee, Lenin said, could hand over the government to another party.

The rebels were only human: they surrendered after a few days' sulking, preferring to play an active part in moulding the new society to being reduced to the status of sterile and frustrated critics. This episode shows incidentally that Lenin was then still willing to concede dissident Bolsheviks a modicum of political existence, on a par with the Mensheviks and Left Socialist Revolutionaries. He even went so far as ostensibly to recognise the right of the proletarian masses, acting through the Congress of Soviets, to arbitrate between opposing socialist parties.

During the years of the Civil War, political opposition to the Soviet government outside the Communist Party became impracticable. The occasional collaboration of prominent Mensheviks and Socialist Revolutionaries in various anti-Bolshevik White Army ventures made it impossible for Bolsheviks, however critical of their own leadership, to join any non-Bolshevik party.

In a struggle for existence such as the one waged during the Civil War, Lenin's dictum 'who is not with us is against us' had some semblance of justification. The situation changed after the central government secured the control of the whole country by defeating its opponents in the field (1920-21). Confronted by the huge task of economic and administrative reconstruction, the Soviet government needed both the goodwill of the masses and the active support of the decimated and dispersed technical, managerial and university-educated intelligentsia. The goodwill, although officially assumed to exist, was in fact far from universal. The workers of both capitals were disaffected because of food shortages, low wages, regimentation and the appearance of Trotsky's army labour detachments in the factories.* The peasants were outraged by the high-handed treatment they had received during the Civil War, and by the attempt to bring the class struggle into the countryside through the establishment of 'poor peasant committees' (*kombedy*), and they were ready to exert pressure to see their demands satisfied. The 10th Party Congress in March, 1921 coincided with widespread unrest in the capitals, particularly in Petrograd.[3] Petrograd workers went on strike and rioted. They appealed for support to the Kronstadt sailors, 'the glamour and the glory of the revolution', as Trotsky once called them. Libertarian traditions were still alive among the ratings of the ice-bound Baltic fleet. They worked out a resolution aboard the battleship *Petropavlovsk* demanding a democratic régime in the soviets, with free and unrigged elections in which all the socialist parties and the anarchists could take part, and an end to the hegemony of the Communist Party as the representative of the

---

*Trotsky planned to use demobilised Red Army men as a labour force subject to paramilitary discipline, and the scheme was partially put into effect.

true interests of the working class. When the Soviet authorities in Petrograd reacted by merely admonishing the sailors to submit to revolutionary discipline, they rose in arms, issuing an appeal to the country for general support in overthrowing the Communist Party dictatorship. Their mutiny, unplanned, ill-organised and lacking experienced leaders, was suppressed after a battle of extermination eighteen days after it broke out.

The political situation which led up to it filled the Bolshevik leaders, especially Lenin, with agonised apprehension. In his statements to the press Lenin dismissed the rising as one more White Guardist adventure, but at the 10th Congress he declared that its political background was more dangerous to the régime than all the White Guardist generals put together. The danger was that of a proletarian revolt against the rule of the Bolshevik Party. Under these circumstances, Lenin claimed, no form of agitation, no appeal to the masses could be tolerated which had not the full sanction of the Party leadership. A small group of Bolshevik leaders was then opposing the Central Committee line on certain matters concerning the organisation of the trade union movement; they were accused at the 10th Congress of forming a splinter group within the Party, and of issuing propaganda for their views independently of the official Party organs. This (the resolution passed at the Congress rightly or wrongly asserted) had helped to inflame the working masses of Petrograd.

The Menshevik leaflets in Petrograd on the eve of the Kronstadt mutiny show ... how the Mensheviks have used the differences of opinion within the Russian Communist Party in order to incite and support the Kronstadt mutineers, Socialist Revolutionaries and White Guardists, while claiming in their statements to be adversaries of the mutineers and supporters of the Soviet régime, wanting to introduce what they call only small corrections.[4]

To prevent a recurrence of such trouble the Congress passed a resolution forbidding the formation within the Party of political groups ('fractions') which adopted and publicised proposals not authorised by the established official Party committees, and forbidding the propagation of such unofficial views independently of publications put out by the Party as a whole. A special periodical known as the 'Discussion Leaflet', where such questions could be ventilated, was planned, but in fact it never appeared.

At the same time the Party decreed that views held by what was then known as the 'Workers' Opposition' should not be permitted to circulate: 'The Congress recognises that the propagation of such ideas [i.e. ideas representing what was called the anarchist-syndicalist deviation] is incompatible with membership of the Russian Communist Party.'[5] But most important, the 10th Party Congress introduced the following rule, in Paragraph Seven of the resolution on 'The Unity of the Party':[6]

In order to enforce strict discipline within the Party and in the work of the Soviet administration as a whole, and in order to achieve maximum unity by eliminating all fractional tendencies, the Congress empowers the Central Committee to apply in all cases of breach of discipline or revival and toleration of fractional activities every kind of Party disciplinary sanction, including expulsion from the Party, and for members of the Central Committee their demotion to candidate status and as an extreme measure, expulsion from the Party. A condition of the application [to members of the Central Committee, candidates of the Central Committee and members of the Control Commission] of such an extreme measure should be the summoning of a plenum of the Central Committee to which all candidates of the Central Committee and all members of the Control Commission should be invited. If such a general meeting of the most responsible leaders of the Party finds by a two-thirds majority that it is necessary to demote a member of the Central Committee to candidate status, or to expel him from the Party, such a measure should be enforced without delay.

Within the Party, this paragraph became the law of the jungle. It was by virtue of it that Trotsky was expelled; it was regularly invoked to condemn any opposition grouping right up to the summer of 1957, when Khrushchev had the 'anti-Party group' consisting of 'Molotov, Malenkov, Kaganovich, and Shepilov, who had joined them', expelled from the Central Committee. In order to appreciate the full significance of this rule we must remember that by the time it was passed no political activity was possible in the Soviet Union outside the framework of the Communist Party. The application of Paragraph Seven to members of the Party and its high administrative organs spelled political death to any oppositionist finding himself in disagreement with majority decisions. Paragraph Seven is so worded as to guarantee its application only in exceptional circumstances, and to ensure an investigation by a large body of high-ranking comrades in case of conflict. In effect, however, it deprives those falling victim to disciplinary action of a generally accepted means of self-defence. The proceedings are confined to a kind of Star Chamber meeting in private; and there is no right of appeal to a full Congress of the Party. Nor can a defendant appeal to the Party rank and file of the primary organisation to which he belongs, and seek their support in organising pressure from below when his case comes up before the Central Committee meeting. In the view of Lenin, embodied in the resolution, such an attempt would be tantamount to engaging in 'fractional' activity and would render the defendant liable to even harsher treatment. An appeal to the largely non-Party proletarian masses would be even more incriminating, for it would be interpreted as a bid to undermine the ruling position of the Communist Party, which claims the exclusive right to represent the 'class-conscious proletariat' (this being in turn defined as those members of the working class who accept the leadership of the Communist Party).

To sum up: the situation brought about by the decisions of the 10th Congress meant that even a leading Party member disagreeing with a majority decision could not appeal to the Party rank and file, nor justify his stand and defend himself before the nation at large. Every time such a Party leader found himself in conflict with the general Party line he was infringing the very resolution of the 10th Congress he himself had once helped to pass. This is what happened to Kamenev late in 1927, when he disagreed with the views of the Party majority as to the role played by the kulaks in the Soviet economy.

> Comrades, as long as such estimates, which become the basis for erroneous practical policy, are possible in the Party, we cannot forbear to criticise such views; we cannot renounce our desire to correct them and to warn the Party—to arouse in it a certain apprehension with regard to such estimates and perspectives. I am convinced that such criticism, carried out in accordance with the statutes, carried out in a framework dictated by the fact that our Party is the ruling party—I am convinced that such criticism helps the dictatorship of the proletariat, that it saves the dictatorship of the proletariat from getting into difficulties and crises. In these conditions it is impracticable and unjustifiable to demand of us a repudiation of our views.[7]

Kamenev's remarks were especially poignant since many of his own followers and Zinoviev's were then in prison for holding the opinions to which he alluded. 'These people,' said Kamenev, 'put their views before their position in society; they were ready to sacrifice their position for a cause which you consider wrong but they consider right, and they did so regardless of the possible consequences to themselves.'[8]

It fell to Rykov to answer Kamenev's plea for the free expression of dissenting views within the Party. He recalled the resolutions of the 10th Congress on anarchist-syndicalist deviation (quoted above) and said: 'As you see, Comrade Kamenev, the traditions of Bolshevism do not allow any member of the Party to defend views which have been recognised as anti-Party and anti-Bolshevik.' 'The very fact,' he continued, 'that oppositionists are ignoring and by-passing this resolution is the best demonstration of how far they have deviated ideologically from the Party.'[9]

In this connection Rykov recalled that the resolution of the 10th Congress was passed against the so-called 'Workers' Opposition' of Shlyapnikov and Myasnikov,[10] who had never gone so far as did the opposition bloc on 7 November 1927. But in making Kamenev personally responsible for the Trotskyite demonstrations of 7 November, Rykov was following the example set by Lenin when he insinuated that the Workers' Opposition of 1920-21 had fuelled the workers' riots of February 1921. Then Lenin claimed that the 'Workers' Opposition' had linked up, however unintentionally, with the Mensheviks, whose leaflets had touched off the Petrograd workers' unrest and the Kronstadt naval mutiny. Now Rykov insinuated that Kamenev's opposition encouraged the student demonstrations in favour of Trotsky which marred the tenth anniversary celebrations of the Great Socialist October Revolution. Going further than Rykov, Stalin said in his speech in condemnation of Kamenev: 'Kamenev assures us that there is nothing in the tradition of our Party, in the tradition of Bolshevism, to justify the demand that members of the Party renounce their views which are incompatible with Party ideology, with our programme. . . . That is a lie, Comrades!'[11] And he recalled Lenin's famous saying at the 10th Congress: 'We have no use for an opposition. We must have an end to opposition, put the lid on it. We have had enough of it.'[12]

Kamenev and his friends went to the 15th Congress with the intention of promising to desist from all organised fractional activities; they sought in return a concession which would permit them not to abjure their political beliefs. Even this last attempt to achieve some kind of status in the Party for members disagreeing with the majority on some question of policy failed completely. The oppositionists were expelled, and the Central Committee was instructed to readmit them only if they renounced publicly and individually the views they had defended during the period of acute opposition struggle. We must therefore regard the decision of the 15th Congress that sealed the fate of the so-called Left or Trotskyite-Zinovievite opposition as that which, going beyond the curbing of 'fractional activities', established the principle of thought control for Party members. It was officially proclaimed to be a Party member's duty to renounce dissenting views as soon as they had been identified as such by the competent Party authorities. In this decision the leaders of the future right-wing opposition, Tomsky, Bukharin and Rykov, fully concurred.

Another novel feature in ideological policy emerged at the 15th Congress. As we have seen, to appeal in Party dissensions to the non-Party masses had always been a grave breach of Party discipline. Shortly before the opening of the 15th Congress, however, there had taken place in Moscow and other cities large-scale workers' and students' demonstrations in favour of Trotsky's policy, allegedly supported by the opposition bloc. The new departure at the 15th Congress was the systematic rallying of non-Party public opinion behind the measures the Central Committee had taken, or was about to take, against the deviationists. For the first time the tribune of the Congress was used for short speeches and informal messages from numerous factory representatives, trade unionists and peasants. Some speakers launched vitriolic attacks on the opposition, spiced with colloquialisms designed to impart an air of spontaneity to these unmistakably staged proceedings. The representative of the workers of *Dneprostroy*,[13] for instance, was repeatedly applauded when he yelled:

> Non-Party workers and employees have asked me to express to the Congress their desire that it should purge the disruptive opposition from their ranks, so that there should no longer

remain in the ranks of Lenin's party a single disruptive oppositionist bedbug. Comrades, one could of course say a good deal more about the opposition, but I am not qualified to do so, having only been educated at a herdsmen's institute. Thousands of shepherds like me proclaim: 'Down with the disruptive work of the opposition! ... Long live the General Secretary of our Party, Comrade Stalin!' And so, Comrades, listen to the voice of the non-Party men—down with the oppositionists!

Such orations revealed that Stalin had decided to reply to what he called the oppositionists' appeal to the street mob on 7 November 1927 by organising a standard, official, non-Party public opinion in support of himself and the majority of the Central Committee.

Well-organised 'spontaneous' demonstrations by the working masses became an important feature of the *mise-en-scène* of the purge trials in the thirties, contributing to their unique atmosphere. Factory demonstrations were widely used to enlarge the scope of the purges. Thus after a show trial one or another factory would demand a full investigation into suspected contacts between persons still at liberty and those already sentenced. When such demands were given publicity in the central press,[14] those on whom suspicion had been cast felt obliged to ask for an investigation of their own accord, thus putting themselves into the hands of the sole authority which could clear them in the eyes of the people. This is how the case against Pyatakov was started in August 1936, after the Kamenev-Zinoviev trial, and how the investigation into Bukharin and Rykov was introduced to the public.* The other function of popular demonstrations was to justify the extreme severity of the sentences,

*After the Kamenev-Zinoviev trial, for example, *Izvestiya*, still ostensibly edited officially by Bukharin, published on 23 August 1936 a resolution passed by the Elektrosila Works in Leningrad in which the workers demanded an investigation into Bukharin's contacts with the 'enemies of the people' already sentenced.

which might have seemed particularly repellent in view of the very close relations subsisting between the accused and their friends still remaining in power.

In 1929, when the dissensions within the Central Committee came out into the open, Bukharin appealed to Stalin to conduct the debate on the Right opposition in the same spirit of mutual respect the two men had hitherto shown towards each other; Stalin retorted that the Party was not a family circle, nor yet a club of private friends. 'We all serve the working class, and if personal friendships conflict with the interests of the revolution, then personal friendships must be relegated to second place.'[15] From then on, Stalin organised popular demonstrations in support of his own policies whilst denying the opposition the right to do the same.

Interlude

The need to create spurious popular enthusiasm for officially accepted policies grew into a source of weakness for the régime. The hypocritical conformism about which Kamenev complained at the 15th Congress became the general pattern of Soviet behaviour in the early thirties. By imposing—on pain of political and physical annihilation—a hypocritical unanimity on Party members, the Party leadership laid itself open to a particularly sinister type of attack. Bukharin, Rykov and Tomsky realised after the fall of Trotsky and the defeat of the Left opposition that to organise splinter groups within the Party, and appeal openly to the masses to support oppositionist views, was both unnecessary and futile. The opposition had no need to ask its followers for vocal support; their silence, or the lip service they paid to accepted policies, did not mean that their hearts were not with the opposition leaders. The opposition could also take public support for granted whenever the government embarked on some policy that inflicted immeasurable hardship on millions. The only thing its leaders had to avoid was becoming identified with unpopular measures. They had to maintain their reputation as oppositionists. But this could be done even by publishing recantations and humiliating self-criticisms. Open propaganda for their ideas, 'fractional' activity and appeals to the masses would only have led to their defeat as it had led to that of the Left opposition. Such were the considerations that inspired their new tactics, i.e., their acceptance of institutionalised mendacity.

We have seen that Bukharin had given his full backing to Stalin's attack on Zinoviev and Kamenev. His speech in condemnation of them at the 15th Conference provided one of the rare occasions when Stalin registered his enthusiastic approval of him. He interjected from his place the words: 'Formidable, Bukharin, formidable. This is not talking but cutting!'[16] However, when the question of the actual expulsion of Kamenev and Zinoviev came before the 15th Congress Bukharin refrained from advocating it.[17] After their expulsion he maintained personal contacts with Kamenev which he did not try to keep secret, and which later became one of the main points in the indictment against him.

Much of what Bukharin had to say against Kamenev and Zinoviev at the 15th Congress was actually in defence of a policy to which he himself was committed—the protection of the peasantry. There seemed to be no dissension between him and Stalin on the issue. But when Stalin, having defeated the leftists, showed a tendency to adopt their radical agrarian programme Bukharin and his friends were faced in their turn with the problem of defending a minority view against the General Secretary. They could not, however, repeat the tactics of the Left opposition and collect signatures for memoranda to the cc, organise pressure groups and directly canvass popular support (or as Stalin preferred to put it, appeal to the 'street mob'). They therefore decided to formulate their views in such a fashion as either to ignore or to minimise their differences in the cc. At the same time they attempted to discredit Stalin personally.

One aspect of this last campaign of internecine warfare is worth recalling because of its subsequent repercussions. This is the matter of the publication of the letter and postscript Lenin dictated on his deathbed, commonly known as his political testament.[18] In 1924, at the 13th Congress, it was agreed between Zinoviev, Kamenev and Stalin that the testament should not be made public, but only shown to members of the cc. At the time, Trotsky raised no objection. But as the struggle between Stalin and the Left opposition grew in intensity, first Trotsky and then Kamenev and Zinoviev joined Krupskaya in demanding that the testament be published. Several leaks took place, and the testament appeared in various versions, of which the most complete was that published by Max Eastman in the *New York Times* of 18 October 1926. The cc forced Trotsky to declare that 'all talk of concealing or violating a will of Lenin's is a malicious invention';[19] but at the plenum of the cc held in October 1927, pressure from Left oppositionists goaded Stalin into demanding that Trotsky and his followers be expelled from the Party.[20] After Trotsky's banishment the campaign for publication of the full text was carried on by the future right-wing opposition, who as much as their predecessors on the left needed to check Stalin's personal power and prestige.

At the 15th Congress, where they backed Stalin in completing the downfall of Trotsky and his followers, the right-wing leaders were in a strong position. At the session of the Congress held on 9 December 1927 they took part in the extraordinary debate on Lenin's testament which to the best of our knowledge has never been wholly elucidated. Ordzhonikidze took the floor for a final statement on the joint report of the Central Control Commission and Workers' and Peasants' Inspectorate. He began by proposing a motion that the testament be published in the *Leninsky Sbornik* (a series of documents pertaining to Lenin's biography and works which appeared between 1925 and 1959). He quoted Stalin, who, he said, had suggested at the plenum of the Central Committee and the Central Control

Commission the previous July that the ban imposed on the testament at the 13th Congress be removed.[21] Ordzhonikidze's motion seems to have come as a surprise to the Congress, and perhaps to members of the Central Committee as well.* When the resolution was passed, at the same meeting, on the report of the ccc and the Workers' and Peasants' Inspectorate, G. I. Petrovsky, who was in the chair, did not read out the passage in the resolution which demanded that Lenin's testament should be published. But when the meeting was resumed after a fifteen-minute interval, he pointed out that 'they had forgotten' to vote on the testament, and reopened the question. Rykov put forward two amendments. These were, firstly, to publish not only the testament but also other letters of Lenin about internal Party affairs dating from the same period (these would incidentally have included Lenin's condemnation of Ordzhonikidze's reign of terror in Georgia) and secondly, to append the text of the testament to the stenographic report of the Congress. The motion, and both amendments, were passed unanimously.[22]

In spite of this unanimity, the resolution, needless to say, was never put into effect, and Lenin's testament was not published in Russia until 1956, three years after Stalin's death. Nor was the decision to include the text in the stenographic report ever implemented, and it does not appear in the published record of the 15th Congress. Finally, the resolution itself was never included in any subsequent edition of the *VKP (b) v rezolyutsiyakh*, nor to our knowledge has it ever been mentioned in the Soviet press. The testament remained the most restless skeleton in Stalin's cupboard throughout the next twenty-five years of his supremacy. At the 15th Congress he had momentarily had his back to the wall, and had even been

---

*Since the text of Lenin's testament had been known ever since its publication abroad by Eastman, Stalin might have suggested its release in Russia in order to counter Trotskyite allegations that it was being suppressed. However, at the plenum of October 1927, only two months before the 15th Congress, he had shown little enthusiasm for the idea.

D

obliged to associate his name, through Ordzhonikidze, with the motion to publish it. Although his powerful *apparat* was able to suppress the dangerous resolution, there can be no doubt that the enmity between Stalin and the Right oppositionists (perhaps even between Stalin and Ordzhonikidze) dates from this attempt to undermine his claim to the spiritual inheritance of Lenin.

Bukharin did not let the matter rest. When, on 24 January 1929, he published in *Pravda* the speech he had made on the anniversary of Lenin's death, in which he had attacked Stalinist policy by quoting copiously from the writings of Lenin, he pointedly headed his article 'Lenin's Political Testament'.

It was part of the oppositionist technique adopted by the rightists to comply with demands for ideological conformity as soon as a majority decision of the Party, even a rigged one, had been adopted. But they refused to be burdened with the reputation of initiators and abettors of Stalin's policies. They fought their utmost to prevent forced wholesale collectivisation; they rejected, on 9 February 1929, the compromise terms proposed by the Politburo;* they resisted even at the plenum of the cc in November 1929. And then, when Bukharin was at long last expelled from the Politburo, they surrendered, and announced their capitulation in *Pravda* on 26 November. In doing so they scored a partial success: whilst they managed to disclaim responsibility for the measures adopted by the cc, they simultaneously prevented Stalin from expelling them from the Party.

Stalin, however, was not a man to be deceived by such

---

*Bukharin was to withdraw his accusations against the cc of carrying on a policy of 'military-feudal' exploitation of the peasantry. Under the terms of the compromise worked out by the cc he was to express regret for entering into negotiations with Kamenev, and to promise not to resign from the editorship of *Pravda* or from the Comintern. In return for this total surrender, the Party leadership offered to withdraw its motion of censure on him and allow him to carry on his normal work in *Pravda* and the Comintern. For the text of the compromise proposal, see Stalin, *Works*, Vol. 12, pp. 6 ff.

manœuvres. As soon as the oppositionists pretended not to be a splinter group with an alternative programme, Stalin set out to describe their clandestine heretical viewpoint himself. In his major speech against them in April 1929 he enumerated the several points of their programme of reconstruction for agriculture and industry, and demonstrated how each one violated the general line of the Party. According to Stalin, Bukharin proposed to allow a free interplay of prices on the open market which might lead to a general increase in the cost of living, slow down the development of collective and state farms while promoting individual peasant farming, and stop the application of 'extraordinary' measures to so-called kulaks; grain to the value of some hundred million roubles would have to be imported, and if this measure depleted the currency reserves, imports of industrial equipment would have to be cut down. This was of course Stalin's own twisted interpretation of 'Bukharin's plan'.[23]

After they had formally surrendered, Stalin was able to force the deviationists to accept implicitly as genuine his own interpretation of their views, even of their motives. Rykov, for example, in his speech of repentance to the 17th Congress in 1934, openly admitted having acted as an 'agent of the counter-revolutionary class of kulaks'. When oppositionists tried to resign from their posts to avoid compromising themselves by having to support the general line, Stalin used every means available to force them to carry on with their jobs. In April 1929, for instance, he inveighed against what he called 'the method of resignations', saying Bukharin's expulsion from the Politburo was inopportune. At the time relations between the two men had reached a point where Stalin could certainly not have hoped for Bukharin's collaboration. His very presence in the Politburo must have been an embarrassment to Stalin; nevertheless Bukharin was forced to stay, so that it could be said that he shared responsibility for the very measures he opposed.

History has shown that in their fight against Stalin the

weapons of the right-wing deviationists were no better than those used by their left-wing predecessors. But let us not be too wise after the event. Bukharin's and Rykov's tactics almost did pay off. They managed to survive, and even be rehabilitated to some degree at the famous Congress of Victors—the 17th, in 1934. Nevertheless they had themselves helped to create the instrument of their own future destruction. They began by joining in the attack on the elementary principles of free thought during the debate with the Left opposition, but far more important was the technique of deceit they applied when they came in conflict with Stalin. An anonymous document published by Nicolaevsky at the time of the Bukharin trial thus describes the atmosphere in which they lived: 'It must be admitted that from the point of view of political morals the conduct of the majority of oppositionists was by no means of a high quality'. True, unbearable demands were made on them, and 'a party which expects such things from its members cannot expect to be regarded as a free association of members of like views united for a common purpose. We are obliged to lie. . . .' Nevertheless there are limits which should not be exceeded, even in lying. Unfortunately the oppositionists and particularly their leaders often went beyond those limits.[24]

What is of particular interest to our study is the fact that the technique of systematic deception used by the right-wing oppositionists reminds us in many respects of the technique of false confessions to which they had recourse at their trials. When they made their earlier political submissions and recantations the oppositionists cooperated with their accuser Stalin and ostensibly accepted his interpretation of their motives thinking they were being clever. What Vyshinsky demanded of them at the trials hardly differed from their confessions, including factual lies such as reports of meetings with certain people at certain times. As the author of 'Letter of an Old Bolshevik' states, not all the opposition leaders went equally far in this technique of deception. Bukharin used it with circumspection, and at the trial he gave a lead in this respect to the less subtle Rykov. In Bukharin's hands, the technique worked to his satisfaction; it was his masterly handling of deception that enabled him at the very end of his trial to make the final plea which (wasted though it was on the ears of many of the journalists and diplomats then in Moscow) may yet be understood by future generations, and reveal to them the agony in which he must have lived out the last ten years of his life. In so doing, however, Bukharin conceded to his adversaries the main and important thing. He connived at the systematic replacement of the factual truth of the situation by the 'network of decorative deceit' which was so familiar to him. He posed as a counter-revolutionary when in fact he was only trying to promote his own way to a socialism far more humane than Stalin's. He accepted the nonsensical description of the peasants crushed in the collectivisation process as kulaks; in a word, he cooperated with the Prosecutor in weaving the web in which he was to be caught, merely in order publicly to refute the monstrous and degrading accusation that he was a spy, and a would-be assassin of his beloved teacher, Lenin.

3. Interpretation of 'class struggle'

Nobody ever doubted that the main reason for the trial of Bukharin, Rykov and the nineteen other defendants was their stubborn opposition in the past to Stalin's policies. Yet it is a sign of the basic perversity of Soviet 'justice' that the deviationists were not tried for their deviations from the 'general line'. Whenever the accused did succeed in hinting at their political ideas, they invariably threw light on the background to the trial; but any attempt they made to explain why they disagreed with Stalin's policy, or to propound some alternative, was always immediately cut short by the prosecutor or the presiding judge. The prosecution was determined not to allow the defendants to publicise their political theories, insisting that they should merely confirm that they had committed acts both treasonable and punishable under Soviet law. In his polemics on the right-wing opposition in the late twenties, and in the *Short Course on the History of the* CPSU (*b*), Stalin maintained that all oppositionist policies were aimed at destroying the achievements of socialism in Russia, and that the oppositionists were turncoats steeped in anti-Communist prejudice. Bukharin's and Rykov's long-term record of political work in the highest councils of the Party and government made the task of sustaining such an accusation a difficult one for Vyshinsky. In order to destroy the prestige of these survivors of the Old Guard he had to show that far back along the road to Communism the accused had been guilty of deception and disloyalty. A number of minor characters among them were willing, after treatment in Yezhov's torture chambers, to provide evidence that the main offenders had taken part in plots, espionage and sabotage. One of the most grotesque allegations (and one of the crowning fabrications in Vyshinsky's indictment) was the story that Bukharin had plotted the assassination of Lenin, Stalin and Sverdlov as early as 1918.

In the second part of this study we shall consider in some detail these entirely fictitious accusations of plotting against Lenin, murdering Gorky and his son Peshkov, spying for foreign powers, putting nails and broken glass in butter and so on. Such allegations were self-defeating, as can be seen from the record of the trial. But we should not forget that behind these figments lay the stark reality of the conflict between Stalin's and Bukharin's economic and historical concepts; although this clash was at the very root of the trials, the two opposing views were never allowed to confront one another in the courtroom. Under the pretence that the accused were either convicted or self-confessed spies, criminals and counter-revolutionaries, Vyshinsky contended that their ideas were not worthy of consideration, let alone of theoretical refutation. In order, therefore, to perceive the underlying canvas on which the procurator embroidered his nightmarish portraits of the accused, we must turn our attention, however briefly, to the preceding political struggles, and especially to Bukharin's systematic opposition to Stalin after 1927.

The main difference between Bukharin and Stalin was that Bukharin regarded the social revolution in Russia as a thing of the past, begun in 1917 with the advent of the proletarian dictatorship and ended with the Soviet government's victory in the Civil War. In his *Way to Socialism and the Union of Workers and Peasants* he stated, 'before the seizure of power the party of the working class is a party of civil war. In as much as the dictatorship of the bourgeoisie has been destroyed, and replaced by the dictatorship of the proletariat ... the party of the working class ... is now becoming the party of civil peace.'[1] According to Bukharin, bitter class warfare was only needed until the Communist Party succeeded in establishing the dictatorship of the proletariat; according to Stalin, the

Party dictatorship must continue and the class struggle be intensified until all class enemies were liquidated.

During the Civil War Bukharin certainly approved, and shared responsibility for, the strongest measures against active enemies of the government. When, however, the military and political victory of the Soviet régime seemed assured, he advocated the gradual integration of the surviving pre-revolutionary economic methods and institutions into the socialist economy planned and administered by the Soviet government. Bukharin accepted NEP not as a temporary retreat on grounds of expediency but rather as a long-term policy. The use of capitalist methods to build new enterprises (through foreign concessions) would bring about a resurgence of economic activity, which would be incorporated into the socialist sector as it gained in strength.

Bukharin's special concern was to avoid the outbreak of class strife between the industrial proletariat and the peasantry as a whole. Bukharin undoubtedly knew and shared Lenin's view that the Russian peasantry was torn by conflicting tendencies, the one inclining towards socialism and socialist forms of production, the other towards private ownership of the land and capitalist methods of agriculture. He saw this conflict, however, as existing not between differing strata of the agricultural population (i.e. the rich and the poor peasantry) but rather in the mind of every Russian peasant, who combined in himself both the mentality of the worker, as one who earned his living by the sweat of his brow, and that of the entrepreneur —as a capitalist using his share of the common land, his livestock and implements for the purpose of economic speculation. In this view he was confirmed by the solidarity shown by the peasants in their opposition to war Communism in 1919-21.

Bukharin's economic programme for agriculture[2] was based on two assumptions: firstly that the individual peasant farmer could be gradually absorbed into the socialist economy without recourse to coercion; and secondly, that the socialist system in the course of its development must preserve both a harmonious economic balance between industry and agriculture and ideological unity of purpose between workers and peasants. His political programme can be summed up as follows: the government and Party should first of all encourage the entry into collective farms of poor and middle-income peasants by giving the collective farms definite economic incentives, and raising their agro-technical standard. No peasants should be forced to join collectives, but the advantages of doing so should be made clear to everyone. As for the richer peasants or kulaks, they should be made dependent on the state and on cooperative organisations, both of which would finance loans for kulak farming. They should be compelled to sell their grain surpluses to the state at a low price, which would be equivalent to an additional supertax. They would thus be made to bear the main burden under the system of 'pumping over' (*perekachka*)* the returns of an agricultural economy for industrial development.[3] The state and Party should give every encouragement to individual peasants to free themselves from their economic dependence on the kulaks; this would apply in particular to those coming together into some form of producers' cooperative. Through all these measures the means of agricultural production would gradually be socialised without any falling-off in output, and without breaking the common front (*smychka*) of workers and peasants. The Bukharinites expressly pointed out that this was not a policy under which the class struggle would 'wither away'. It was a method of absorbing peasants still dominated by the property-owning mentality into the socialist economy without impairing their usefulness as producers.

Stalin, in his broadside against the right-wing deviationists delivered at the CC plenum in April 1929, quoted Bukharin's *Way to Socialism* . . . where the following passage can be found: 'The basic network of our peasant organisations will consist of cooperative cells, not of the kulak but of a labour type of cell, which will grow into the system of organs of our state as a

---

*'Reshuffling resources from agriculture to industry by the way of direct taxation or voluntary peasant savings.'

whole and will thus become links in the one chain of a socialist economy. On the other hand the cooperative nests of kulaks will also grow into this system through the medium of banks and so on, but they will remain to a certain extent a foreign body, like for instance, concessionary enterprises.' This meant, Stalin continued, that both kulaks and concessionaires would grow into socialism, however much they remained foreign bodies. The Marxist theory of the class struggle was therefore completely perverted by Bukharin's theory of a peaceful growing of capitalists, both kulaks and concessionaires, into socialism. This type of nonsense was 'a betrayal of socialism worthy of such liberals, camouflaged as socialists, as Brentano and Sydney Webb'. Rozit, a follower of Bukharin, protested violently at what he called a misrepresentation of Bukharin's views. Class struggle was not to be stopped, but would take the form of incorporating the residual elements of the capitalist economy into the socialist planned system. 'The point is' (interjected Rozit during Stalin's speech) 'that growing into [socialism] presupposes according to Bukharin the existence of a class struggle.'[4]

At the time of the crisis in grain supplies in 1927-29 Bukharin wanted to rely completely on the workings of the free market, with the state interfering only to influence prices. Instead of being coerced, peasants should be induced to sell their produce by being offered plenty of consumer goods (the famous *sitets*, or cotton dress fabric). In order to regulate prices and satisfy the needs of expanding cities, Bukharin proposed that grain be purchased from abroad.[5] This would of course put a strain on currency reserves badly needed for forced industrialisation. But Bukharin thought it would be wrong to speed up industrialisation to the point where agricultural production fell off. This would inevitably happen if the government was to apply 'extraordinary methods' (i.e. requisitions or reprisals) to the richer surplus-producing section of the peasantry in order to secure food supplies for the rapidly-developing industrial centres.[6] Bukharin was an enthusiast of mechanisation and of the use of modern machinery in agriculture. What he wanted to avoid was an over-precipitate development of heavy industry, resulting in over-production of heavy agricultural machinery before the peasants had been given time to learn how to use it.

Some of Bukharin's faith in the future of cooperative socialist agriculture stemmed from his view that even the richer Russian peasants were hardly prosperous enough to be classified as bourgeois or capitalist. For him a kulak was, at worst, a man who hoped to improve his lot by becoming something of a capitalist. We know he felt this way both from what Ruth Fischer reports of her conversations with him[7] and from the attack on the Right opposition Stalin launched at the plenum of April 1929, when referring to Bukharin he angrily exclaimed: 'For him a kulak is not a kulak; a middle peasant is not a middle peasant, and poverty reigns everywhere in our villages.... This conception of the peasantry is wrong, and incompatible with Leninism. Lenin said that the individual peasantry was the last capitalist class.'[8]

The way Stalin and Bukharin argued about the status of the Russian peasantry is highly characteristic of both men. To Bukharin the question of the peasants' social status was a question of fact, answerable by finding out how poor they were. To Stalin it was a question of doctrine—whether or not they were to be regarded as property-owning economic units, the last bastion of capitalism according to Lenin's teaching. This difference of approach conditioned many disagreements between the two men when they confronted the practical problems of economic organisation in the countryside.

Bukharin's economic programme was published in his 'Notes of an Economist', which appeared in *Pravda* on 30 September 1928,[9] at the height of the crisis in grain supplies that so greatly influenced the future of Soviet agriculture. The leftists, who had consistently advocated an economic policy of 'super-industrialisation', even at the expense of agriculture, declared that the grain shortage was due to hoarding by rich peasants. The Bukharinites, on the other hand, explained the drop in production by pointing to the reduction in the area under cultivation. In 'Notes of an Economist' Bukharin remarked: 'Today every child knows that the [Left] opposition fairy-tales about the "frightfully tremendous" grain reserves held back by the villages, the legends of the 900 million poods* of grain that have been stored away, have burst once and for all like soap bubbles. Nobody believes these fairy tales any longer.'[10] As long as Stalin's main preoccupation was the defeat of the Left oppositionists, he allowed Bukharin to attack them on the economic question, and at the 15th Congress, which sealed the political fate of Trotsky and his followers, a number of resolutions embodying Bukharin's economic policy were passed.

Yet no sooner were Trotsky and the 'superindustrialisers' defeated than Stalin made his enemy's theories his own, and Bukharin's economic programme was already in danger of being abandoned. Discussion of the question in the cc must have started immediately after the 15th Congress. In his article on the results of the July 1928 plenum of the cc, Stalin, without mentioning names, attacked men who did not understand how to exert pressure on the peasantry, and said such people were not proletarian revolutionaries but 'peasant philosophers'—a transparent allusion to Bukharin.[11]

The existence of these disagreements was kept secret from the public. Speaking at an open gathering on 19 October 1928 on the dangers of Right deviationism, Stalin said there were in the cc some most insignificant elements which were adopting a policy of appeasement towards the Right opposition. But he asserted emphatically that 'it is time to stop the gossip being spread by those who wish the Party no good, and by all sorts of oppositionists, that there exists a rightist deviation or an appeasing attitude towards it in the Politburo of the cc.'[12] From a note first published in the eleventh volume of Stalin's *Works* (it appears as an abridged version of what Stalin said, and should therefore be treated with circumspection) we learn that at the joint meeting of the Politburo and the Presidium

*1 pood = approximately 15 kilograms.

of the CCC held at 'the end of January/beginning of February' 1929, Stalin allegedly stated that the Politburo had decided the previous autumn to inform the CC of their complete unity of purpose and absence of all disagreements.[13] If such was indeed the case, and Bukharin, without withdrawing his programme, did assent to such a general declaration, he must thereby have signed the warrant for his own execution in 1938. It is clear that he must have done something of the kind, since otherwise he could have contradicted Stalin's statement of 19 October. But he had certainly not renounced his views, which he continued to propagate without directly attacking Stalin's policy, now gradually gaining momentum.

A debate within the Party on economic policy could not be conducted on a purely factual basis, using objective conditions at a given date as a starting-point and working out a programme for future changes. Instead, every practical proposal had to be backed by quotations from Marxist authorities, to give it the semblance of orthodoxy and brand all alternatives as deviationist. Bukharin embarked on this war of quotations and interpretations with all the *brio* of an accomplished Party polemicist. He had the backing of Krupskaya, who encouraged him to some extent by recalling the ideas on collectivisation expressed by Lenin in his article 'On Cooperation'.[14] Bukharin's most representative article* was published both in *Pravda* on 24 January 1929 and as a separate pamphlet. In it he presented a systematic exposé of all the relevant later writings of Lenin ('Pages from a Diary', 'About Our Revolution', 'How Should We Reorganise the Rabkrin?', 'Better Less but Better', and 'On Cooperation'). He summed up his reading of the sacred text as follows: 'The main guarantee of our work of socialist construction is the care we take to obtain the most favourable combination of class forces, which will make it possible for us to continue to build up socialism—the care we take to coordinate the "proletarian revolution" and the "peasants' war" in a new and this time constructive form'. According to Bukharin, Lenin

*Suggestively entitled 'Lenin's Political Testament'.

thought the main task of the CC was to prevent a conflict between the proletariat and the peasantry. The development of the two main forces of industrialisation and peasant cooperation would guarantee the advent of socialism.

Newspapers and magazines of 1929 were full of covert polemics, with both sides claiming Lenin as the supreme authority for their views. But while Stalin's theory of intensified class warfare and anti-kulak measures was openly mooted, and a crude appeal was made for the backing of the Party rank and file, Bukharin, having accepted the legend of a 'united Politburo', was forced to resort to Aesopian language, advancing his views by means of allusions intelligible only to enlightened Party intellectuals and those familiar with the details of his conflict with Stalin.

On 30 June 1929 *Pravda* published an article, once again with a somewhat sensational title, which Bukharin had sent from a rest home in Sochi. It was called 'Theory of Organised Uneconomics'—an allusion to the wanton mess Stalin was about to impose on the country with the first Five-Year Plan. The article purported to be a review of a book by Dr Hermann Bente, *Organisierte Unwirtschaft. Die ökonomische Gestalt verbeamteter Wirtschaft und ihre Wandlung im Zeitalter des gesamtwirtschaftlichen Kapitalismus.** In this review Bukharin attacked systems, whatever their structure, which were based on state interference, petty regulation and bureaucracy. 'The essence of organised uneconomics,' he wrote, 'amounts to the fact that the organisational links which should be the means to achieve economic ends degenerate into an end in themselves.' After desultory criticisms of the book, he concluded: 'Bente's work takes full measure of the problem of the *apparat* as such, and treats it as a scientific problem. Bente shows us clearly how urgent this problem has become for them [i.e. economists

*The ponderously repetitive title may be translated as 'Organised Uneconomics. The Economic Structure of a Bureaucratised Economy and Its Modifications in the Era of Total Economic Capitalism'—Jena, 1929.

working in a totalitarian capitalist society]. For us, the task of building up socialism raises similar problems with even greater insistence.' We may wonder whether Bukharin was already conscious of what it would cost him to tackle the problem of the *apparat,* fast becoming the main instrument of Stalin's power.

At this point it may be useful to recall what the measures were which Bukharin and his friends were fighting. The same issue of *Pravda* that contained Bukharin's article on 'Organised Uneconomics' also carried a decree of the Central Executive Committee (TSIK) and Council of People's Commissars, signed incidentally by Rykov. By the terms of this decree, where an assembly of the whole village voted to share out the burden of grain deliveries to the state, the village soviets were given special powers of coercion. (Kulaks and other class enemies, while excluded from the assembly, were nevertheless obliged to abide by its decisions.) Should any household fail to contribute its grain quota, the local soviet could exact a fine amounting to five times its value. If this were not paid, it could seize outright all the property of those concerned, auction it, and use one quarter of the proceeds to collectivise the holdings of the poorer peasants. It can well be imagined how petty village vendettas must have been inflamed by the abuses inherent in this monstrous regulation.

As early as the winter of 1928-29, reports of a desperate situation in the villages were being circulated by members of the Right opposition. Stalin mocked crudely at these when he spoke of Bukharin's and Rykov's 'ludicrous lamentations' over the miserable lot of the peasantry.

Yes, Comrades, a class is a class. You really cannot get away from it. The most fashionable word now in the Bukharinite ranks is the word 'overbending' (*peregib*), applied to methods of securing grain supplies. They say: 'We are of course not against pressure on the kulaks, but we are against the over-bending which occurs in this connection, and which affects the middle peasants.' Then follow stories of atrocities caused by this 'overbending'. Letters from peasants are read . . . and then the conclusion is reached that our policy of pressure on the kulaks must be abandoned.[15]

But the conditions of 1928 and 1929 were only the beginning of a process which ended in the early thirties with the extermination of the kulaks as a class.[16]

4. The Comintern incident

However obvious it must have seemed to the initiated, the disagreement between Bukharin and Stalin over collectivisation and grain supplies did not become public knowledge until the end of 1929. The fiction of unity in the Politburo was kept up for the benefit of the Party rank and file and of the masses, who understood nothing of the quarrel.

The differences between Stalin and Bukharin on internal politics and the way to achieve socialism were real and fundamental. Divergences of this kind are hardly to be overcome by persuasion. In countries where political ideas are allowed to compete freely for the popular suffrage, such a contest is ultimately decided either by a majority vote in favour of one or another alternative, or by a compromise. Under Soviet conditions it can be decided only when one of the contestants is declared a 'deviationist'.

Stalin's position was a strong one. From the outset he commanded the backing of a majority of the Politburo, and although the existence of a rift was concealed from the Central Committee for some time, he hoped to manœuvre that body into declaring Bukharin's theories identical with the much-discussed rightist deviation. Bukharin, however, had one advantage: his position as chairman of the Communist International. In that capacity he could influence Communist opinion abroad, and by enlisting the active support of fraternal parties strengthen the opposition in Moscow. Before striking his main blow, and openly branding Bukharin as the head of a Right deviationist group, Stalin therefore had to ensure that the debate would not reach the Third International, and that even if it did Bukharin would meet with the same fate there

E

as previous oppositionists such as Trotsky, Sapronov or Zinoviev.

In 1928 a number of sordid intrigues were set afoot in Third International circles. The occasion arose at the 6th World Congress of the International in July. No political arguments were officially permitted at the Congress, and Stalin emphatically denied rumours of dissensions between himself and Bukharin.[1] Nor were any such dissensions reflected in the official minutes. But things looked different in reality. An American participant, Lovestone, described the conditions in which the delegates worked: 'There were two congresses,' he said, reporting to his colleague Gitlow in New York. 'One was the official Congress over which Bukharin presided, whose plaudits he received, and the decisions of which were passed unanimously. Then there was the corridor congress, called together by Stalin. It took place in the corridors. Through it, a devastating campaign was carried out against Bukharin as a right winger.'[2] A whispering campaign emanating directly from Stalin developed in all the foreign Communist parties. The American delegate Foster wrote from the Congress to Gitlow that

> Stalin informed him [in a confidential interview] that Bukharin was a right winger, and supported the right-wing elements generally in the Communist International. He told Foster that this accounted for the support which Bukharin gave to the Lovestone group. He [Stalin] informed Foster that his differences with Bukharin extended over a long period of time, but that the time had come when Bukharin's right-wing deviations could no longer be tolerated. He further let Foster know that he was ready to support him in the American party.[3]

At the Congress Thälmann, secretary of the German Communist Party, staunchly supported Stalin's line, and may well have received the same kind of promises as Stalin dangled before Foster. A later intrigue bringing Stalin and Bukharin into conflict over Thälmann's position in the German party was instrumental in obtaining Bukharin's dismissal from the Comintern. Relations between the German and Russian parties had been strained ever since the Left faction had been expelled from the German party by the direct intervention of Bukharin himself, who travelled to Berlin expressly for this purpose in 1926.[4]

Soon after the end of the 1928 World Congress a sensational corruption affair broke out in the German Communist Party. Thälmann's brother-in-law, a certain Wittorff, an organiser of the important Hamburg branch, had embezzled a large sum of Party money. To prevent the scandal from becoming public, Thälmann took it upon himself to repay the embezzled sum, an action which made him guilty of 'family-mindedness' and nepotism, grave sins for a Bolshevik. Wilhelm Pieck demanded his and Wittorff's immediate expulsion from the Party. The German CC, however, voted to suspend Thälmann from his Party posts pending investigation of his case, a decision published in the Communist paper *Rote Fahne*. Stalin acted swiftly to rescue his protégé from this predicament. On the evening of the following day the organiser of the English department of the Comintern, the courier Petrovsky-Bennett, arrived in Berlin from Moscow with a message from Stalin ordering the German CC to reverse its decision on the affair, and reinstate Thälmann.[5] The German Party complied. Bukharin, however, was obviously nettled by Stalin's direct interference in matters he himself should have handled, and put forward a resolution in the Comintern condemning Thälmann's behaviour. This Stalin refused to countenance. Alluding to the affair in his speech of 24 April 1929 censuring the Right deviationists, he said Bukharin's attempt to condemn Thälmann a second time for a single offence was one of the reasons for the decision to recall him from the Comintern. He also implied that Bukharin wanted to exploit the whole affair in order to oust Thälmann from the leadership, and make over the German Party to the right-wing deviationists.[6]

Although Bukharin was recalled from the Comintern at the

beginning of 1929, his dismissal was not announced immediately. It took several months to obtain the agreement to it of all the member parties; the honour of revealing Bukharin's implication in the right-wing deviation fell to the German Party as represented by Thälmann himself. On 21 August 1929 *Pravda* carried a resolution passed by the 10th plenary meeting of the Executive Committee of the Communist International (ECCI). This mentioned Bukharin by name and accused him of 'stooping to a policy of class collaboration with capitalist elements'. It also publicly alleged for the first time that he had tried to enter into an unprincipled alliance with former Trotskyites in order to combat the CPSU and the Comintern. The resolution revealed that at a meeting of the Russian CC and CCC held on 23 April, he had been removed from various posts. On 23 August 1929, *Pravda* published a note of the Central Committee of the German Communist Party approving this measure of the ECCI, and describing Bukharin's conduct as a classic example of 'cowardly opportunism'. Next day *Pravda* printed an announcement ominously headed 'On the Mistakes and Deviation of Comrade Bukharin'.

From that day on Bukharin was branded as an oppositionist and a deviationist, and became fair game for every denunciator and slanderer. Any reply from him would have been interpreted as an attempt to camouflage his deviation and perpetuate 'fractional' activities. The only way to retrieve his position in the Party was to confess his mistaken views, and promise to amend them. This Bukharin postponed, however, until after the plenary meeting of the CC of 10-17 November 1929. Rykov, who had supported him in the councils of the Politburo and at the plenary meetings but had never compromised himself by publicising his own deviationist views, tried to manœuvre so as to avoid being identified with the opposition. On 21 September 1929 he had made an ambiguous speech which was tantamount to approval of Stalin's programme of swift industrialisation and full-scale collectivisation. But it was already far too late, and at the November plenum

Stalin repeated the charges he had made the previous April, saying: 'The oppositionists have gone mad, and do not understand what classes mean.'* The November plenum decided to expel Bukharin from the Politburo.

On 26 November *Pravda* carried a short note signed by Tomsky, Rykov and Bukharin admitting their responsibility for the opinions of the right-wing deviationists and acknowledging that on all the counts on which they had disagreed with the cc majority, they had been in the wrong.

> During the last year and a half there subsisted between us and the majority of the Central Committee of the All-Russian Communist Party differences of opinion on a number of political and tactical questions. Our views were expressed in a number of documents and speeches at plenary and other sessions of the Central Committee and the Party itself. We regard it as our duty to state that in this controversy the Party and the Central Committee have been proved right, while our views, as set out in certain documents, have proved mistaken. We confess these mistakes and shall for our part endeavour with the whole Party to struggle with all our might against all deviations from the Party line.[7]

*By this time Stalin's policy had already ushered in a state of 'cold' civil war in Russia. Extraordinary measures applied to kulaks, and to kulak underlings as well (*podkulachniki*, which could mean almost any peasant in a Russian village) were creating an atmosphere of violence and terror. Murders of village soviet officials by resentful peasants were regularly reported in the press, with inflammatory commentaries about the truculence of the class enemy and the necessity for ruthless repression.

5. Stalin's offensive begins

By recanting, the right-wing leaders obtained the same respite as had previous oppositionists: their total liquidation was postponed. Rykov kept his post as Chairman of the Council of People's Commissars for another year; Tomsky managed to keep his as head of the All-Union Central Council of Trade Unions (AUCCTU) for some time. But the oppositionists were already discredited in the eyes of the Party rank and file, unable as they were to defend or protect their former followers, who stood accused of the very sins their leaders had now abjured. The official capitulation of 26 November was certainly vague enough to allow all the rightist leaders to go on professing certain views they had not explicitly renounced, but this may well have been exactly what Stalin desired. After a short break during preparations for the election of delegates to the 16th Party Congress, the persecution of the Bukharinites was renewed.

The Congress, which took place from 26 June to 13 July 1930, was the next stage in the campaign against them. Its delegates (and those attending the 16th Party Conference that preceded it) included a large number of representatives of the Party *apparat,* now increasingly becoming a tool of Stalin's secretariat. The central organs of the Party and the Comintern were nevertheless represented as usual, and delegates from these included a good many right-wing sympathisers. Bukharin did not come to the Congress. He was reported to be ill and out of Moscow, which did not prevent scurrilous attacks from being made on him from the rostrum. The other right-wing leaders, Uglanov, Rykov and Tomsky, all made speeches in which they repeatedly denied having engaged in subversive activities, drew attention to their previous recantations and complained about the continuing campaign of slander and defamation to which they were subjected. Uglanov in a frequently-interrupted speech[1] while refuting the charge of subversion admitted he had made political mistakes. His protestations failed to satisfy his unruly audience. After his speech he found it necessary to address a special letter to the Congress presidium (published at the end of the stenographic report of the Congress proceedings) admitting that he *had* engaged in subversive activities. In particular, he had tried to play off against the Central Committee the Moscow Party organisation of which he was the head. This was a fatal admission to make because of the role he had played in suppressing the uprising of 7 November 1927. On that occasion he had organised gangs from the Moscow Party Committee to break up Trotskyite demonstrations. It was not in Stalin's character to trust a man who had helped him to maintain himself in power at a difficult juncture; the head of a Praetorian guard could easily try to turn king-maker and oust his master at the next opportunity. The safest course was to eliminate him, thus gaining direct control over his underlings. Uglanov's fate was sealed at the 16th Congress: he was not even reelected to the Central Committee.

Tomsky, in a long speech, advanced some surprising arguments to prove the sincerity of his repentance. Sometimes his remarks seemed to contain an undercurrent of bitter irony. Why, he asked, could one not doubt the sincerity of his confession? Because (he replied) the only reason for making an insincere confession would be to gain time and an opportunity for further manœuvring. But after the political lessons which the Party had learned, he exclaimed, further manœuvring was impossible. Speaking of his personal attitude towards Stalin, Tomsky said there was no such thing as personal politics in the Communist Party. If someone pursued the right policy, he also had the right personality. If his policy was a good one he was also a good comrade. Tomsky nevertheless expressed resentment at the repeated calls for renewed, additional repentance. It is hard enough, he said, to admit one's mistakes, and he and his comrades had done so sincerely. Why should it now be demanded of them that they 'repent, repent and repent without cease'?[2]

There was less defiance and subtlety in Rykov's statement to the Congress.[3] He betrayed his fear by trying to dissociate himself from his former political allies, protesting against Uglanov's use of the pronoun 'we', with its implication that perhaps he, Rykov, was also a member of the right-wing caucus. He repeated his assurances that there had never been any right-wing 'fractional' activities, and complained bitterly of the violent campaign being waged against him, and more especially of the adverse criticism of a speech he was said to have made while on a tour of the Urals.[4] While he disapproved of the Bukharin-Kamenev conversations,* he said, he was unwilling to criticise Bukharin for views they had held in common, and which both they and Tomsky had solemnly repudiated. He also took great exception to allegations by his Party comrades that he had been in contact with counter-revolutionaries. Of course counter-revolutionaries like the American renegade Lovestone might well make use of his name in order to defame him and stir up Party strife, but it was wrong to accept their testimony at its face value.

Rykov's fears were undoubtedly justified, as became obvious from the speech of the GPU official Vareikis, who levelled the most damaging accusations at the right-wing deviationists. He said Uglanov, Rykov and Tomsky had made a written statement defending the 'unheard-of and provocative actions of Bukharin' (meaning his meetings and conversations with Kamenev). 'You have been and you remain agents of the kulak class', Vareikis exclaimed to the deviationists.

The next speaker, one Sheboldaev from Astrakhan, continued in similar vein.[5] We quote his statement in full, as it

---

*As time went on they began to be referred to as 'negotiations', e.g. in Kamenev's speech at the 17th Congress.

helps us to understand the standpoint of the Right opposition in 1930, which Vyshinsky twisted during the trial into an organised conspiracy. He said:

I have today been given a document concerning a group of Party members and non-Party men in our Lower Volga region who have formed an outright counter-revolutionary organisation. I shall read to you a number of passages from the testimony of one old Party member, a leading worker of our organisation in the region, who was heading this business. This is what Ulyanov says: 'I was in agreement with the platform of the rightists, Bukharin, Rykov and others. I believed it was impossible for me to warn the Party of such dangers [he means dangers to the dictatorship of the proletariat caused by the Party's policy of speeded-up collectivisation and industrialisation] as this could lay me open to expulsion from the Party and to reprisals. It became obvious to me that the dissatisfaction with the course chosen by the Party was leading to a peasant rebellion against the Soviet régime, and that this threatened the conquests of the October Revolution. It was therefore necessary to give a lead to the spontaneous peasant movement, and to work for a change in our present leadership, so that the Party and the Soviet régime should be headed by Bukharin, Tomsky and Rykov.

Sheboldaev went on:

When he was asked 'What would happen if attempts to change the leadership were unsuccessful?' Ulyanov declared, 'Zaletov and I answered,* in the last resort one can seize

*Sheboldaev's statement is somewhat confused. He has obviously been given material incriminating the opposition just before making his speech, so as to be able to substantiate the charge of counter-revolutionary activities. He quotes the protocol of an interrogation of Ulyanov from which it is not clear to whom the reply about the possible use of force was made—to an investigating officer, or to Ulyanov's followers before his arrest. Zaletov's name did not recur in any investigation, but an Ulyanov described during Bukharin's trial as a 'Polish spy' may be identical with the one mentioned by Sheboldaev.

power by force of arms.' On the question of a programme
he said, 'There is no written programme and no need to
invent one, since we already have one—Bukharin's platform.'

Here Sheboldaev was interrupted by delegates shouting from
the floor of the hall: 'But these are obvious counter-revolutionaries!' He continued, 'Yes, they are obvious counter-
revolutionaries, and among them are Party members. You see,'
he remarked sarcastically, 'as Ulyanov writes, these people
started "wavering" and "doubting" the Party line on collectivisation of the land, industrialisation and wage matters. "As
a peasant by origin," Ulyanov said, "I am still unable to accept
the Party line on intensive collectivisation. I understand that
there are two methods of development, one capitalist, the
other socialist. I believe that for collectivisation to succeed we
need a technical base—tractors and so forth." ' 'I do not propose
to quote further,' concluded Sheboldaev, without protest from
his audience and to the great loss of historians of the period.

The most vicious attack on the opposition at the Congress
was reserved for the second intervention of E. Yaroslavsky, who
could be regarded as a precursor of Vyshinsky in formulating
the theory of the rightists' subversive underground activities.
'It is necessary to state,' said Yaroslavsky, 'that the right-
wingers were daydreaming of a wide bloc of oppositionist groups
of the type which the Trotskyites and the "Leningrad"
opposition* tried to bring together.' Yaroslavsky even quoted
from the deposition of a member of an organisation in the
North Caucasus calling itself (to the amazement of the Congress)
the Bureau of Right-Wing Deviationists. The quotation ran:
'In discussing the question of what kind of régime we should
have we came to the conclusion that: monarchy is a thing of
the past, anarchy has been defeated. The present-day Soviet
régime oppresses the people. What is most acceptable now is
the Right deviation—Bukharinite policy.' This quotation was

*Meaning the opposition of the Leningrad Party organisation led by
Zinoviev in 1926–27.

greeted with laughter, but not so the remark of Yaroslavsky's that followed it: 'These, Comrades, are facts which prove that whether Bukharin or Rykov desire it or not, the matter is reduced to the simple truth that if you start a row against the Central Committee of the Party, the one and only proletarian party, it means that your programme will tomorrow become the programme of a class hostile to the proletariat.'[6]

On 21 July Stalin rounded off the debate on the right-wing opposition by outlining to the Congress the role in which he had cast them.[7] It was a most revealing performance. Having terrorised the opposition by means of Vareikis' and Sheboldaev's denunciations, Stalin boasted that this pressure had produced the desired results—it had already brought the letter of repentance from Uglanov mentioned above. He said the oppositionists need not fear harsh treatment provided they agreed to do three things: first, recognise the abyss that divided their political line from that of the Party, by openly acknowledging that their policy was leading straight to capitalism; second, state explicitly that their policy was incompatible with Leninism (this, obviously, to counteract the effect of Bukharin's article 'The Political Testament of Lenin'); third, join the Party majority in the struggle against the right-wing deviationists (i.e. betray their own supporters). If they did all this, Stalin said, they need have nothing to fear. 'That is why I think all that talk of Comrade Tomsky's about someone wanting to send him to the Gobi Desert to eat locusts and wild honey is nothing but the empty patter of a provincial vaudeville act, having nothing in common with the dignity of a revolutionary.'

Stalin dismissed opposition objections to his agricultural policy in the same jeering way. 'Take, for instance, the question of extraordinary measures against the kulaks. Do you remember the fits of hysterics with which they were greeted [referring to the debates on grain requisitioning in 1928-29]? And now we are carrying out a policy of liquidating the kulaks as a class, compared with which the extraordinary measures against the kulaks were a mere trifle. Well, what of it? We are still alive.'

So he was; so were the millions of peasants who were to die in the 1932 famine caused by the collectivisation drive; so were the oppositionists who were to be shot eight years after the 16th Congress for trying to avert this disaster.

The mood of the Congress was certainly hostile to the opposition, but this did not affect elections to the Party organs—Bukharin, Rykov and Tomsky were all elected to the Central Committee. But the speeches of Vareikis and Sheboldaev foreshadowed not only the purge of right-wing deviationists, which assumed mass dimensions in the autumn of 1930, but also the situation that arose in the Party in 1934.* Towards the end of 1930 a new drive was launched against right-wing and other deviationists which surpassed in intensity anything previously seen. Among other victims of the Party purge (for the time being, it did not always entail arrests) were such staunch Stalinists as Lominadze and Syrtsov. Lominadze had been one of Stalin's chief agitators behind the scenes at the 6th World Congress of the Third International, but was now expelled from the Party along with Syrtsov for deviationist views. At the same time the campaign of terror against the intellectuals was stepped up, and the theory of large-scale sabotage by the class enemy was reinforced by the trial of members of the Industrial Party.†

*We shall return to these speeches when analysing the trial proceedings.
†The 'Industrial Party' (*Prompartiya*) was itself one of the great achievements of Vyshinsky's political mythomania. When, in the late twenties, a large number of intellectuals (economists and engineers) who helped to run the Soviet economy were subjected to a wave of terror, they were accused not merely of sabotage but also of collusion with the capitalist powers and anti-Soviet Russian émigrés; gradually the unfounded and almost wholly unbelievable notion of a conspiratorial, anti-Soviet, 'Industrial Party' took shape during a number of trials culminating in the trial of the 'Industrial Party' itself (25 November to 7 December 1930). The five principal accused, who all confessed, including the scholar and engineer Ramzin, were sentenced to death, but had the sentence reduced to ten years' imprisonment. During the Second World War Ramzin, by then a free man, was awarded the Stalin Prize for outstanding services to the motherland.

The 16th Congress adopted without protest Stalin's plan for the total collectivisation of agriculture, the first 'experimental' instalment of which was carried through in the North Caucasus. Rykov was denounced for his ambiguous attitude towards the plan by a certain I. Schmidt in *Pravda*.[8] On 19 November he was downgraded to the post of People's Commissar for Communications (equivalent to that of Postmaster-General) and stayed there until 1936, when Yagoda succeeded him. The North Caucasus experiment might have made it impossible for Rykov to remain in a post where he would have to share responsibility for the campaign. This is suggested by the fact that the day after his demotion, *Pravda* published an article by another member of the Politburo, Andreev, boasting of the success of collectivisation in the Northern Caucasus. Simultaneously with his demotion from what was nominally the post of premier, Rykov left the chairmanship of the Council for Labour and Defence which he had held from the inception of that body in 1918.

Even at this late stage in 1930, protests were still being voiced by some oppositionists. It was reported for instance that on 16 November Uglanov, then in exile in Astrakhan, had objected to the description of the Right opposition as 'unprincipled', and denied cooperating with the Trotskyites. But as time went on public protests of this kind became impossible. The country was in a state of civil war induced by the coercive methods used in collectivisation,[9] and all overt criticism of the Party line was at once denounced as giving comfort to the class enemy. By the end of 1930, all opposition seemed to have been finally driven underground. Most of the left-wing oppositionists had been sent into exile; the right-wing oppositionists on the other hand, both those expelled from the Party and those who had lost their state and Party posts, were absorbed into the swelling ranks of industrial management. A number of them were helped to find such posts by Ordzhonikidze, who although to all appearances fully supporting Stalin in the Politburo (to which he was himself promoted in 1930) still extended his protection to victims of the purge. Bukharin himself was given a job in the Ministry of Heavy Industry then headed by Ordzhonikidze. Buber-Neumann reports that he assisted Lominadze when the latter was expelled.[10]

In the next two years Stalin's economic policy (and especially the implementation in four years of the Five-Year Plan and wholesale collectivisation) played havoc with the economic life of the country. The full story of the resulting disorganisation, particularly to industry, has now been told by N. Jasny.[11] More has also come to light through the study of documents from the Smolensk Party archives which fell into German hands during the Second World War and were salvaged by the United States Army.[12] This source reveals the catastrophic effect of the organised starvation of rural populations over large areas, of mass deportations and of the systematic dispersal of families, involving hundreds of thousands of households and millions of people.

The oppositionists' worst fears were realised in 1932, when they saw the results of Stalin's policy exceed their gloomiest prognostications. We know little about their attempts to organise resistance to this totalitarian administration run amok. They may have united in small groups to discuss how to stop the growing madness. Such evidence of this as is provided by the great trials must however be treated with circumspection. The information published in Trotsky's *Bulletin of Opposition* would seem equally biased and exaggerated, although many of those who emigrated from Russia after the Second World War also claim that such pockets of resistance existed. As Stalin's 'revolution from above' developed, many of those not actually involved in opposition must have sympathised with the men who had prophesied disaster and suffered demotion in consequence. In the face of the vast calamity that befell the country in 1932 even the sharp contradictions between the Right and Left oppositions must have faded to some extent. But much of what Stalin was doing had been advocated in somewhat milder form by the left-wing oppositionists. It is no coincidence that just as Bukharin and Rykov were being exposed as deviationists left-wingers like Serebryakov, Drobnis and others were beginning to publish their recantations and sue for readmission to the Party. Contemporaries have compared the situation in 1932 to the crisis leading up to the Kronstadt revolt; this time, though, the whole country was involved. A revolutionary situation was ripening, and any group determined to lead a popular uprising might have stood a chance of success.

In this turmoil the position of leading right-wing oppositionists was doubly precarious. On the one hand their influence in the supreme organs of the Party and state was waning, although they were never completely eclipsed. Social changes they had all desired were being brought about without their participation and by methods they regarded as highly prejudicial to the resulting social order. On the other hand among the people, and even more among rank-and-file members of the Party and administration, their prestige must have increased considerably. They had predicted the disastrous consequences of Stalin's policy, and those who had been carrying it into practice could note its effects on the population at close quarters, and must gradually have become 'crypto-Bukharinites'. We know from Sheboldaev's speech at the 16th Congress what a Party worker could think in 1931. It was even easier to think that way in 1932 and 1933. Bukharin himself had retired from active politics and become head of the Research Department of the Ministry of Heavy Industry, where he published philosophical essays on the economic and social effects of technical progress. His position gave him the opportunity to travel to the large provincial centres and to place his followers in various points of vantage in industry. His own experience and the reports he received from supporters all over the country must have shown him a tragic picture. Words were thus hardly necessary to effect an understanding between a critical and thinking official in a provincial town and a visiting ex-oppositionist like

Bukharin. At the trial with which we are concerned another defendant, Ikramov, described a similar meeting with Bukharin in Moscow.[13] The prosecution tried to represent the unspoken understanding between them as seditious conversations and plotting.

The realisation that so many people were moved to the same reasonable and decent outrage at Stalin's recklessness may have lulled the opposition leaders into a false sense of security. They seemed to hope that Stalinism would blow over, like a storm. The chaos caused by the constant 'stepping-up of the class war', the ruinous result of interfering with traditional methods of agricultural production, the frustrations aroused by increased interference from Moscow in the affairs of the union republics, and all the other consequences of Stalin's policy would sooner or later (they argued) lead to the overwhelming rejection of his régime. And then in spite of a disastrous start the socialist order could be established on a workable basis and the achievements of the October Revolution be salvaged. Nurturing such hopes, the majority of the opposition thought it madness to organise resistance to Stalin's social and economic campaigns, or to rouse popular support for such resistance. Such action, in their view, could only lead to an intensification of what Stalin called the class struggle, to further arrests and purges of 'class enemies', 'saboteurs' and 'foreign agents', perhaps even to civil war and counter-revolution.

In considering the accusations made at the trial that the right-wing leaders were directing underground agitation and sabotage, we should remember that whatever the truth in these charges the overt conduct of the opposition leaders was to accept their political defeat and pay lip service to the success of Stalin's line. By this means they hoped to work their way back into policy-making positions in the Party. As the immediate crisis passed, many of them imagined their strategy to be successful. Gradually a number of oppositionists of both left and right wings were brought back to the capitals, and given jobs in the less sensitive departments of the administration.

Bukharin as a young man

2. Tomsky in 1925   3. Rykov, c. 1930

4. Lenin's funeral : Kamenev, Tomsky, Zinoviev, Bukharin, Kalinin

In this they were helped by a number of men who had survived the purge of 1929-32. Possibly Stalin himself, faced with mounting difficulties, thought it best to call a halt to Party warfare and prevent the demoted Communist leaders from linking up with disaffected sections of the Party and populace.

The 17th All-Party Congress of 1934 was the outward manifestation of this precarious truce. Once again leaders of both oppositions indulged in a war of words which must have gratified Stalin: he had always maintained that oppositionists were most useful when they exposed one another's mistakes, so that his own middle road stood out as the only reasonable policy.* Kamenev admitted in a long speech that the Kamenev who had opposed the Party and its leadership between 1925 and 1933 was a political corpse, whereas he, the true Kamenev, having abjured his errors and sloughed off his old skin, would march forward with the rest of the Party. At the same time as he renewed his quarrel with Bukharin Kamenev even enlarged the scope of his self-accusations. According to his analysis the difficulties the Party had just overcome were caused not solely by him but by the combination of Trotskyites and rightists to which he had 'opened the floodgates'. The left-wing opposition as a whole had opened the floodgates to successive waves of the counter-revolutionary peril. The first wave was Trotskyism, 'that typical ideology of the petit-bourgeois intelligentsia, with its blend of revolutionary phrases and profoundly counter-revolutionary essence'.[14] The second wave, to which Kamenev confessed he had personally 'opened the floodgates', was the kulak ideology. Here he made an allusion to his conversations of 1928 with Bukharin that was later used against both of them.

I refer to the negotiations I entered into in 1928 with the representative of the rightists, Comrade Bukharin. We are

*Particularly in his speeches on the opposition at the 15th Party Conference.

F

not concerned now with formalities, but with the essence of this matter*—that is, with the question of being faced with the typical ideology of the kulak, who, terrified by the proletarian offensive, attempts to salvage what is left of his position. The rightists' utopian theory of the 'acclimatisation of the kulak to socialism'—a concept utterly ridiculous from a theoretical point of view, theoretical gibberish, a concept contradicting the most fundamental principles of Marxism— meant under existing class conditions an attempt by the kulak to defend himself against proletarian dictatorship. It meant that the kulak, with the rightists as his mouthpiece, said: 'Do not touch me; I will become acclimatised,' while in fact thinking: 'Do not touch me; I will engulf the proletarian dictatorship.'

And, Kamenev declared, his sycophancy becoming even more explicit:

Comrades, if this *bloc* of our group with Comrade Bukharin has not been allowed to develop, has not become a new and loathsome malady of our party, it is due exclusively to the vigilance of the Central Committee, to the theoretical maturity of its leader Comrade Stalin—to his ideological intransigence, emulating the best aspects of the ideological personality of Lenin. Only this ideological intransigence, which at once exposed this *bloc* and revealed to the Party as a whole its real class significance, made it possible to nip it in the bud.[15]

---

*In opposing the 'formalities', the 'essence' of the Bukharin-Kamenev conversations, Kamenev was foreshadowing the trials, at which the defendants accepted the prosecution's gloss on a particular event as equivalent to a literal description of it. By maintaining that the defence of the kulak was the 'essence' of the talks, Kamenev sought to forestall Bukharin, who on purely 'formalistic' grounds would have been quite justified in saying that the kulak question did not even enter into the talks.

Rykov also contributed to the theory of the class origin of the Right opposition when he said that one of the obstacles the Party had encountered on the thorny road between the 16th and 17th Congresses was right-wing deviationism, 'of which I was one of the leaders, and which is an agency of the petit-bourgeois and kulak strata in our country, resisting the socialist offensive of the Party and the working class.'[16]

Bukharin's speech to the Congress is perhaps even harder to fathom than the confessions of Kamenev and Rykov. He avoided identifying himself with 'an agency of the petit-bourgeois and kulak strata.' Yet he admitted that 'Comrade Stalin was entirely right when by a brilliant use of Marxist-Leninist dialectics* he destroyed a number of theoretical assumptions of right-wing deviationism formulated first and foremost by myself'. After listing these, he continued: 'It is clear that Stalin was right in smashing every manifestation of fractional activity based on the theories of the Right opposition, and right in destroying it root and branch.' Bukharin further admitted that, after the rightist leaders had recanted, underground groups still continued to function, tending indeed to become progressively more counter-revolutionary. They included a number of Bukharin's former pupils, who had been 'punished', he said, 'as they deserved'. It was the duty of every Party member to combat such groups, and to rally round 'that incarnation of the will and intelligence of our Party, Comrade Stalin'. He ended by professing his faith in the victory won through the comradeship-in-arms of courageous revolutionaries, led by the glorious Field-Marshal of all proletarian forces, of the 'best of the best', Comrade Stalin.[17] Bukharin was one of the few former oppositionist speakers to receive the plaudits of the assembly.

---

*Bukharin's allusion to Stalin's dialectical brilliance looks like flattery with a sting in the tail. It sounds like a reference to the part of Lenin's testament in which Lenin cast doubt on Bukharin's understanding of dialectics. In his speech at the plenum of April 1929, Stalin had made use of this passage in order to discredit Bukharin.

It is doubtful whether Stalin was taken in by such flattery. Bukharin's speech betrayed a considerable difference in tone from the currently-accepted propaganda jargon. He equated the struggle for socialism with the struggle for technical, scientific and cultural progress, for the happiness of mankind. To talk of Stalin as 'the mighty harbinger of technical and scientific progress on our planet' had a slightly ironical ring, even then. Again, the extravagances of the Hitler régime gave Bukharin the chance to attack certain totalitarian symptoms without direct reference to Stalin or his régime. He quoted National-Socialist writers—one Hilscher, for example, who had written: 'To become more rustic means to become poorer and more primitive, perhaps wilder and more barbaric, but at the same time more Germanic. Barbarism is its own justification.' In a country where cases of cannibalism had recently occurred in the villages and even been reported in the press, this was rather a daring allusion. Bukharin went further. He quoted the Nazi poet Jost: 'The people ask for priest-leaders who let flow blood, blood, yet more blood, who thrust and stab!' 'That', he said, repeating the quotation in German, 'is the bestial face of the class enemy'.

The speeches of the opposition leaders found a curious echo in the words of Kirov, the last speaker in the debate on the report of the Central Committee. Kirov pointed out the plight of the oppositionists: they were like soldiers of an advancing army who had sat out the decisive battle in the rear, he said. Now that only 'mopping-up' operations remained to be done, they tried to join in the triumphal procession; but 'they are out of tune; they are out of step'.[18] Kirov, whilst professing sympathy for these men in their predicament, warned the Party rank and file by his metaphor not to fall into the same trap as these pathetic and slightly contemptible figures. He also warned them against being intolerant of criticism, and quoted Stalin as his authority. Those who engaged in self-criticism, said Kirov, should not be afraid to carry their heart-searching to the limit. 'It can do no harm; it can only help to repair the damage.'

The implication is clear. After the struggles of the last few years a new life had suddenly become possible, in which there was room for everyone. To confess past mistakes was no longer dangerous.

After the standard hymns of praise to the victory of socialism, the abject confessions of oppositionists lured into repentance, Kirov's speech, with its buoyant ring, took the Congress by surprise. With the high spirits of one who has surmounted a crisis and feels himself invigorated by it, he exclaimed: 'Our successes have indeed been great. By God, to say it in a human way, how glorious it is to live and be alive!' There is something of the Karamazovs in Kirov's zest for life; it seems the more intense because these words were spoken before his death a mere ten months later.

6. The Kirov murder and its consequences

Nineteen-hundred and thirty-four could be described as the year in which an attempt was made to restore some kind of normality to Soviet political life. There were many reasons for this. Hitler's rise to power in Germany brought with it the threat of a major conflagration in the face of which even Stalin could no longer afford to preach unlimited class warfare. Some sort of national unity was an obvious prerequisite for the conduct of a successful war policy, and Stalin could not publicly dispense with the services of the many able 'old' Bolsheviks who, having repented of their sins, were now ready to bury the hatchet and help repel the Fascist onslaught. Henceforth he could prolong his feud with the various oppositions only by claiming that they were in the Fascist camp, i.e. by accusing them of outright, conscious collaboration with Hitlerite Germany. But both Left and Right oppositionists were convinced that the Soviet Union and the world Communist movement were the irreconcilable enemies of all Fascist régimes, the stoutest defenders of the ideals of human progress and the ordained leaders of the peoples of the globe against Nazism. This throughout the thirties was the basis of Litvinov's official line in the League of Nations, and a source of the appeal of Popular Front movements. It was a dominant theme of the Soviet press, where Radek and Bukharin were its star propagandists. The governments of the Western democracies were denounced for their policy of appeasement, and the masses were advised to look East for a lead in the struggle against the Nazi and Fascist peril.

In internal politics, a similar closing of ranks and relaxation of tensions could be observed. The excesses of the collectivisa-

tion campaign had left even convinced Communists exhausted
—some disappointed and ashamed as well. Even men such as
Kirov, who purported to look on forced collectivisation as a
historical necessity, were resolved that nothing of the kind
should ever happen again. Meanwhile the new industrial and
agricultural structure that had sprung into being required a
great deal of organising, and the younger generation of Soviet
intellectuals went to work with a will. Kirov was to a certain
extent its spokesman. He was also, as we have seen from his
speech of the 17th Congress, a potential peacemaker. Unlike
Stalin, he harboured no personal grudge against the oppositionists, had no skeleton like Lenin's testament to hide in the
cupboard. Nor had he any obvious reason to fear Stalin,
whom he had backed throughout both the political struggles
of the late twenties and the industrialisation and collectivisation campaigns. His support of Stalin, while it certainly compromised him in the eyes of the public, could only raise his
standing within the Party since it ruled out accusations of
'demagogy', i.e. of courting the popularity of the wavering
masses. His success at the 17th Congress was spectacular; he
got an ovation as impressive as that arranged for Stalin. His
assurance to those who courageously fulfilled their duty of
self-criticism that they had nothing to fear was a bold attempt
to win the approbation of all sections of the Party. His line
seemingly prevailed, for the new Central Committee elected at
the Congress reflected all shades of Party opinion.

The 17th Congress also introduced certain changes into the
workings of the Party constitution. As the late Boris
Nicolaevsky pointed out in his article[1] on the Kirov murder,
the post of General Secretary was apparently not renewed, and
Stalin, the last incumbent, was elected merely as one of a
number of Party secretaries. He certainly suffered no public
eclipse at the Congress, which was staged after all as a
triumphal celebration of his policy. Nevertheless a good deal
of the triumphant talk may well have been conscious hypocrisy.
Many of those who lauded Stalin's victory in the struggle for

socialism may have hoped in creating for him a position as a kind of supra-political figurehead that he would now prove unable to launch out on insane policies, or pursue private vendettas by influencing Party elections and appointments.

The work of the new Central Committee proceeded more or less smoothly all through 1934. But this, it was felt, was merely a beginning; a definitive return to normality would require some major constitutional act to restore legality and scotch all attempts to rekindle class strife. In November 1934 the Central Committee decided to transfer Kirov from his position as Leningrad Party boss to Moscow. It was intended that he should play an active role here in the work of the CC Secretariat, a body hitherto completely dominated by Stalin. On 1 December 1934, following his return to Leningrad, Kirov was killed by a Party member, Nikolayev, in his office in the Smolny. This act of terrorism produced a tremendous impression, and its repercussions were immeasurable. The pistol-shot in the Smolny can only be compared in terms of world politics with the shot in Sarajevo.*

In terms of intra-Party strife it opened up the era of the great trials. The charges levelled against the oppositionists largely duplicated those they had already faced at earlier Party congresses, but before the trials they had not been liable to extreme interpretations. Then the Party had refused to treat opposition leaders as counter-revolutionaries, although it had tolerated mud-slinging tantamount to charges of counter-revolution. The banishment, deportation and execution of

*In introducing this bold comparison we wish to convey that, if the policy of Party reunification introduced in 1934 had triumphed, such Party leaders as Kamenev, Zinoviev, Radek and Bukharin would never have tolerated a pact with Germany, and the Second World War might not have become inevitable. Boris Nicolaevsky goes even further, tending to interpret the *Yezhovshchina* and the purges as a necessary prerequisite of the radical change which took place in Soviet foreign policy in 1939. Without going so far we must agree that had the opposition remained active, the Molotov-Ribbentrop pact could hardly have come into existence.

oppositionists certainly took place even before Kirov's murder, but always on some such pretext as bourgeois-nationalist deviation, conniving with foreign secret services, or sabotage. The mere fact of being an oppositionist did not in itself make a Party member guilty of these crimes, or place him on a par with such flagrant counter-revolutionaries as former White Army officers, for example. At the Congresses accusations of 'counter-revolution' sounded like hollow threats, they lacked vitality. The vitality was provided by a transfusion of Kirov's blood.

The murder marked the beginning of a campaign of terrorism by the régime in which the show trials were merely episodes. The question is, who started the campaign? The theories that have been advanced can be grouped under three headings. According to the first theory (Stalin's official one), the murder was the result of the combined propaganda and organisational efforts of all the existing opposition groups, the Trotskyites included. Among those charged at successive trials with having prepared, perpetrated or assisted in the crime were agents of foreign powers, Trotskyites, left-wing deviationists, right-wing deviationists, and followers of all these who had infiltrated into the security services. The number of people shot for alleged participation, whether direct or indirect, in the murder must have run into several thousands.

The Stalin theory does not hold water, however. That terrorist ideas were current just then in oppositionist circles is very plausible. That they should have been directed against a man like Kirov is wholly fanciful. The oppositionists, whether of Left or Right, could have nothing to lose from Kirov's growing power in the Party and government. True, Kirov was Zinoviev's successor in the Leningrad organisation, and he sometimes showed a strong hand there. But the venom of the leftists' resentment was reserved for Stalin; to perpetrate an act of terrorism against one of Stalin's closest aides would have seemed to them the height of folly, if only for the reason that it would instantly have betrayed any plan to assassinate Stalin himself.

The second theory, advanced by Ouralov, is that the assassination was a typical *crime passionel*. Kirov is said to have had an affair with the extremely attractive wife of Nikolayev. The jealous husband surprised them together, and shot Kirov on the spot.[2] This story does not agree with such facts as can be ascertained. The murder took place in Kirov's office—some reports say in his study, others in an adjacent corridor, neither place one where Nikolayev could easily surprise a pair of lovers. Ouralov also says Nikolayev had returned from an assignment in the north immediately before committing the murder. This is contradicted by two independent sources, both of whom favour yet a third theory.

According to this version Kirov's assassination was planned by the Leningrad GPU on instructions from higher authority. This was directly alleged by Khrushchev (assuming the US State Department's version of his secret speech to be authentic). 'There are reasons for the suspicion,' Khrushchev is reported as saying, 'that the killer of Kirov, Nikolayev, was assisted by someone from among the people whose duty it was to protect the person of Kirov. A month and a half before the killing Nikolayev was arrested on the grounds of suspicious behaviour, but he was released and not even searched.' Khrushchev goes on to reveal that the day after the murder, Kirov's personal bodyguard was killed in suspicious circumstances, 'in a road accident in which no other occupants of the car were harmed.'[3] Khrushchev's theory, which must be well founded, is singularly corroborated by the evidence of Elizabeth Lermolo in a book written before Khrushchev made his speech.[4] Lermolo claims, as did Bulanov in his confession at the Bukharin trial,[5] that this bodyguard, a certain Borisov, died in a car crash while being taken to be interrogated by Stalin. She says that Nikolayev, exasperated by the petty persecution of the Leningrad security organs, had been led to believe that Kirov was at the root of his troubles. She names a GPU officer, Rogachev, who was supposedly assigned to liquidate Kirov but was driven to suicide by the mental anguish this occasioned him. Finally she asserts (and other sources bear her out) that immediately after Kirov's murder and the passing of decrees to curb terrorist activity, Stalin went to Leningrad to supervise the investigations in person. The evidence of Khrushchev and Lermolo taken together seems to indicate that even if Stalin did not actually instigate the murder, he exploited it to break the political truce Kirov had obviously desired (though not achieved), and to renew the struggle against his enemies, this time to the death. If this is true Stalin took his time over the task; it was completed only in 1938, with the Bukharin trial and the few subsequent executions of prominent Bolsheviks disclosed for the first time in Khrushchev's secret speech.

Khrushchev's and Lermolo's revelations throw even more light on the Kirov murder if they are taken in conjunction with the evidence put forward at the trials. As the purge developed, the role of the security organs in the murder grew increasingly apparent. The Leningrad office of the GPU was not only implicated, it was said to have acted on direct instructions from Moscow. Yagoda admitted that he had issued instructions not to prevent an act of terrorism against Kirov,[6] claiming to have done this at the behest of Yenukidze, of the 'Bloc of Rights and Trotskyites', and of Rykov in particular. By and large, however, he was markedly reticent on the whole affair, and was allowed to make a full statement on it only at a closed session of the court. This was not surprising: in mentioning Yenukidze (by then already liquidated without public trial) he was putting the onus for the murder on persons who had been very close to Stalin. Bearing in mind Khrushchev's remark that the investigation into the murder remains incomplete and also that it was conducted by Stalin in person (who went to Leningrad on 2 December and was there when Borisov died) the conclusion is well-nigh inescapable that Stalin had some reason for concealing the truth about the crime. We still do not know whether he wanted merely an *attempted* assassination to set the purge in motion or whether he was anxious to eliminate in Kirov a potentially dangerous rival. Whatever the solution to these questions, the great trials can never be understood completely until there has been a full and honest enquiry into the circumstances of Kirov's death. This seems also to have been the view of Khrushchev, when he declared at the 22nd Congress that:

> Now, as they say, we cannot bring the dead back to life, but it is necessary that all this be recorded truthfully in the history of the Party. This must be done so that phenomena of this sort can never be repeated in the future. (*Stormy, prolonged applause.*)
>
> You can imagine how difficult it was to solve these questions when the Presidium of the Central Committee included people who had themselves been guilty of abuses of power, of mass repressions.[7]

Intra-party strife was resumed on the very day of Kirov's murder with the enactment of special regulations for dealing with acts of terrorism. Under their provisions Zinoviev, Kamenev, Bakaev and Evdokimov, all prominent left-wing oppositionists, were arrested almost immediately, brought to trial after a short investigation and convicted of creating a moral atmosphere conducive to the murder. They were given the relatively mild sentence of ten years' imprisonment. The lightning blow struck against the leftists must have served as a warning to other oppositionists not to toy with terrorist ideas. On the other hand, the comparative leniency of the punishment meted out to Kamenev and Zinoviev may well have been intended to convey the impression that Kirov's policy of reconciliation was not to be abandoned. Stalin indeed claimed that the normalisation campaign would continue, and that other oppositionists not directly inculpated would play a prominent part in it. The means of achieving this normalisation was to be the new Soviet constitution. This was to abolish the differences in legal status between the former classes by officially announcing the emergence of a society in which mutually antagonistic classes had been superseded. It was to provide guarantees of individual freedom and personal security immeasurably superior to those existing in any other country in the world. In February 1935 the Seventh All-Union Congress of Soviets elected a commission to draft this constitution. It included both Radek and Bukharin who actively participated in the work under the chairmanship of Stalin. In view of what actually took place a year later when the constitution was introduced, the commission appears to have been ingeniously devised by Stalin to divert the energies of his opponents. These must have hoped in vain that a legal order would now emerge in which they could pursue their own policies whilst protected by constitutional safeguards.

The oppositionists were thus lulled into a false sense of security. At the same time they were given every opportunity to compromise themselves through their contributions to the daily press. Such seemingly innocuous matters as the denunciation of Fascism in Germany, Italy and later Spain gave ample scope to their journalistic temperaments. Bukharin continued to maintain his contacts with such high officials in the provinces as secretly shared his views; but he was deprived of the help of the majority of his disciples, whose active support of him in 1932 and 1933 had led to their being arrested without so much as a public protest on his part—even, as we have seen, with his approval.[8] When in 1936 the constitution was about to be published in draft form, a nation-wide discussion on it opened in all the papers. By that time, however, Bukharin was already aware that it was going to be a great deception.

In the spring of 1936 something happened which casts light on the bizarre relationship subsisting between Stalin and his adversaries. Bukharin, with Stalin's express permission, was sent abroad to negotiate the purchase of archive material for the Marx-Engels-Lenin Institute with émigré Menshevik circles and German Social Democrat exiles. In view of what happened some two or three months later this assignment must be regarded as an ingenious trap. Bukharin, however, as we shall

see, did not fall into it as completely as Stalin probably hoped
he would. Full of lively impressions, he returned to Moscow,
where the radiant official prophecies of a new era ushered in
by the constitution contrasted grimly with a campaign of
mounting terror.

Though nominally editor of *Izvestiya,* Bukharin can hardly
be held responsible for all its leading articles. The contrast
between his approach to Soviet reality and that of the official
propagandists is illustrated by the last signed article he ever
published. It appeared in *Izvestiya* on 6 July 1936, known as
the Day of Stalin's Constitution, and was entitled 'Highways
of History—Thinking Aloud'.[9] It began by deploring the fact
that the real importance of Stalin's constitution was not
universally grasped:

> Everybody is talking about Stalin's constitution. It is the
> sensation of the day, the greatest political event of our time.
> Those who are used to petty gossip on the lines of 'the dog
> bays at the moon' would like to see in it only a clever
> manœuvre, because they weigh everything up on their miser-
> able shopkeepers' scales. But every serious person realises that
> we are dealing with the political expression of a colossal
> change in the entire inner structure of our nation and its
> life.

He went on to describe the consolidation of Soviet society, of
the Soviet nation, of the 'monolithic Party' and of the 'single
and united Stalinist leadership'. He ridiculed those who maintained that it was impossible to achieve socialism in one
country; they were deluded, he said, by a false conception of
history. 'Real history is not that symbolised as Fate, the master
of gods and men; real history is made by live men, by millions
of these live men,' and this real history had made possible
the creation of a socialist state the very existence of which had
become a factor of the greatest international significance. 'Anyone with the least historical sense' realised that the original,

best-organised, most consistent fighter against Fascism was the USSR. This was a fundamental fact of international politics.

Bukharin's article attacked the Russian émigré group known as the Eurasians (*Evraziitsy*), whose adherents combined a geopolitical theory of a Eurasian sub-continent with Slavophile and Pan-Russian traditions. To this he opposed his own concept of a Eurasia where 'the proletariat has become the vehicle of the national idea, where internationalism is the standard-bearer of national culture, where the Russian people, through its proletariat, has become the symbol of international brotherhood'. Carried away by his argument, Bukharin claimed that it was conservative Russian thinkers who had inspired the pseudo-academic group among the German Fascists. This gave him an opportunity to attack Fascist ideas. Fascism, he said, despite its claim to abolish classes, in fact reinforces the class mentality; this leads to a kind of 'apotheosis of the hero' indistinguishable from 'beastly bullying, oppression, violence and war'. Criticising Fascist régimes, Bukharin used the following remarkable and fateful phrase: 'A complicated network of decorative deceit in words and action is a highly essential characteristic of Fascist régimes of all stamps and hues.' He then proceeded to contrast the Fascist with the socialist society:

We must not forget that the most crucial moment in history is the moment of historical change in the human being himself. On the type of human being depends his actions and his 'effectiveness'.

Thus we may affirm that Fascism, with all its attempts at organisation, creates a depersonalised mass subject to a blind discipline, to the cult of Jesuitical obedience, to the oppression of the intellectual faculties.

Socialism exalts the mass as a complex unit, constantly enriching the content of the personality and increasing its thinking capacity.

So, concluded Bukharin, the socialist masses, 'which have ceased to be mere talking slaves, *instrumenta vocalia*, and have become a conscious mass of conscious personalities, will be able to attain and indeed surpass the achievement of every other country in the world'.

The article concludes with a mild panegyric of Stalin and of his successes in the field of industrialisation and collectivisation—poor amends for its concealed insolence and subtle innuendoes. For Bukharin was in fact telling those who were able to read between the lines that there were people capable of seeing through Stalin's latest fraud—the introduction of 'the world's most democratic constitution'. He was equating Stalin's régime with the 'Fascist régimes of all stamps and hues', régimes characterised by their 'complicated network of decorative deceit'. He was declaring that the anti-Fascist attitude of the Soviet Union was an immutable one, which enabled it to give a lead to the nations resisting Nazism; finally, he was condemning Stalin's concept of discipline and of the necessity to sacrifice the intellect to the state. In short the article was really saying that Stalin's régime was a Fascist régime, and that socialism would conquer in spite of, not because of it.

Six weeks later the first show trial, that of Kamenev and Zinoviev, took place. Bukharin said nothing. Radek published panicky articles confessing his former links with the accused and with Trotsky, and protesting that he had mended his ways. Bukharin said never a word, not even when factory meetings started to pass resolutions asking for a complete investigation into his own and Rykov's associations with the 'condemned monsters'. Ouralov has alleged that at a plenary meeting of the Central Committee Bukharin succeeded in defending himself. It was after this meeting, according to Ouralov, that a notice appeared stating that he and Rykov had been cleared of suspicion.[10]

Bukharin's name was printed on the masthead of *Izvestiya* until 16 January, 1937. A week later the second trial began, and new accusations were levelled at Bukharin and Rykov.

5. Kamenev

6. Zinoviev

7. The Trial building

Bukharin must have been already under arrest by then, and little was heard of him until his appearance at the trial. The only reliable clue to what became of him after his arrest is provided by an indiscretion of Khrushchev's. Khrushchev was one of the most vocal leaders of the 'hate campaign' against the defendants, using the rostrum of the Moscow Party organisation which he then headed in order to attack them. *Izvestiya* reported on 17 March 1937 that the decisions of a plenary meeting which took place at the beginning of the month had been discussed at a session of Moscow Party activists held from 12 to 16 March. At this session Khrushchev again attacked those accused in the second trial, and said Rykov and Bukharin had both been present at the plenum. 'But,' he said, 'they came to the plenum to deceive . . . they did not tread the path of repentance.' And he concluded that the Party was now entitled to deal with them 'as the interests of the revolution require'.

G

PART II

The trial

7. The prosecutor and his case

Viewed in historical perspective, the Moscow trials of 1936-38 marked Stalin's final victory over his political opponents. All of them were closely interconnected. Both the Kamenev-Zinoviev trial (August 1936) and later the Pyatakov trial (January 1937) foreshadowed that of Bukharin and his twenty co-accused. The proceedings against Bukharin were said to be the last of their kind. The gradual unfolding of the prosecution's case, the accumulation of charges, the choice of the accused—all these point to the fact that the trials were planned as a whole, and were intended to continue until all coherent political opposition to Stalin had been destroyed. It is possible, however, that the proceedings against Pyatakov were for some reason interposed between the trials of the Right and Left oppositions as a kind of intermediate stage, and were not foreseen in the original plan. The same may be true of the intervening massacre of Red Army generals in the summer of 1937 and the numerous executions without public trial, such as those of Yenukidze and Karakhan. The success of the first trial and its acceptance by a wide public may have encouraged Stalin and the state prosecutor to go further than they had originally intended, if not in the choice of the accused then in the gravity of the charges they made. By and large, however, the three public trials should be seen as a single manœuvre designed to establish the undisputed autocratic rule of Stalin.

The master mind behind the operation was the state prosecutor, Vyshinsky. Vyshinsky had studied at Kiev University before the revolution. His ambition to pursue an academic career was thwarted because of his revolutionary activities, and a prison sentence in 1905. He was a Menshevik, but joined the Bolshevik Party in 1920. He belonged to a small number of lawyers who, soon after the revolution, placed their talents at the disposal of the People's Commissariat of Justice. The place of law and legality in the revolutionary socialist régime was a subject of speculation and polemics. Vyshinsky, basing himself on a few quotations from Lenin, and later Stalin, maintained that state and law formed a necessary 'superstructure' during the socialist period of transition to Communism. But his main achievement lay in his forensic activities as a procurator assisting the far less intelligent, poorly-educated Krylenko (People's Commissar of Justice).

In 1946, before leaving his lawyer's career for the far more exalted one of diplomat and Minister of Foreign Affairs, Vyshinsky summed up his theory of legal proofs and judicial procedure in a work which was awarded the Stalin Prize, First Class. In this he claimed that the discovery of his new method of legal proof went back to the philosophical works of both Lenin and Stalin.

Our task in the legal field and particularly in procedural law does not consist in eliminating the [personal] conviction of the judge, which remains the most important and decisive factor in assessing proofs, trying to replace it by some mechanical force such as Bentham's thermometer of validity or Ferry's sphygmography,* but in grasping the real content, the actual process of the formation of the inner conviction of a judge, to assist this formation, and to secure the most favourable conditions for it.

This task can be properly and successfully fulfilled only on the basis of a really scientific methodology, of a real science. Such a really scientific methodology is dialectical materialism. Such a real science is Marxism-Leninism, the great teaching of Marx, Engels, Lenin and Stalin. Only on this basis can the doctrine of proofs be raised to the level of a

*Measurement of the pulse rate.

scientific theory, able to solve the tasks with which procedural law and practice are faced.[1]

There is more in Vyshinsky's writings in the same vein, praising the Marxist dialectical method as the 'granite foundation of science', and claiming that the Soviet (read : Vyshinsky's) legal theories go back to the revelations of Stalin's work on dialectical and historical materialism. What the application of this 'scientific method' amounts to is clear from a remark on page 233 of the book quoted above:

> It is inadmissible, on the other hand, to attempt to prove in court or during the investigation propositions which imply contentions which are considered immoral, politically harmful, criminal; for instance, to dispute in a Soviet court the anti-social character of a criminal act, the immorality of the exploitation of man by man, to try to prove the reasonableness of the capital system and its advantages over the socialist system.

Still, Vyshinsky claims that all that is best and scientifically validated in the procedural law of other nations has been adopted by Soviet procedural law and digested in accordance with the new historical requirements of the socialist state of workers and peasants. 'The Soviet system of proofs is based on the principle of the inner conviction, i.e. the socialist conviction, of the judge, armed with socialist legal consciousness, and truly scientific Marxist-Leninist methodology.'[2]

The 'true scientific method' visualised by Vyshinsky amounted to a wide application of indirect proofs of guilt. There is little theoretical justification for this in Vyshinsky's writings, but he was certainly a master at handling indirect proofs in court. In May 1936 his performance as a prosecutor was given wide publicity in the Soviet press in connection with a case of murder committed on Wrangel Island, far in the Arctic. Vyshinsky never tired of quoting himself and recalling his triumph at that trial, in which he demonstrated his ability to wrest confessions from defendants in the absence of direct material evidence or witnesses. Even before judgment in the case had been pronounced, *Izvestiya* commended him in the following terms: 'The vivid and convincing speech of the prosecutor was listened to with rapt attention. His profound analysis of the suspicious circumstances left no shadow of doubt about the guilt of the accused.'[3] Vyshinsky himself later cited his performance at the trial as a classic example of what the work of a public prosecutor should be.

Vyshinsky explicitly claimed the legitimacy of circumstantial evidence in cases of conspiracy against the state when he made his main speech at the Pyatakov trial, in January 1937:

> You cannot demand that cases of conspiracy, of *coup d'état*, be approached from the standpoint: give us minutes, decisions, membership cards, the numbers of your membership cards; you cannot demand that conspirators have their conspiratorial activities certified by a notary. No sensible man can put the question in this way in cases of state conspiracy. In fact we have a number of documents to prove our case. But even if these documents were not available, we would still consider it right to submit our indictment on the basis of the testimony and evidence of the accused and witnesses and, if you will, circumstantial evidence. In the present case I can quote such a brilliant authority on the law of evidence as the well-known old English jurist William Wills, who in his book on circumstantial evidence shows how strong circumstantial evidence can be, and how not infrequently circumstantial evidence can be much more convincing than direct evidence.[4]

Not only did Vyshinsky conduct the prosecution in person at the preliminary hearings and in court; he also remodelled the Institute of the State Prosecutor's Office so that it could handle the legal side of the purge efficiently. On 1 June 1936, in connection with the discussions on the constitution, he published in *Izvestiya* an article proposing certain juridical reforms relevant to the conduct of legal terror. Having praised the Soviet judicial system as one based on the principle of proletarian democracy, administered exclusively by the workers in the full light of publicity, he suggested a number of changes. The system could be improved by turning the law in defence of socialist property and that against treason to the motherland into the cornerstone of 'our entire criminal legislation'. The main guarantee of the accused, he said, would be the professional competence of the investigating judges. 'It is necessary to establish a firm rule whereby certain categories of legal case demanding specially complex investigation techniques are dealt with exclusively by the investigating judges.' With these changes, 'the newly reconstructed Soviet judiciary will continue to work selflessly to rid the Soviet nation of all sorts of crimes which bring shame on our motherland and impede the work of socialist construction'.

Vyshinsky's reorganisation of the judiciary met with some degree of opposition, both from Soviet legal theorists such as Pashukanis and more surprisingly from NKVD officials. In July 1936 a prominent Party member, Antonov-Saratovsky, published in *Pravda* an article entitled 'A People's Commissariat of Justice or a People's Commissariat of Tribunals'. It criticised the plan to let the State Prosecutor's office function independently of the Commissariat of Justice. Otherwise 'we would have only a lopsided People's Commissariat of Tribunals'.[5] Even more pointed was an article by an NKVD man, R. Katanyan, published as a 'contribution to a discussion' (a phrase which in effect absolved the editorial staff from responsibility for the author's views). Katanyan stated that sooner or later the question of admitting defence counsel at preliminary investigations would have to be squarely faced. Quoting Dicey's *Law of the Constitution,* he reminded his readers of *habeas corpus* and the principle of inviolability of the person—a principle which he said had long formed an integral part of Comrade Stalin's teaching. Vyshinsky, needless to say, never condescended to respond to these feeble attempts to defend liberal principles, contenting himself some months later with branding Pashukanis an enemy of the people.

As regards the organisation of the Prosecutor's Office, he was given the independent authority he wanted. In an interview published in *Izvestiya* on 17 November 1936, he explained the basis on which his office was organised, stating that a special department had been set up to inspect the work of the NKVD. This of course meant that in the last resort it was Vyshinsky who was responsible for the excesses of the security police under Yezhov.

From Vyshinsky's standpoint, the trial of Zinoviev and Kamenev (19-24 August 1936) was a success. The accused obligingly introduced the names of future victims, and on 21 August he was able to announce that in view of the court testimony implicating Rykov, Bukharin, Tomsky, Uglanov, Radek, Pyatakov, Serebryakov and Sokolnikov he had given orders that investigations into their activities should begin. Criminal proceedings against Sokolnikov and Serebryakov had already started, and the evidence against them ostensibly proved them guilty of counter-revolutionary crimes.

The investigation of Tomsky was never carried out, since he committed suicide while the Kamenev-Zinoviev trial was still in progress. That of Rykov and Bukharin was cancelled by the announcement, quoted earlier, which the State Prosecutor's Office issued on 10 September 1936. This said that no judicial basis for proceedings against them had been found, and that their case was therefore considered closed. The publication of Khrushchev's secret speech at the 20th Congress brings to light another explanation for the announcement. For Khrushchev disclosed that in a telegram Stalin and Zhdanov sent to Kaganovich and the Politburo on 25 September, they insisted that Yagoda be replaced by Yezhov. The telegram ran : 'We deem it absolutely necessary and urgent that Comrade Yezhov be nominated to the post of People's

Commissar for Internal Affairs. Yagoda has proved himself definitively incapable of unmasking the Trotskyite-Zinovievite bloc. The OGPU is four years behind in this matter. This is noted by all Party workers and by the majority of representatives of the NKVD.'[6] By this time the Trotskyite-Zinovievites of the first trial had been not merely exposed, but summarily executed, and those of the impending Pyatakov trial were under investigation. Yagoda's incompetence could therefore relate only to Bukharin and Rykov, who had temporarily eluded Vyshinsky's net. It was for the lease of freedom now granted them that Yagoda was being held responsible.

Khrushchev's secret speech suggests that there was a conflict of policy between Yagoda and Vyshinsky. Vyshinsky's carefully-worded announcement clearing Bukharin and Rykov stated:[7] 'The investigation has failed to establish a judicial basis for the proceedings against Bukharin and Rykov, and the legal investigations into the present case have consequently been dropped.' The expression 'has failed to establish . . .' etc., sounds like either an admission of inefficiency or (which is more likely) a charge of collusion. Vyshinsky was proclaiming Yagoda's inability (or unwillingness) to help him execute Stalin's plans for exterminating his political rivals. He had every reason to be furious with Yagoda for some of the slipshod evidence produced at the Kamenev-Zinoviev trial. The testimony regarding the Hotel Bristol in Copenhagen,* for instance, which must have been supplied by the NKVD, caused an international scandal very humiliating to him.[8] There was not much praise in the Soviet press for Yagoda's contribution to the investigation of Kamenev and Zinoviev; this contrasted sharply with the acclamation that greeted Yezhov after the third trial. We must therefore assume that a personal conflict existed between the state prosecutor and Yagoda; Vyshinsky naturally won, since it was he who was carrying out Stalin's plan. Yezhov replaced

---

*The Hotel Bristol had ceased to exist long before the meetings were alleged to have taken place there.

Yagoda as People's Commissar for Internal Affairs on 27 September 1936. Yagoda became Commissar for Communications in place of Rykov, who was relieved of this appointment without being given a new one. The next Commissar for Communications was appointed on 6 April 1937, and no mention of Yagoda was made on that occasion. He had been arrested a few days previously.

After the announcement of 10 September 1936, a fresh investigation into the case of Bukharin and Rykov could only be launched if some new and weighty piece of evidence materialised. The second trial, that of Pyatakov in January 1937, provided this. Both men were again shown (mainly through the testimony of Pyatakov and Radek) to be implicated in counter-revolutionary activities, this time even more seriously. In his final plea Radek said, 'I knew that Bukharin's position was just as hopeless as my own, because our guilt was the same, if not juridically, then in essence. But we are close friends . . .' and so on.[9] The accusations were left deliberately vague so as to allow full scope for elaboration by Vyshinsky, but the threads connecting Rykov and Bukharin to the convicted traitors were carefully exposed. Pyatakov, for instance, testified: 'I had had connections with Bukharin until 1934 . . . but when he was transferred to *Izvestiya* this connection passed to Radek. He maintained and continued counter-revolutionary connections with him.'[10] And Radek introduced the following remark into his evidence on the Kirov murder: 'Bukharin informed me that in their centre there were many who considered that it would be frivolous and cowardly to give up terrorism altogether because of the results of the Kirov murder.'[11]

A month after the Pyatakov trial ended, at the February-March plenum of the Central Committee, Bukharin and Rykov were expelled from the Party. Stalin's two speeches at the plenum are important to our understanding of further developments.

In his first speech he claimed the Trotskyites had been forced to conceal their programme: to have disseminated it openly would have alienated the masses. Why did Kamenev and Zinoviev deny they had any political platform? he asked. 'They feared such a platform would arouse the aversion of the working class.' The defendants at the second trial at least had the merit that they admitted their criminal schemes. Pyatakov, Radek and Sokolnikov had owned that they had a programme —one advocating the restoration of capitalism, the liquidation of the collective farms, the reintroduction of exploitation, the dismemberment of Russia, defeatism in the event of war, terrorist action against individual Soviet leaders and sabotage and espionage on behalf of Fascist states. They were naturally forced to conceal such a programme from the working class, and in so doing had ceased to lead a working-class political movement and degenerated into 'an unprincipled band of wreckers devoid of ideas, diversionists, intelligence agents, spies, murderers, a band of sworn enemies of the working class in the hire of the intelligence organs of foreign states'. Stalin summed up: 'Political leaders concealing their platform not only from the working class but from the Trotskyite rank and file, not only from the Trotskyite rank and file but from the Trotskyite upper leadership—such is the physiognomy of contemporary Trotskyism.'[12]

In his second speech, delivered on 5 March 1937 and published three weeks later (and it may be assumed in a carefully edited version), Stalin said the only difference between present-day wreckers and diversionists and the counter-revolutionary wreckers of the Shakhty trial* was that the latter had acted directly against the Party, whilst the former were bootlickers who tried to ingratiate themselves. It had become

---

*The Shakhty trial, in which forty-three mining engineers and officials from the Donbass were accused of sabotage and contacts with foreign powers, took place in May-July 1928. Eleven of the accused were sentenced to death, and the proceedings can be regarded as an early example of a show trial.

clear to everyone now that the present-day wreckers and diversionists, no matter what disguise they adopt, whether Trotskyite or Bukharinite, have long ceased to represent a political trend in the labour movement; they have been transformed into a gang of professional wreckers, diversionists, spies and assassins devoid of principles and ideals. These gentlemen must of course be ruthlessly crushed and extirpated as enemies of the working class, as traitors to our country. That is clear and needs no further explanation.[13]

This was the final blow that Stalin struck in person at his political opponents. The rest was left to the state prosecutor and the executioner. Stalin's analysis of the Pyatakov trial served as a blueprint for the last trial of March 1938. The words he used in his two speeches were echoed in Vyshinsky's perorations and in the official indictment. In accordance with his instructions, Vyshinsky kept a sharp look-out for attempts to introduce political discussions into the proceedings, and suppressed them at once. For example, when Rakovsky referred to the defeatist attitude of the opposition, the following exchange took place:

Vyshinsky: What opposition? When was that?

Rakovsky: This was in the middle of 1935, when Laval was on a visit to Moscow.

Vyshinsky: In this case what opposition are you talking about?

Rakovsky: I am talking both of the Rights and the Trotskyites.

Vyshinsky: But what kind of an opposition are they? They are a bandit gang of counter-revolutionaries.

Rakovsky: Citizen procurator, you must excuse me, for a long time this term . . . [dots in text].

Vyshinsky: In your explanations today you are generally permitting yourself to use quite a number of such expressions, as if you were forgetting that you are being tried here as a member of a counter-revolutionary, bandit, espionage, diversionist organisation of traitors. I consider it my duty to remind you of this ...[14]

A few days after Stalin made his speeches, as we have seen, the February-March plenum of the cc expelled Rykov and Bukharin from the Party. We learn from Khrushchev's indiscretion that both men were allowed to make a statement in their own defence, and were given an opportunity to endorse Stalin's indictment and repent of the crimes of which they were accused. But, as Khrushchev tells us, they were stubbornly unrepentant, and therefore had to be dealt with 'as the interests of the Revolution require'. According to another report,[15] they were brought into the cc meeting under guard. Bukharin is said to have denied all guilt and wept, rousing Stalin to the stinging comment, 'that is not the defence of a revolutionary. You must prove what you say, and that you can do equally well in prison.' Such behaviour seems incompatible with Bukharin's rather dignified and consistent manner at the trial a year later; Krivitsky confirms, however, that he refused to accede to Stalin's demand for total surrender. From then on he and Rykov were in the hands of the secret police.

All through 1937, Vyshinsky worked to assemble the evidence to substantiate the indictment outlined by Stalin. The *Yezhovshchina** was at its height; every citizen feared for his life as Vyshinsky's investigations gradually dragged in more and more people. Some of the defendants at the impending trial had to be induced to come home from abroad (Bessonov, in his final plea, described his unsuspecting return from Berlin in February 1937); others had to be removed from high positions in the Union republics, where they enjoyed the support of their local Central Committees (Khodjayev, Ikramov,

---

*The reign of terror that lasted from early in 1937 to August 1938 will go down in history under this name. Of the many thousands who perished without public trial, the majority were members of the Communist Party. The show trials were in a sense only the visible tip of the iceberg represented by the terror operations of the secret police.

Sharangovich). In the summer of 1937 there occurred the purge of the Red Army part of which was revealed by the announcement on 12 June of the execution of Tukhachevsky and other military leaders. Also arrested at this time was another prominent member of the CC who had been particularly close to Stalin, Abel Yenukidze. It was stated in the Bukharin indictment that Yenukidze had been tried on 15 December 1937; he was shot a few days later. His death and that of Tukhachevsky overshadowed the courtroom debates of March 1938. As convicted conspirators they were deemed to have been in league with the accused, and the secret proceedings against them must have played some part in the preparations for the show trial.

Another pre-trial arising from a complicated intrigue involving the medical staff of the Kremlin clinic went on all through the summer of 1937, in preparation for the charges of 'medical murder' to be brought at the trial. Again, a future co-defendant of Bukharin's, Bessonov,* was given a preliminary hearing *in camera* before a Moscow tribunal in August. When the trial finally opened in 1938, the general outline of the indictment and the arguments expounded by Vyshinsky were in accord with Stalin's directives of March 1937.

The trial lasted from 2 to 13 March 1938. The composition of the court was almost the same as it had been during the Pyatakov trial. It was presided over by V. V. Ulrich, President of the Military Collegium of the Supreme Court of the USSR, with I. O. Matulevich, Vice-President of the Collegium, and B. I. Yevlev, member of the Collegium, as his assistant judges. Yevlev was replacing N. M. Rychkov of the Pyatakov trial. Once again the prosecutor was Vyshinsky, and the defence was represented by I. D. Braude and M. V. Kommodov. None of these except Vyshinsky, and to some extent Ulrich, ever emerged from the background of the proceedings. There were twenty-one defendants:

*See below, pp. 120 ff., 219 ff.

Bukharin, Nikolai Ivanovich, born 1888
Rykov, Alexei Ivanovich, born 1881
Yagoda, Genrikh Grigorievich, born 1891
Krestinsky, Nikolai Nikolayevich, born 1883
Rakovsky, Khristian Georgievich, born 1873
Rosengoltz, Arkady Pavlovich, born 1889
Ivanov, Vladimir Ivanovich, born 1893
Chernov, Mikhail Alexandrovich, born 1891
Grinko, Grigori Fedorovich, born 1890
Zelensky, Isaac Abramovich, born 1890
Bessonov, Sergei Alexeyevich, born 1892
Ikramov, Akmal, born 1898
Khodjayev, Faizulla, born 1896
Sharangovich, Vasily Fomich, born 1897
Zubarev, Prokopy Timofeyevich, born 1886
Bulanov, Pavel Petrovich, born 1895
Levin, Lev Grigorievich, born 1870
Pletnev, Dmitry Dmitrievich, born 1872
Kazakov, Ignaty Nikolaevich, born 1891
Maximov-Dikovsky, Venyamin Adamovich
    (Abramovich), born 1900
Kryuchkov, Pyotr Petrovich, born 1889*

As at previous trials, the accused were persons of very different standing and calibre. The chief defendant was undoubtedly N. I. Bukharin, and after him, A. I. Rykov. It was essentially at them that the trial was aimed. Most of the other accused, including the former People's Commissar for the Interior and Chief of the GPU, Yagoda, could have been shot without any publicity as countless others had been. But the elimination of Bukharin and Rykov had to be explained to the country, and that of the diplomats Krestinsky and Rakovsky to the world at large. This was the main purpose of the indictment and the so-called evidence. The other accused

*See Appendix II for biographies of the defendants.

H

functioned as witnesses against the principal defendants. As they were at the same time alleged accomplices, they had necessarily to be self-confessed criminals, and it was obviously their willingness to collaborate with the prosecution that determined their presence in the dock.* For there were a considerable number of persons either under arrest or shot in the recent past who would have made more convincing witnesses than those actually selected. For instance, Karakhan, who was said to have negotiated with the Germans on behalf of the rightists, would have been better qualified than either Krestinsky or Rosengoltz to substantiate the charge of collusion with potential enemies of the USSR. Zaporozhets and Yenukidze would have been more useful than Yagoda in reinforcing accusations that Bukharin and Rykov had engineered Kirov's murder. Rudzutak, whom Vyshinsky had cast in the role of a direct link between the Trotskyites and the Right opposition, never appeared in court. The unexplained absence of such important witnesses, who had all been in the hands of the NKVD shortly before the trial, made it necessary for Vyshinsky occasionally to introduce hearsay evidence. In Soviet conditions this did not of course invalidate his case against the accused, but it inevitably increased its tortuous absurdity.

If we take note of the way the indictment was framed we can group the defendants according to the role the prosecution assigned them. The basic charge against all of them was that they were members of a conspiratorial group named the 'Bloc of Rights and Trotskyites' formed on the instruction of foreign intelligence services in order to carry out acts of sabotage, wrecking, diversion and terrorism within the USSR, undermine the country's defence capacity and bring about its dismemberment. This part of the indictment was to be backed by the evidence of the ex-diplomats Rakovsky, Rosengoltz, Bessonov

---

*This is proved by the Krestinsky incident at the beginning of the trial. When he denied having spoken the truth at the preliminary investigation he explained that he had done it in order to appear in open court, where he could renounce his confessions. See below, p. 120.

and Krestinsky, who actually testified to the Bloc's connection with foreign powers, and with the Trotskyite organisation abroad.

The charge of attempting to dismember the USSR was reinforced by accomplice-witnesses who were formerly Party leaders in the federal republics—Sharangovich (from Byelorussia), Grinko (from the Ukraine), Khodjayev and Ikramov (from Uzbekistan).

Confessions of 'wrecking' were made by defendants holding key posts in the economy—Zelensky, Chairman of *Tsentrosoyuz*,* Rosengoltz, People's Commissar for Trade, Chernov, People's Commissar for Agriculture, and Grinko, People's Commissar for Finance. The regional Party leaders already mentioned also admitted they had carried out wrecking activities in their respective regions.

The second part of the indictment dealt with the organising of terrorism in the Soviet Union. As there had been only one successful attempt on the life of a Communist Party leader, namely that on Kirov, the accused were taxed with having ordered the assassination. The charge was supported by the former GPU chief Yagoda, but strenuously denied by both Bukharin and Rykov. However, four years had now elapsed since the murder, and it had already produced so many self-confessed terrorists as to have become incapable of further exploitation. In the absence of any new acts of an obviously terroristic kind allegations were made that the deaths of a number of prominent Soviet figures had been criminally expedited by their doctors. Three doctors, Levin, Pletnev and Kazakov, were charged with having contributed to these deaths on instructions issued by the Bloc of Rights and Trotskyites through Yagoda and Yenukidze. Kryuchkov and Maximov-Dikovsky, secretaries to two of the 'victims', were accused of being accessories to the murder of their employers. Besides these 'successful crimes', a number of terrorist projects were

*The central organisation of all consumer cooperatives of the USSR.

mentioned, the plan to spray Yezhov's study with poisonous substances being the most spectacular. Yagoda's secretary Bulanov, whose testimony served to confirm his master's guilt, described how together they had plotted Yezhov's demise.

A final section of the indictment attempted to answer the question of how and why a close collaborator of Lenin like Bukharin could have degenerated into a 'counter-revolutionary bandit'. For reasons which will emerge later, Bukharin found it necessary to confirm the story of his gradual degeneration and admit his alienation from Communist ideals. But the prosecution could not afford to admit that a distinguished Bolshevik could have become thus alienated at a time regarded by theorists as one of triumphant socialist success. To have probed more deeply into the causes of this degeneration would inevitably have led to political analysis and debate, and thence to a critical examination of Stalin's policy. The prosecution therefore concocted its own theory: no decline had in fact taken place. Bukharin had been a traitor to the Party from an early date. The fantastic charge was even made that he had planned the assassination of Lenin, Stalin and Sverdlov in 1918. Vyshinsky argued this point with especial thoroughness, calling a number of witnesses to his aid. None of the charges against him was more strongly resisted by Bukharin than this one. For Vyshinsky's fabrication was in fact a distorted version of a real historical occurrence connected with the activities of the so-called Left Communists of 1918, of whom Bukharin had been the chief.

Vyshinsky's indictment taken in its entirety is a remarkable example of the way statements of fact can be exploited in order to inculcate in the minds of the people the acceptance and indeed approval of a given political line. The political line the trial of Bukharin and the rest was designed to promote was of course the total acceptance of Stalin's leadership in both internal and foreign politics, particularly as regards the integrity of the state and the wholesale collectivisation of agriculture. This acceptance naturally entailed renouncing all criticism of

Stalinist measures, both retrospectively and in the future. A mere promise on the defendants' part that henceforward they would not attack these measures, a mere expression of regret that they had attacked them in the past—this would not suffice. The criminal and debased nature of any attitude critical of Stalin's decisions had to be demonstrated to the people. This is why the monstrous phantasmagoria of the indictment had to be invented. It was couched in factual terms and in the indicative mood, but its real purpose was to serve as a categorical imperative justifying emotions of hatred and abuse, of blind rejection of all that the principal accused had ever stood for.

The defendants, already previously subjected to many months of cross-examination in prison, were familiar with the method whereby a travesty of the facts was used in order to destroy them morally. Some cooperated with the prosecution, even reinforcing the indictment by actively embracing the roles assigned to them. Others, primarily Bukharin, tried to cause the whole fabric of the indictment to disintegrate by endorsing the opprobrium heaped on them by the prosecutor while at the same time demonstrating the absurdity of the facts with which they were charged. More than once, Bukharin insisted that when he denied having done something or other, he was not seeking to whitewash himself or shrug off responsibility; it was dangerous and unnecessary for the prosecution to stretch the facts, concoct spurious conspiracies, claim they had proof of personal meetings which could never have taken place, or extort nonsensical confessions in order to destroy his own and his friends' moral and political prestige. He offered to do the job himself without resorting to the chimeras of the indictment. This Vyshinsky naturally rejected as the ultimate in vileness and treachery. He would accept no correction from people who, by their own confession, were disillusioned Communists, let alone hear their rational explanations of the black magic he employed to conjure up the 'factual' basis of the indictment.

The Russian writer Mikhail Bulgakov illustrates this point

in his magnificent satire, 'Master and Margarita',[16] a remarkable work written during the tragic years of the trials but not published until some thirty years later. A practitioner of black magic is allowed to perform on the stage of a Moscow variety theatre, on condition that he afterwards reveals the secrets of his art. But when at last the performance is over, he has given away valuable presents and distributed a fortune in banknotes to the audience, and he is asked to explain his magic, he abruptly claims that there is nothing to explain, blackmails all those who protest into silence, and transfers his mischievous devilry to the streets, apartments and offices of the capital. Like Vyshinsky himself, Bulgakov's magician accurately takes the measure of the Soviet public whose members, well schooled in the art of living in a world of make-believe, will take at face value any statement of fact, no matter how implausible or absurd, provided it justifies the political behaviour expected of them by the authorities.

Even Bukharin cannot be completely exonerated of sharing this attitude of the ordinary law-abiding Soviet citizen. For in attacking Vyshinsky's lies he did not simply argue against them by saying they *were* lies, but emphasised in addition that by employing such blatant falsehoods Vyshinsky was undermining the lasting political effectiveness of his case. Whether or not he did this (as is sometimes assumed) tongue in cheek, his behaviour during the trial failed to dissipate the smog of mystification and lying which is one of the greatest scourges of Soviet public life.

8. Opening moves

The preliminary investigation

A record of Vyshinsky's preparation of the evidence for the 'Trial of the Twenty-One' was contained in the report on the 'preliminary investigation', which consisted of the minutes of the interrogations of the accused and the witnesses in the case. The report has never been published or made available for research, but some fifty volumes of it were lying on a table in the courtroom throughout the trial. Its suppression is a particularly grave matter, since time and again during the trial it was alleged that this or that charge had been *proved* in the course of the preliminary investigation.

The cardinal importance of the preliminary investigation was one of the tenets of Vyshinsky's theory of prosecution under Soviet criminal law. In his article in *Izvestiya* of 1 June 1936, quoted above, Vyshinsky said the prosecution should bring before the court only cases in which the guilt of the accused had been proved at the preliminary investigation. Such a procedure, he argued, was the Soviet citizen's guarantee that he would not be unjustly prosecuted. In fact the reverse was the case: it created a presumption of guilt against any accused person finding himself in court.

The whole procedure of the Bukharin show trial, like that of those that went before it, was based on the assumption that the men in the dock would fully bear out the evidence they had already given during the preliminary investigation; this would, in fact, have been a condition of their appearance in court. Krestinsky claimed at the opening of the trial that he had accepted the charges brought against him at the preliminary investigation solely so as to be able to appear in the courtroom and deny his guilt publicly.[1] Bukharin protested when allegations were made against him which he said had never been mentioned at the preliminary investigation.* It is clear that at the end of the preliminary investigation Vyshinsky obtained from each of the accused a promise to stand by the minutes of his interrogation, every page of which he had signed in the presence of the prosecutor. All the accused abided by this rule with one temporary exception. Krestinsky, at the beginning of the trial, repudiated every word of his preliminary evidence and pleaded not guilty. A closer analysis of this incident throws some light on the methods used by Vyshinsky in preparing his case.

At the opening session Krestinsky said he had deliberately deceived his interrogators so that he could appear in court and make a public protest to the Party. Vyshinsky, caught off balance,[2] hastily turned to other defendants for some damaging piece of evidence with which to counter this. The first witness to be called was Bessonov. He unhesitatingly described an alleged meeting between Krestinsky and Trotsky in Meran in October 1933, and claimed Krestinsky had enlisted him the following December to work for the Trotskyites. Later, in his final plea, Bessonov, recounting how he had been induced to confess, made some illuminating remarks which brought him as close as any defendant ever came to describing the methods of coercion used against him, and showed how he had been trapped into entangling himself and Krestinsky in a tissue of lies. After ten months of denials, Bessonov said, he was shown Krestinsky's testimony implicating him as the liaison man between the 'Bloc of Rights and Trotskyites and abroad and Trotsky' (sic). Bessonov continued: 'I no longer had the energy and did not attempt to maintain my former position of disavowal; I only asked for a few days to think things over, and these were granted to me.'[3] What kind of 'energy' was it that was needed to maintain that what he said was the truth? And who were the people entitled to grant 'a few days to think things over' to a man in prison awaiting trial?

*See Appendix I, 3.

The implication is clear. Without those few days, Bessonov would not have been able to 'think things over'—that is, he would have been tormented as he had been tormented for the previous ten months. Bessonov also indicated that he had surrendered not only because of the treatment he had received but because of Krestinsky's accusations. Krestinsky had incriminated him recklessly, intending to deny his preliminary evidence in court. Nevertheless his accusations caused Bessonov, who until then had resisted his interrogators, to surrender in his turn. Bessonov having thus become state's witness for Vyshinsky then proceeded in court to break the morale of Krestinsky, so encompassing their mutual destruction.

Krestinsky's morale did break, though he stuck to his position all through the first day of the trial. He must have hoped to carry his co-defendants with him in a sweeping repudiation of all their preliminary evidence, and if he had succeeded in doing so, it is hard to say what would have become of the trial. But Vyshinsky, by his cross-examination of Grinko, Chernov and Rosengoltz, was able to demonstrate that the rest of the accused would do nothing but repeat their prepared evidence against Krestinsky. When his fellow-diplomat Rosengoltz accused him of lying, Krestinsky was considerably shaken. He said he felt ill, and asked for some pills before he could go on.[4]

By the next morning he had surrendered. Vyshinsky must have sensed that the situation was under control, for he would not let him speak the whole of that day. When, at the evening session, Krestinsky offered to make a statement and 'shorten your labours', Vyshinsky replied: 'I have no need to have them shortened, all the more because the statements you made yesterday do not testify to a desire on your part to shorten the trial.'[5] Only late in the evening session was Krestinsky, obviously impatient to confess and have done with it, allowed to stand up and repeat in a weak voice that a feeling of 'false shame' at the thought of his crimes becoming known to the world had overcome him the previous day and made him lie to the court.[6]

For at least two of the defendants, the preliminary investigation had involved a pre-trial held *in camera* during the summer of 1937. One, as we have seen, was Bessonov; the other was one of the medical defendants, Professor Pletnev. In both cases the pre-trials ended inconclusively, and both men escaped the death sentence in March 1938.* Bessonov described his pre-trial in his last plea. The court had consisted of 'approximately the same members as at the present trial', he said, and in view of his persistent denials of guilt it had ruled to send him back for further investigation.

Professor Pletnev's pre-trial received more publicity, and was probably the opening shot in an NKVD campaign to 'collect' medical defendants. On 8 June 1937 an article in *Pravda* entitled 'The Sadist Professor' described the relations of Professor Pletnev, a man of 66, with a woman patient who had accused him of assault. During an examination in his surgery he had bitten her. The bite had become infected, and caused a permanent disease of the breast which the Professor had treated incompetently. In her desperate efforts to induce him to cure her, the woman had followed him around in the street and written him excited letters, from one of which *Pravda* quoted extensively. In a tone of righteous indignation, the article commented that the sadistic professor had threatened to denounce his patient to the police if she continued to pester him, and had actually asked for police protection against her. Within a few days of the appearance of the article, the central press published declarations from groups of Pletnev's colleagues and workers in medical institutions expressing their horror and indignation at his crimes, and dissociating themselves from him. One such declaration was signed by Pletnev's future co-defendant, Dr L. G. Levin. At a trial held *in camera* on 17 and 18 July, Pletnev was found guilty of attempted rape, and sentenced to two years' imprisonment.

*The only other defendant to do so, Rakovsky, was probably spared because of his friendship with a number of leading French intellectuals who were making protests on his behalf in the Western press. The Soviet government was anxious to secure their backing for the French Popular Front.

The tribunal, however, announced that, in view of his sincere confession and repentance and the improbability of a repetition of the offence, sentence would be suspended.

Only once at the Bukharin trial was this incident referred to, even obscurely. This was at the very end of Pletnev's evidence, when Vyshinsky provocatively asked him whether his career as a scientist and physician was beyond reproach. From the exchange that followed, it is clear that Pletnev wanted to reaffirm his innocence in the rape case, but was outmanœuvred by the prosecutor.

Vyshinsky: How many years did you say was your standing as a physician?

Pletnev: Forty.

Vyshinsky: You consider your standing as irreproachable?

Pletnev: Yes, I do.

Vyshinsky: Irreproachable?

Pletnev: Yes, I think so.

Vyshinsky: During those forty years you have never committed any crime in connection with your profession?

Pletnev: You are aware of one.

Vyshinsky: I am asking you because you state that for forty years your work was irreproachable.

Pletnev: Yes, but since I denied that time ... [dots in text]

Vyshinsky: Do you think that the sentence in the case which is well known to you, the case of an outrage which you committed against a woman patient, is a blot on your reputation?

Pletnev: The sentence, yes ... [dots in text]

Vyshinsky: Is that sentence a blot on your reputation or not?

Pletnev: It is.

Vyshinsky: So there were moments of disgrace during these forty years.

Pletnev: Yes.

Vyshinsky: Did you not plead guilty to anything?

Pletnev: I cannot say I did not plead guilty to anything.

Vyshinsky: So you did plead guilty to something?
Pletnev: Yes.
Vyshinsky: Is this a blot on your reputation?
Pletnev: Yes.
Vyshinsky: So during those forty years there were blots?
Pletnev: Yes.
Vyshinsky: I have no more questions.[7]

No one ever suggested that Pletnev's evidence against his co-practitioner Dr Levin when the latter was accused of having expedited Menzhinsky's death, might have been motivated by a desire for revenge.

Whilst little is known about the use on the defendants of physical torture, except that it was then the general practice of the NKVD,[8] the trial itself provides some evidence of the psychological pressures to which they were subjected during their stay in prison. Rakovsky, who had refused to confess for eight months, described in court how an adroit use of news of the international situation eventually broke down his resistance:

I remember, and will never forget as long as I live, the circumstances which finally impelled me to give evidence. During one of the examinations, this was in the summer, I learnt, in the first place, that Japanese aggression had begun against China . . . I learnt of Germany's and Italy's undisguised aggression against the Spanish people. I learnt of the feverish preparations which all the Fascist states were making to unleash a world war. What a reader usually absorbs every day in small doses in telegrams, I received at once in a big dose. This had a stunning effect on me. All my past rose before me . . . and it became clear to me that I myself was a party to this, that I was responsible, that I myself had helped the aggressors with my treasonable activities . . .[9]

In his last plea Bukharin hinted at the psychological pressure to which he had been subjected. He mentioned that he had 'happened by chance to get Feuchtwanger's book[10] from the prison library. There he refers to the trials of the Trotskyites. It produced a profound impression on me.'[11] Bukharin went on to criticise Feuchtwanger's remarks about Trotsky, but an examination of the book suggests that the 'profound impression' must have been made by something quite different. *Moscow 1937* is perhaps the most nauseating of the Western apologias for the Moscow trials. Feuchtwanger came to Moscow late in 1936, was an eye-witness of the Pyatakov trial, and had two widely-advertised interviews with Stalin.

It has been alleged that Feuchtwanger acted as an *agent provocateur* in the preparation of the Pyatakov trial.[12] Feuchtwanger guaranteed (supposedly) Stalin's promise to keep Radek alive, and thus induced Radek to act as a denunciator at the trial. In his book Feuchtwanger reports a conversation with Stalin about Radek, during which Stalin spoke of Radek bitterly and with feeling. 'He described his friendly relations with the man. "You Jews," he said, "have created one eternally true legend—that of Judas." It was strange to hear a man otherwise so sober and logical utter these simple and emotional words' (sic). He also reports that Stalin said Radek had written a long letter to him protesting his innocence, and the very next day, under pressure from witnesses and the evidence, he had confessed. Curiously disturbing is Feuchtwanger's description of Radek parting from his co-defendants after sentence had been pronounced: 'He turned around, raised a hand in greeting, shrugged his shoulders very slightly, nodded to the others, his friends who were condemned to death, and smiled. Yes, he smiled.'

Feuchtwanger's sugar-and-cream description of the tragedy of the second trial was not only objectively wrong but subjectively dishonest. While describing to the West the quiet, dignified atmosphere of the court, Feuchtwanger was giving advice in Moscow on how to make it palatable to Western public opinion. In a statement published in *Izvestiya* on

30 January 1937 he wrote: 'Abusive epithets and noisy indignation, however understandable they are, cannot explain to the
end what is going on in the souls of these people [the
defendants]. Only the pen of a great Soviet writer could explain
to Western Europeans the crimes and the punishment of the
defendants.'

However, the tone in which he presented the trial to the West
will be clear from the following passage describing Radek's confession: 'He was quite free from pose when he spoke his conclud-
ing words, in which he admitted why he had confessed, and despite
his apparent imperturbability and the finished perfection of his
wording, this admission gave the impression of being the self-
revelation of a man in great distress, and it was very affecting.'[13]
Feuchtwanger assured his readers that the men who stood
before the court were not tortured and desperate people facing
their executioner. There was no justification of any sort, he
continued with unbelievable effrontery, 'for imagining that there
was anything manufactured, artificial or even awe-inspiring or
emotional about these proceedings'.[14]

This was the book which was given 'by chance' to Bukharin
to read in prison before his trial. Obviously his interrogators
wanted to show him how his trial would be presented to
left-wing circles abroad. They meant to destroy all hope that
the proceedings would be correctly understood by Westerners,
and to discourage him from trying, through public statements
in court, to convey a message to sympathisers and followers in
the world outside. The book did indeed produce a profound
impression on him, though probably not quite the one intended
by those who put it into his hands.

Confessions

Having selected a group of accused persons who would support
the charges in the indictment, Vyshinsky was at last able to
produce them in open court. The aim of the proceedings was

not so much to prove the guilt of the defendants, since according to Vyshinsky this had already been done during the preliminary investigation, as to demonstrate to the court, the nation and the world that proof of it existed. This explains why, with a few exceptions, Vyshinsky did not consider it necessary to call other witnesses than the co-defendants to buttress his edifice. The value of the trial as a demonstration of actual guilt was further reduced by the fact that Vyshinsky regarded it as forming only a part of a whole complex of trials, some of them secret, the findings of which he took as generally accepted.

The cross-examination of the accused did not open with the principal defendant, Bukharin, but with a relatively minor figure, Bessonov. This was not fortuitous. Shortly after the Pyatakov trial an article entitled 'Judicial Investigation', by a certain S. A. Golunsky, had appeared in the magazine *Sovietskaya Iustitsiya*.[15] The author stated that it was not always advisable to open a trial with an examination of the principal defendant, especially if he was a clever criminal who could easily attract the sympathies of the 'attendant public'. For, Golunsky went on, 'it may not always be possible to dispel this first mistaken impression in the course of later proceedings'. Let us ignore the outrageousness (from the legal standpoint) of Golunsky's reference to the public. The importance of his article lies in its implicit admission that even among legal theoreticians the propaganda function of criminal proceedings was paramount. During his trial, in 1937, Pyatakov was cross-examined first, and Golunsky's criticism may have applied principally to him. In March 1938 Bukharin was not called upon to give the main body of his evidence until sixteen of his co-defendants had already given theirs.

It soon emerged that the various confessions were not in harmony with one another. Whilst all the accused admitted in a general way that they had perpetrated heinous crimes, their confessions differed considerably on points of detail. Some vehemently and convincingly denied every particular of the charges against them, at the same time maintaining that the co-defendants accusing them had themselves committed the crimes in question. As had been the case at previous trials, some of the accused willingly and indeed systematically aided the prosecution, and would obviously have said anything required of them. Bukharin openly called two of them* *agents provocateurs*.[16] Many others were equally pliant tools in the hands of the prosecutor. The difference between men like Rosengoltz, Krestinsky, Grinko and Chernov and the two named by Bukharin was merely that the latter had probably acted on police instructions even before their arrest whereas the former became accomplices of the police only after they had been broken in during the preliminary investigation.

The attitude adopted by Bukharin put him into a special category at the outset. At the preliminary investigation he had made far-reaching general admissions, and these he confirmed throughout the trial. But when it came to the concrete details which were to substantiate his guilt, he made difficulties. By denying the details, he threatened to undermine the whole edifice so carefully constructed by the prosecution. The fact that he did this without any attempt to save his life or his reputation, freely confessing his villainy and even assuming responsibility for certain actions of alleged accomplices of which he claimed to have no direct knowledge, merely strengthened his position in court. Indeed Vyshinsky sometimes fell into the traps Bukharin laid for him. Nowhere was this so obvious as during the cross-examination of Ivanov, when Bukharin forced Vyshinsky to concede that the term 'counter-revolutionary' in relation to the activities of the Right opposition meant no more than resistance to the majority Party line—i.e. the Stalinist line.

When Ivanov alleged that Bukharin had spoken to him in 1928 of leanings towards insurrection among the kulaks and the Cossacks of the Northern Caucasus Bukharin objected. No

---

*Sharangovich and Ivanov.

8. Bukharin

9. Vyshinsky

10. Rykov

11. Yagoda

insurrections were planned before 1932, he said. In 1928 'I spoke about a suitable social base for the Right organisation, about recruiting members for the Right *counter-revolutionary* organisation'. The term 'counter-revolutionary', applied to an organisation which was not planning insurrection, startled Vyshinsky. He enquired what was the aim of this counter-revolutionary organisation. It was to create 'a mass basis for the struggle against the Party line', explained Bukharin. Vyshinsky, feigning indignation, asked what kulaks and Cossacks could have to do with a struggle against the Party line. Bukharin for his part pretended not to understand. Vyshinsky suggested that kulaks and Cossacks could not struggle against the Party line, this being an intra-Party affair, though they could do so against the Soviet power. To which Bukharin triumphantly rejoined: 'The struggle against the Party line is the struggle against the Soviet power.' Vyshinsky was caught in a trap. Bukharin pusued in a professorial tone:*

> I think that the Citizen Procurator, the Citizens Judges and the whole country are interested in seeing how out of certain deviations monstrous conclusions are formed by the logic of the struggle. That is why I want to preserve a certain time-proportion in this respect. In 1928 the anti-Party platform was formulated. At the end of 1928 and the transition to 1929 the slogan was issued to form an illegal organisation. In the course of the further intensification of the struggle all this led to what you know.[17]

Thus Bukharin, by proclaiming his own definition of the word 'counter-revolutionary', hoped to take the sting out of all his admissions of 'counter-revolutionary activities'. 'Counter-revolutionary', to him, meant no more than 'opposed to the Party line', i.e. Stalin's line. His confessions, and to a large extent those of Rykov, must be understood in this sense.

*The context of Bukharin's declaration will be found in Appendix I, 1.

Later in the trial Bukharin mentioned a conference of young people which had met in the summer of 1932 on the initiative of his pupil, Slepkov, to discuss the Ryutin Platform. Vyshinsky asked him whether the meeting had been illegal, and Bukharin readily replied : '[It was] illegal. The conference was illegal, the work was illegal, the reports were illegal and the reports were about illegal work.' Vyshinsky retorted: 'The conference was counter-revolutionary, the reports were counter-revolutionary, and the reports were about counter-revolutionary work.' Bukharin agreed: 'Yes, the whole thing was counter-revolutionary.'[18] The term 'illegal' as used by Bukharin meant 'unauthorised by the Party'. We know that the Ryutin Platform was a document circulating in Moscow in 1932.[19] It was written by a former member of the Central Committee who had been in exile or under arrest since 1930, and called for uncompromising resistance to Stalin's personal rule. During his interrogation in court Bukharin several times attempted to report on the contents of the Ryutin Platform.[20] In order to gain a hearing he was obliged to describe it as eminently counter-revolutionary, and to pretend to make disclosures about counter-revolutionary activities. On each occasion he was stopped by Vyshinsky, who managed to block every attempt to publicise the document. Bukharin of course went very far in describing the platform as counter-revolutionary. In fact a meeting of political oppositionists such as the one which gathered to discuss the Ryutin Platform was not necessarily even seditious.

All the accused confessed their guilt, but they can be divided into two groups according to the nature of their confessions. The first group consented to play the roles assigned to them by Vyshinsky, and corroborated the facts on which the prosecution founded its case. The second group, led by Bukharin, admitted general responsibility but denied the facts on which the prosecution charges were based.

There were of course intermediate attitudes. During the preliminary investigation Rykov had obviously given in to a much greater degree than had Bukharin. But during the courtroom confrontations he rallied to Bukharin, even disputing Vyshinsky's interpretation of his previous admissions.

Yagoda's attitude, too, was noteworthy. People who saw him in court had the impression that he had undergone considerable suffering.[21] He seemed to regard himself as out of place in the dock, as if he knew that his fate would be decided irrespective of what happened there. He held aloof from the other accused, and once even remarked that Bukharin was a chatterbox who knew nothing about 'real politics'.

Yagoda fulfilled the design of the prosecution by linking Bukharin and Rykov with the Kirov murder[22] and revealing the secrets of the medical assassinations. When, however, the professor of medicine Kazakov and his secretary Kryuchkov accused him in their turn of planning to kill Gorky's son Maxim Peshkov, Yagoda objected that all they had said was lies.[23] Confronted by Vyshinsky with his own statement during the preliminary investigation, Yagoda said he had lied on that occasion, but refused to explain why. This prompted Vyshinsky to ask him whether he had registered any protest or complaint regarding the preliminary investigation, or wanted to now. But Yagoda declined to do so.

All in all his demeanour at the morning session of 8 March was somewhat truculent, and Vyshinsky was clearly incensed. However, at his formal cross-examination the same evening he was much more subdued, and admitted much of the substance of the indictment. Touching briefly on the Kirov murder he said Yenukidze had ordered him 'not to place any obstacles in the way of the terrorist act against Kirov'.[24] But when it came to the assassination of Peshkov Yagoda refused either to plead guilty or to answer questions, and asked that what he had to say on this subject be heard *in camera*. Vyshinsky agreed, but only because, as he put it, 'I have in mind that the results of this [secret session] should be announced at an open session.' In a short note on the session held *in camera* on the evening of 9 March the published report says Yagoda 'fully admitted to organising the murder of Peshkov'.[25]

The casual, detached, slightly bored manner of Yagoda during the trial is easily explained. His position in the dock was very different from that of the other accused, and his interrogation in court by Vyshinsky even had its absurd side. He had served for so long in the NKVD that there could be nothing secret for him about the methods used in staging the trial and extracting confessions, let alone about the aims of the Procurator; in fact for a long time he had actually collaborated with Vyshinsky, and the two men knew more about each other than any third party could. Yagoda may well have regarded his role in the whole performance as both superfluous and farcical. True, his fate was sealed, but he could have been done to death without having to appear at the show trial; no one, in the Moscow of 1937, would have been surprised to hear that the head of the secret police had been quietly liquidated.

The position of the other principal accused, like Bukharin and Rykov, was entirely different. People knew what they stood for, and a bullet in the head would not have lessened the threat they represented to Stalin's policies. In their case the protracted ritual of vilification and degradation performed in public with their own participation was fully justified from the angle of Stalinist politics. Odium had to be cast on their ideas, their personalities, even their very names. Anything even remotely connected with them had to become the object of horror and fear. This was to be achieved both through the interrogation of the accused and of selected witnesses, and by means of 'legal expertise'. It would be futile at this stage, thirty years after the trial, to apply the criteria of truth and falsehood, or even of greater and lesser probability, to Vyshinsky's manifold accusations. Such an approach would merely mislead, and obscure the real aim of the trial. We shall rather try to ascertain what it was that the prosecutor was actually alleging, i.e. what he was asking the public to believe and the defendants to confirm. We shall also attempt to discover what those accused who tried to counter his charges were trying to convey, both by their demeanour in court and the way they interpreted Vyshinsky's allegations when making their diverse admissions and confessions. Bukharin was in a sense the leader of this opposition to Vyshinsky in court, supported, though only partially, by Rykov; most of the other accused acted as mere tools of Vyshinsky. In the chapters that follow we shall look at the various counts in the indictment as these were reflected in the court proceedings.

9. The Bloc of Rights and Trotskyites

The chief count in the indictment, which gave its name to the trial, was that a conspiratorial organisation known as the 'Bloc of Rights and Trotskyites' had been formed in the Soviet Union; this had set itself the aim of overthrowing the socialist government, restoring capitalism and the power of the bourgeoisie, dismembering the country and severing from it for the benefit of foreign powers the Ukraine, Byelorussia, the Central Asian republics, Georgia, Armenia, Azerbaijan and the Maritime Region of the Far East.

According to the prosecution the existence of this organisation had already been 'well established' at the preliminary investigation. Most of the accused spoke of it as though its existence could be taken for granted. Krestinsky listed the adherents of its 'leading centre'. 'I learnt from Pyatakov', he said, 'when he spoke to me about this in February 1935 that an organisation had been formed which united the Rights, Trotskyites and military men, and which set itself the aim of preparing for a miltary *coup*. I also knew that the leading centre included Rykov, Bukharin, Rudzutak and Yagoda from the Rights, Tukhachevsky and Gamarnik from the military and Pyatakov from the Trotskyites.'[1]

No evidence, even in the form of confessions, was brought by the prosecution to support its claim that the Bloc had been formed at the behest of foreign powers. On the contrary both Bukharin and Rykov said the conspiracy had grown out of the activities of the various opposition groups within the Communist Party.

At an early stage in the trial Bukharin started to undermine the theory of a conspiratorial 'bloc'. While Rykov was being interrogated about his alleged contacts with representatives of various bourgeois-nationalist counter-revolutionary organisations, Bukharin interposed the following comment: 'I must say, since there is some confusion and misunderstanding here concerning this question: the point is that the "Bloc of Rights and Trotskyites" was an organisation that had not taken final shape. It took final shape only in this contact centre [by which he meant the association between himself, Rykov and Tomsky].' Therefore, Bukharin argued, persons coming in contact with members of the centre could not be regarded as accredited representatives of any particular organisation. 'One could speak of representatives only with regard to an organised body, but with regard to the Bloc this question did not arise.'[2]

When Bukharin was summoned to give the main part of his evidence he first asked the court's permission to make 'an analysis of the ideological and political stand of the criminal "Bloc of Rights and Trotskyites".'[3] Vyshinsky, alarmed, launched out on a minute cross-examination of Bukharin on the various points of the indictment. He elicited the information that the Bloc had been formed about 1928. From then on, declared Bukharin, he assumed responsibility for 'the crimes committed by this counter-revolutionary organisation, irrespective of whether or not I knew of, whether or not I took a direct part in, any particular act.'[4]

Vyshinsky proceeded to ask questions about the restoration of capitalism, the forcible overthrow of Soviet power and the dismemberment of the USSR. Bukharin was impatient to make his prepared statement, while Vyshinsky wanted to extract his confessions without giving him time to put his own interpretation on them. When he was finally allowed to speak without interruption Bukharin began with an astonishing statement. So great, he said, was his responsibility for the nation's political and counter-revolutionary disturbances in the past that he could not be suspected of 'wanting to wriggle out of or repudiate responsibility even if I were not a member of the Right and Trotskyite organisation'.[5] As for the 'Bloc', it was an insurrectionary band bent on terrorism, wrecking and treason, and the overthrow of 'the valiant leadership of Stalin'.

All this was the outcome of an ideological change in Communist circles originating with Right deviationism in 1928. In 1932 the Right deviationists carried their position one step further by accepting the Ryutin Platform,* which called for radical opposition to Stalin's policies on industrialisation and collectivisation.

Our programme was—the prosperous peasant farm of the individual, but in fact the kulak became an end in itself. We were ironical about the collective farms. We, the counter-revolutionary plotters, came at that time more and more to display the psychology that collective farms were music of the future. What was necessary was to develop rich property-owners. This was the tremendous change that took place in our standpoint and psychology. In 1917 it would never have occurred to any of the members of the Party, myself included, to pity White Guards who had been killed; yet in the period of the liquidation of the kulaks, in 1929-30, we pitied the expropriated kulaks from so-called humanitarian motives. To whom would it have occurred in 1919 to blame the dislocation of our economic life on the Bolsheviks and not on sabotage? To nobody. It would have sounded as [sic] frank and open treason. Yet I myself in 1928 invented the formula about the military-feudal exploitation of the peasantry, that is, I put the blame for the costs of the class struggle not on the class which was hostile to the proletariat, but on the leaders of the proletariat itself. This was already a swing of 180 degrees. This meant that ideological and political platforms grew into counter-revolutionary platforms. Kulak farming and kulak interests actually became a point of [the] programme. The logic of the struggle led to the logic of ideas and to a change of our psychology, to the counter-revolutionising of our aims.[6]

*See above, p. 130, and n. 19 on p. 239.

Bukharin's explanations were becoming too pointed for the court, and he was again interrupted.

After a brief skirmish on the subject of espionage, the duel between Bukharin and Vyshinsky reverted to the question of the formation of the Bloc. Bukharin said the 'quest for blocs' had begun with his conversations with Kamenev in 1928. He explained, 'I regard these three attempts [i.e. conversations with Kamenev and Pyatakov in 1928] as quests for criminal connections and a criminal bloc against the Party leadership and the Party with those circles which were grouped around Kamenev and Zinoviev on the one hand, and the Trotskyite Pyatakov on the other.'[7] This was certainly not what Vyshinsky had meant in the indictment by 'Bloc of Rights and Trotskyites'. Bukharin's conversations with Kamenev had been common knowledge for years, and were mentioned by Kamenev himself in a speech to the 17th Party Congress (the very Congress at which Bukharin had been elected a candidate member of the Central Committee!). Bukharin's interpretation of his talks with Kamenev as having constituted the beginning of the Bloc amounted to an implicit rejection of Vyshinsky's claim that a formal, counter-revolutionary, 'Bloc of Rights and Trotskyites' actually existed. According to him, from the very beginning of the class struggle against the kulaks the three Right leaders, Rykov, Tomsky and Bukharin himself, had constituted a centre of resistance to Party policy. 'The trio became an illegal centre,'* he explained, 'and therefore whereas this trio had previously been at the head of the opposition circles, now it became the centre of an illegal counter-revolutionary organisation. And inasmuch as they, I repeat, were illegal in relation to the Party, they became thereby illegal in relation to the Soviet authorities.'[8]

When he was given the freedom of the last plea Bukharin struck his final blow at the prosecution's case. He declared that he had never known his alleged accomplices, Sharangovich,

*Cf. above, pp. 70 ff.

Maximov, Pletnev and Kazakov, never discussed counter-revolutionary matters with Rakovsky, Rosengoltz or Zelensky.

> Consequently the accused in this dock are not a group. They
> are confederates in a conspiracy along various lines, but they
> are not a group in the strict and legal sense of the word.
> All the accused were connected in one way or another with
> the 'Bloc of Rights and Trotskyites', some of them were also
> connected with intelligence services, but that is all. This,
> however, provides no grounds for asserting that this group
> is the 'Bloc of Rights and Trotskyites'.
>   Secondly, the 'Bloc of Rights and Trotskyites', which
> actually did exist and which was smashed by the organs of
> the People's Commissariat of Internal Affairs, arose
> historically . . . I have testified that I first spoke to Kamenev
> as far back as 1928 . . . How then can it be asserted that the
> Bloc was organised on the instructions of Fascist intelligence
> services? Why, this was in 1928! . . . I categorically deny
> that I was connected with foreign intelligence services . . . ![9]

It is in the light of this passage that we should read Bukharin's
references all through the trial to the 'Bloc of Rights and
Trotskyites' : just as we should see his use of the term 'counter-revolutionary' in the light of his own definition of it, already
discussed.

Bukharin and the other accused, adopting the prosecution's
terminology, consistently referred to the 'Bloc of Rights and
Trotskyites'. Although almost all the prominent Trotskyites had
already been sentenced at the first two show trials, Vyshinsky
nonetheless managed to produce a few individuals, such as
Rakovsky, capable of being tarred with the Trotskyite brush,
and introduced them in court as members of the 'Bloc'.
Krestinsky and Rosengoltz were made to serve as direct links
between the Bloc and the arch-villain of all the trials, Trotsky.
Vyshinsky said they had maintained personal and postal

contacts with Trotsky through Bessonov and others. The chief piece of evidence in support of this was Krestinsky's reported interview with Trotsky in Meran, in October 1933. Krestinsky testified that the meeting had been arranged by Bessonov, and described in some detail how he had seen Trotsky and talked with him at the Hotel Bavaria.[10] This hotel, he stressed, was still in existence—a not unreasonable remark in view of the embarrassing incident of the Hotel Bristol, Copenhagen, during the trial of Kamenev and Zinoviev.*

When Trotsky heard of Krestinsky's evidence, he immediately retorted that in October 1933 he was staying in Bagnères-de-Bigorre in the French Pyrenees, where he was under police supervision and where his uninterrupted sojourn could be confirmed by a number of people.[11]

Bessonov mentioned having been in touch with members of Trotsky's family in Berlin in 1931-32. His account of how he transmitted letters from Pyatakov to Trotsky's son Sedov in May 1931 is belied by the details he gave of the circumstances. He claimed that at this time the Berlin gutter press was writing a great deal about Trotsky and his children because of 'something that had happened to Sedov's sister'. As Trotsky pointed out, nothing had as yet happened to his daughter, who did not arrive in Berlin until the end of 1931 and did not become the subject of comment by the Berlin press until two years later, when she committed suicide. Again, Bessonov claimed to have met Sedov in Karlsbad in 1934, whereas Trotsky said he could provide documentary proof that Sedov did not leave France after 1933.[12]

Lastly Bessonov claimed to have transmitted a letter to Trotsky through a certain Johannson 'in December 1936, or perhaps in the early part of January 1937—more exactly in December 1936'.[13] 'Within a few days,' he went on, 'I received a reply from Trotsky.' The date of this communication obviously caused Vyshinsky some headaches. Two days later Krestinsky,

*See above, p. 107, and n. 8 (Chapter 7), p. 238.

giving evidence about the letter, said 'the reply apparently came at the end of December, or perhaps in the beginning of January'.[14] Vyshinsky suggested: 'Or perhaps in the middle of December?' Krestinsky either did not understand or engaged in a bit of sabotage, for he answered, 'No, it could not have been the middle of December . . .' The point is quite important, for Trotsky wrote (in the March 1938 issue of the *Bulletin of Opposition*) that on 18 December 1936 he was taken by the Norwegian police on board the tanker *Ruth,* which left Oslo on 19 December and arrived in Tampico, Mexico, on 9 January. Trotsky could not have maintained any correspondence during the voyage, since he was not allowed to use the telegraph system. These facts were reported in the Oslo *Dagbladet* on 7 March 1938, with the added information that from the beginning of December 1936 until his departure, Trotsky's mail was censored by the chief of the Norwegian Central Passport Bureau, and all letters to and from him were copied.

It seems clear that the Soviet diplomats' evidence about their links with Trotsky does not withstand Trotsky's determined and largely substantiated denials. But this is not the main point. The main point is that even if the diplomats *had* been in league with Trotsky, Vyshinsky could still produce no proof that Bukharin or Rykov were aware of this. Krestinsky and Rosengoltz said they had received instructions from Pyatakov, Karakhan, Radek, Serebryakov, Smirnov and Rudzutak, and obtained from them information about the Bloc; but only at one point does the evidence mention direct conversations between either of them and the two Right leaders. Rosengoltz described a conversation he claimed to have had with Rykov in November 1936. Rykov conceded that he knew Rosengoltz—'I spoke to Rosengoltz once or twice'—but denied ever having said that the subject of their conversation was the Tukhachevsky plot.[15]

That was the sum total of the evidence adduced for a link between the centre of Rights (i.e. Bukharin, Rykov and

Tomsky) and Trotsky. Bukharin did of course concede that he had planned, or wished, to coordinate his activities with Trotsky or the Trotskyites, especially in 1932.[16] But he always made it plain that he learned of Trotsky's plan and activities through some third party such as Pyatakov, Radek or Tomsky. In giving an account of their conversations about Trotsky, he would always end up by saying that he personally regarded himself as detached from and in no way responsible for Trotsky's acts. For example, 'I was against territorial concessions ... I did not consider Trotsky's instructions as binding on me',[17] and 'Radek ... confirmed at a confrontation with me ... that I considered it essential that he, Radek, should write and tell Trotsky that he was going too far in these negotiations [i.e. negotiations with the Germans], that he might compromise not only himself, but all his allies, us Right conspirators in particular, and that this meant certain disaster for us ...'[18]

Bukharin lent some support to the prosecution's case by talking as though it were an established fact that Pyatakov and Radek had been in correspondence with Trotsky at times when, according to Trotsky, no such correspondence could have taken place. However, he was doing no more than backing up the confessions and self-accusations which Pyatakov and Radek had already made. Vyshinsky for his part never even attempted to prove the existence of direct contacts between the leaders of the two main trends of the opposition, which he asserted had united to form a bloc of Rights and Trotskyites.

10. The charges: Collusion abroad

Defeatism and negotiations with the Germans

The charge that the accused held defeatist views and had negotiated with 'the Fascists' was formulated by the prosecution as follows: some time after 1933 (Vyshinsky alleged) the Right centre had despatched Karakhan to Germany to negotiate with official circles. In the course of the negotiations Karakhan had discussed certain proposals made to the Germans by Trotsky. The chief tenor of these was that the Germans should assist the treasonable efforts of the Rights and Trotskyites to undermine the Soviet defence potential and unleash the war. If war broke out, the Bloc, with the aid of Tukhachevsky's military group, would throw open the front to the Germans. The Bloc, having first frustrated the establishment of a military dictatorship by accusing the generals of responsibility for defeat, would come to power and proceed to form a government which would agree to yield certain territory to Germany, Poland, Japan and Great Britain.

Bukharin and Rykov contributed their share to this fantasy by conceding that Karakhan had indeed gone to Germany and reported the conversations he had had there to Tomsky, who had in turn informed them.[1] They also admitted that a conversation, or conversations (the evidence varied) took place between themselves and Tomsky in which the expression 'to open the front' was used. It is noteworthy that, although the prosecution could easily have produced Karakhan in court to confirm the story of his negotiations with the Germans, they did nothing of the kind. Karakhan, presumably shot at the same time as Yenukidze, was not even included in the indictment's list of people investigated in connection with the Trial of the Twenty-One.

Rykov began by giving a 'general exposition of the question' which backed Vyshinsky's thesis up to a point but gave no specific details. He said that the Rights had tried to 'intensify' their dealings with the Germans in every way, but that what he called 'connections' were maintained exclusively through Karakhan. He also stated explicitly that Bukharin had 'formulated' the idea of opening the front in his presence.[2]

Questioned about Rykov's evidence, Bukharin said: 'Rykov's memory is failing him here.' He admitted discussing with Tomsky 'the idea of opening the front'; Tomsky had 'inclined to the opinion' that the front would or should be opened in the event of war, but he, Bukharin, had objected. Rykov immediately took his cue from Bukharin, saying: 'I only want to tell of what actually occurred in my presence. [*To Bukharin*] It is from you that I first heard the term "opening the front".'[3] Probably alarmed at the possibility of Rykov's recantation, Vyshinsky urged him to own that Bukharin held defeatist views and favoured opening up the front to the enemy. Rykov tried to back out of the admissions he had made at the preliminary investigation, when he was quoted as having said: 'As for our defeatist position, Bukharin shared it fully.' He hedged, and said: 'Knowing Bukharin as I do, I should say that perhaps he did not consider it [i.e. the defeat of the USSR] the only thing, but he considered it something which could be discussed, something that could be realised under definite conditions.' Pressed harder, Rykov made bold to propose a change in the wording of his previous admissions.[4] Vyshinsky accused him of trying to ease Bukharin's position, and insisted that he repeat his preliminary testimony as it stood. But Rykov had managed to show Bukharin that he was ready to help him to the best of his ability, and Vyshinsky preferred to drop the interrogation.

The question of opening the front came up once more during the cross-examination of Bukharin. Bukharin said the term had first been used by Tomsky in conversation with him. As long as he was allowed to speak uninterrupted, he explained that he and Tomsky had been discussing the alternatives of whether to seize power in time of peace or in time of war. If war came, a Soviet defeat was a possibility to be envisaged, and it was in this connection that the question of opening up the front had arisen. At this point Vyshinsky broke into Bukharin's narrative, and using the minutes of his preliminary investigation tried to force him to acknowledge that he and Tomsky were prepared to throw open the front and agree to peace terms involving the cession of large areas. Bukharin resisted. Finally he said he and Tomsky disagreed about the desirability of war. Moreover Tomsky had not said that the military leaders *ought* to open the front but merely that circumstances might oblige them to do so. This led to a confused debate on the interpretation of the Russian word *dolzhna*, which may mean either 'must' or 'ought'.[5]

Bukharin's admission of defeatist talk with Tomsky amounted to no more than this. Rykov's evidence went no further, for all he had heard was Bukharin's account of his conversation with Tomsky. Neither man conceded that he had had any negotiations with the military leaders whom the prosecution taxed with preparing to adopt a defeatist stand in the event of war. The negotiations with Tukhachevsky* and his followers, they said, were carried on by Yenukidze and Karakhan.

Vyshinsky's efforts to prove that Bukharin and Rykov had maintained contacts with the German government via Karakhan met with the same discomfiture as his attempt to prove Bukharin a defeatist. Everyone in court seemed to be agreed that at some unspecified date between 1933 and 1937, presumably after Hitler's rise to power, Karakhan had gone to Germany and negotiated with somebody. Those with whom he had dealings were vaguely described as belonging to 'government circles', and no circumstantial details about the talks were given. Vyshinsky tried to demonstrate that Karakhan's mission was decided upon by the joint leadership of the Rights, and

*On Tukhachevsky, see below, pp. 161, 165.

12. Krestinsky

13. Rakovsky

14. In the courtroom, 15 March

15. Moscow workers listening to a resolution denouncing the traitors, 15 March

that he was being briefed by the Right centre during his talks with the Germans. But both Bukharin and Rykov said they knew nothing of the negotiations until after his return, when they were told about them by Tomsky. Rykov, embarrassed by his own preliminary testimony, was obliged to concede that they had 'endorsed' the Karakhan mission *post facto*. Bukharin obviously did not want to risk a quarrel with his co-defendant, and concurred.[6]

Karakhan's negotiations were allegedly concerned with the relations between Germany and a future Bloc government which would grant her trade and industrial concessions and in the event of a war territorial gains as well. Bukharin objected to Vyshinsky's suggestion that he had agreed to these terms. He granted that Rykov's evidence on ceding territory to the Germans might be correct in as much as there had been talk along these lines, but maintained that the idea had been put up to the Germans by Trotsky; Karakhan knew of it not from Trotsky or his followers but from what the Germans had told him of Trotsky's offers.

Thus both main props of Vyshinsky's charge of collusion with the enemy collapsed during the courtroom examination. The prosecution case was rendered still more absurd by the fact that Karakhan, the only witness who could have provided first-hand evidence, was never produced in court. Just as Bukharin's interrogation was coming to an end, and Vyshinsky was saying he considered the question of 'opening the front' was clear, Bukharin put in the following remark, which sums up his whole attitude during the trial: 'I forgot to say and mention that when Trotsky was negotiating with the Germans, the Rights were already a component part of the "Bloc of Rights and Trotskyites", and that consequently they were partners to these negotiations, even in spite of the fact that Trotsky did this on his own initiative, independently of any preliminary arrangement . . .'[7]

By this remark Bukharin wanted to say that he was being made responsible, and accepted responsibility, for an action

K

Trotsky had undertaken without his knowledge or consent. He had moreover only heard of it indirectly—Karakhan had told Tomsky that he had heard from some (unnamed) Germans that Trotsky had approached the German authorities. The absurdity of the whole situation must have been clear to many people in court, and the verbatim report shows that Vyshinsky must have been raging at that moment.

Espionage and dismemberment of the USSR

Conscious of the lameness of his evidence in support of high-level contacts between the Right leaders and governments who might become enemies, Vyshinsky resorted to allegations that leaders of the national republics had collaborated with the intelligence services of various countries. These charges all followed a similar pattern.

The vaguest charge concerned the Ukraine. Vyshinsky's witness here was Grinko, a former member of the *Borotba* party* who had joined the Communist Party and occupied high-ranking positions in the republic. Just before his arrest he had been People's Commissar for Finance of the USSR. Grinko said he had been connected with Pyatakov, Gamarnik and Rykov (hardly surprising, since as heads of government departments they would naturally have turned to a minister of finance on certain occasions) and had joined the Bloc in 1935 as official representative of a Ukrainian national-Fascist organisation. Rykov took exception to this, saying that Grinko had joined as an individual, and Bukharin backed him by explaining that the Bloc was not a formal organisation designed to include 'official representatives' of any party.

Ivanov and Sharangovich gave more circumstantial accounts of their links with foreign intelligence agents in Byelorussia and the Northern Region (an administrative unit comprising

---

*Ukrainian left-wing nationalists who had joined the Bolsheviks in the twenties.

the northern provinces of European Russia). Sharangovich, who had never actually met either Bukharin or Rykov, said that through Goloded, then Chairman of the Council of People's Commissars of Byelorussia, and Chervyakov, a prominent member of the Byelorussian Communist Party, he had received instructions to 'strengthen relations' between their group and the Polish General Staff. On comparing the instructions to the Byelorussian counter-revolutionary organisation emanating from the Polish General Staff with those originating with the Right centre, said Sharangovich, he had found them to 'coincide'.[8] Rykov, who must have made some compromising statements during his preliminary investigation, conceded in general terms that he knew connections did exist between the Byelorussian organisation and the Poles. But Bukharin categorically denied knowing of them,[9] and Rykov, when urged to admit he had told him about espionage, refused to do so, maintaining that his preliminary testimony was being misread by the prosecutor.[10]

Ivanov testified that in 1934 he went to the Northern Region to work in the timber industry. He said Bukharin had set him 'the task of proceeding to prepare the way, through the forces of the Right organisation, for the defeat of the Soviet power in case of intervention, in a war with the capitalist Fascist states'.[11] Ivanov remembered (with amazing exactitude) that Bukharin had told him: 'You must, with the help of the Party organisation, give every assistance to the residential agent who will be sent there, so as to fulfil the requirements of the British intelligence service.' Following the example of Sharangovich, Ivanov confessed: 'I performed services for, I sent material to and received instructions through this residential agent, and the directions received from the British intelligence service fully coincided with the directions I received from the Right centre.'[12]

Ivanov and Sharangovich failed either to name these intelligence agents or produce their instructions, and Bukharin treated their evidence with the contempt it deserved, referring at one point to both men as *'agents provocateurs'*.[13] He had never met Sharangovich before the trial, and knew nothing of his activities.[14] Ivanov he had certainly met, and in accordance with his system of defence he admitted that as far back as the 10th Party Congress he 'really did advise Ivanov, believing him to have counter-revolutionary views, to continue anti-Party work'. (This sentence illustrates Bukharin's characteristic use of the term 'counter-revolutionary' to mean 'oppositionist'.) But he emphatically denied knowing anything about the intelligence activities of the British in that region.[15]

The fourth region where the Rights were said to be working for secession, and trying to establish links with foreign intelligence, was Uzbekistan. Bukharin's alleged accomplices in the area, Khodjayev and Ikramov, were men of very different calibre from Sharangovich and Ivanov. Both had distinguished themselves during the revolution, and after it had taken a leading part in the development of their native land. They had been fiercely opposed to each other in the twenties over questions of Uzbek local policy. Politics in Central Asia have always been characterised by extreme violence. Although either Ikramov or Khodjayev could have been liquidated at home in Uzbekistan in a manner wholly compatible with the political traditions of the region, they were nevertheless brought to Moscow to underwrite Vyshinsky's charges against the right-wing opposition. Their interrogators at the preliminary investigation must have scored a success with them, for at the trial they spoke more convincingly of Bukharin's seditious plans than their co-defendants with their feeble formula about the 'coincidence' of the Rights' instructions with those of foreign agents. Bukharin was particularly indignant about them, and eager to controvert their evidence, for he could not treat it with the same contempt he had shown for that of Sharangovich and Ivanov.

Khodjayev's evidence centred on a conversation he had had at his country house in Chimgan with Bukharin in August 1936. The timing and circumstances of this meeting are of special significance. It was the month of the Kamenev-Zinoviev trial, and criminal charges had for the first time been publicly levelled against Bukharin and Rykov. Bukharin had lately returned from a journey to France and Czechoslovakia, brimful of impressions on the international situation. His veiled reflections on it were expressed in the article *'Marshruty istorii'* quoted above.* According to Khodjayev, Bukharin criticised the ineffective way in which Stalin's policy was being resisted in Uzbekistan. 'He said that we were working badly, that this was not the way to work. Of course, he did not abuse me, and could not do so, but just said plainly that this was bad, that this was inadequate, that allies ought not to work like this.' There was talk of organising terrorist groups, and then, said Khodjayev, of establishing connections with England. 'Bukharin said that an agreement had been reached with Fascist Germany, and that one was impending with Japan. But in regard to the Central Asiatic Republics, the nearest powerful country was England. . . . Bukharin said that when it is a matter of capitalist countries assisting us Rights to seize power, and you [the Uzbeks] to obtain your independence, we have to promise something, to give something.' 'Give what? Promise what?' asked Vyshinsky. Khodjayev explained: 'To give means accepting a British protectorate, that is, as a minimum. I need not mention economic things, which are natural. Uzbekistan with its 5,000,000 population could not become an independent state between two colossuses—the Soviet Union on the one side and Great Britain on the other. We must make fast on some shore; if you sail away from one shore, you must make for another shore.' 'Is that what Bukharin said?' asked Vyshinsky. 'That is how I understood him', answered Khodjayev. He repeated this formula—'that is how I understood him'—several times while Vyshinsky urged him to repeat Bukharin's exact words. Vyshinsky even prompted him to formulate certain of Bukharin's remarks in the same terms as the other defendents, citing the example of Sharangovich.

*Pp. 94 ff.

But Khodjayev preferred to keep his version of the conversation with Bukharin on a loftier plane. Once he said he had 'understood' him to speak in praise of Fascism.[16] Bukharin was not asked to comment on Khodjayev's testimony that day.

The conversation with Khodjayev came up again during Bukharin's own interrogation. He said he had a number of corrections to make to Khodjayev's report of their talks.[17] Vyshinsky tried to get him to confirm Khodjayev's version, but Bukharin was determined to use the opportunity to explain the views he had held on international politics in 1936.

The stenographic report of this part of the proceedings is most revealing. Bukharin began to explain that in foreign policy he was 'oriented ... exclusively on the neutralisation of Japan and Germany and on their assistance, which, however, did not preclude the necessity of taking advantage of the international contradictions ...' Here Vyshinsky interrupted him, and Bukharin protested, 'I beg your pardon, it is I who am speaking and not you'.[18] After further heated exchanges Bukharin said he was using 'the same words which I used in my testimony during the preliminary investigation', making it clear that in preventing him from speaking, Vyshinsky was breaking the agreement on which the trial procedure was based. This brought a flood of abuse from Vyshinsky, who shouted at Bukharin: 'you are ... hiding behind a flood of words, pettifogging, making digressions into the sphere of politics, of philosophy, theory and so forth—which you might as well forget about once and for all, because you are charged with espionage and, according to all the material of the investigation, you are obviously a spy of an intelligence service.'[19] Finally he uttered his direst threat: if this behaviour continued he would cut short the interrogation. Bukharin persisted in denying that he had ever instructed Khodjayev to get in touch with British spies. Harrassed and out of temper, Vyshinsky tried a different approach:

Vyshinsky: Did you say that it was necessary to orientate your-

selves in your foreign relations towards various foreign states, and to make use of the internal contradictions and international contradictions in the interests of the struggle of your group?
Bukharin: I did.
Vyshinsky: Hence, Khodjayev is right when he says that you spoke to him about connections with British spies.
Bukharin: But there was nothing of this.
Vyshinsky: Was it so, Khodjayev?
Khodjayev: It was.
Bukharin: But this is nonsense, because assistance is not determined by spies . . .
Khodjayev: I do not say spies, but resident agents.[20]

With his correction Khodjayev seemed suddenly to realise what the wrangle between Bukharin and Vyshinsky was all about. Bukharin, however, was not impressed with the change of terminology. When Vyshinsky in desperation finally asked, 'Do you choose to admit before the Soviet Court by what intelligence service you were enlisted—the British, German or Japanese?' Bukharin replied, 'None.' The session was adjourned.

Ikramov's evidence introduced hardly anything new on the subject of espionage. He had no direct knowledge of any connections between the Rights and foreign agents, but could only claim to have heard from Antipov, one of Bukharin's emissaries, 'about the German-Japanese orientation and about the connections with the Germans and Japanese'.[21] In the detailed account he gave of his own conversations with Bukharin he made no mention of the subject of spies.

From the welter of evidence it emerges that in August 1936 Bukharin did discuss with Khodjayev the international situation and its possible implications for Russia. By interrupting and threatening to terminate the interrogation, Vyshinsky succeeded in keeping dark what Bukharin had actually said on that occasion. Khodjayev did not repeat what Bukharin had said, but merely recorded what he had 'understood' him to say. 'Understood when?' we may well ask. In 1936, when Bukharin was talking to him, or in 1937, when Khodjayev was face to face with his interrogator? Bukharin was not told during his preliminary investigation that charges of spying would be preferred against him in this form.

We shall not concern ourselves here with the admissions of the two Uzbeks that they had led subversive nationalist groups, but we should at least point out that the liquidation of Ikramov must have caused lasting resentment in Uzbekistan. At a public meeting in Tashkent in 1957 the secretary of the Uzbek Party Central Committee, Mukhitdinov, said steps were being taken to rehabilitate him posthumously, and this statement was later reported in the local press,[22] both Uzbek and Russian. The edited version of Mukhitdinov's speech published in the central press omitted it.

The prosecution tried to reinforce the regional leaders' espionage confessions with parallel ones from some of the accused diplomats. In surrounding Bukharin with alleged confederates from the Bloc, all freely admitting that they were intelligence agents, Vyshinsky hoped to discredit Bukharin's own denials of espionage. Such internationally-known diplomats as Rakovsky, Krestinsky and Rosengoltz were compelled to say they had been foreign agents.

Rakovsky was preeminent among this group; he was accused of having entered the service of the British, German and Japanese intelligences successively.[23] The part assigned to him in the trial by Vyshinsky is not altogether clear. He did relatively little to compromise his co-defendants. He had been under suspicion for years as a genuine friend of Trotsky's, who resisted Stalin with more tenacity than most Trotskyites. An article over his name was once even published in the *Bulletin of Opposition*.[24] He had returned to Moscow from exile only in 1934, and had not been actively engaged in politics for years.

In his evidence[25] Rakovsky stated that in 1924 he had been blackmailed by two British agents, Armstrong and Leckart, who had forced him to become an informer for British intelligence. Naturally Vyshinsky could hardly imply that the Right opposition, not yet in existence, had played a part in this affair. Rakovsky's work as a spy was bound up with Trotsky; he claimed that it was Trotsky who had instructed him to let himself be blackmailed and so establish the link with British intelligence.[26]

The history of the case is not without interest. According to Rakovsky, the two Englishmen produced a document ostensibly signed by himself and datelined Berne, October 1915 in which (to the best of his recollection) he was supposed to have written that he was supplying his correspondent with 'a list of Rumanian commercial firms and newspaper offices which should be won over to the side of Germany in order to draw Rumania itself into the war on the side of Germany'.[27] Rakovsky maintained at some length that he had protested that this document was a forgery, and demanded proof of the blackmailers that they were acting on behalf of the British government. Whether the story of the letter contains any vestige of truth it is difficult to say. We must however bear in mind that in 1915 the Germans were making strenuous efforts to induce Rumania, if not to fight on their side then at least to stay neutral. At that date Rakovsky was pursuing an openly anti-war policy, and may easily have been cooperating with German 'pacifists'. A document in German Foreign Office files of the period certainly suggests intimate contacts between Rakovsky and the German Government during the First World War.[28]

Only one other self-accusation of Rakovsky's merits attention. He stated that in September 1934, when he was a delegate to the International Red Cross conference in Tokyo, he discussed with the Japanese Trotsky's suggestion that the Soviet Maritime Province should be ceded to Japan if the Japanese, in return, would back the oppositionists in the event of war. This was the only mention at the trial of negotiations between a defendant and the Japanese. Rakovsky taxed Yurenev, then Soviet ambassador to Japan, with being privy to the plot. This accusation, like the rest of his evidence, sounded like a well-rehearsed lesson repeated by a terrified man, and bore little

relation to the rest of the trial. Rakovsky had never claimed
more than a casual acquaintance with Rykov and Bukharin,
and did not pretend to know whether or not they were aware
of his negotiations with the Japanese on behalf of the
Trotskyites. The manner in which he testified may have served
as an example to the other accused of how to behave in order
to save their skins. He was not sentenced to death, and uncon-
firmed reports have it that he died a natural death in prison
during the Second World War.

When Krestinsky and Rosengoltz tried to substantiate their
confessions of espionage for the Germans, they fell back on a
reinterpretation of the negotiations which the Russians and the
Germans had conducted during and after 1920. These had
resulted in the Von Seeckt agreement, under which (it is now
known)[29] part of the German rearmament programme was
carried out in the Soviet Union. They were entered into with
the full knowledge of the Soviet government, and could not
have been undertaken otherwise, but Krestinsky and Rosengoltz
referred to them as 'partly legal and partly illegal'. They
claimed Trotsky had promised to make certain disclosures about
the Soviet armed forces in return for financial aid for his group,
and that even after his exile, German military circles continued
to lend him powerful financial support. Once again the only
proof offered was the confessions of the accused, and the Right
opposition was totally unconnected with the affair.

When it was his turn to give evidence, Chernov vitiated
by one detail his claim to have been a German spy. He saw
fit to drag in the name of the veteran Menshevik leader Dan,
whom he said he had met in Berlin in 1928. Both during
cross-examination and in his final plea, Chernov accused Dan
of being a German agent, and of luring him into the German
secret service network. Nothing roused socialists abroad to
greater indignation than this gratuitously silly charge.[30] The
attack on Dan was being prepared even before the trial, for in
the autumn of 1937 *Humanité* published an article making
the same allegations against him as those subsequently made

by Chernov. Dan sued the paper for defamation, and on 16 October 1937 obtained full redress under a decision of the *Cour Correctionnelle* in Paris. *Humanité* was ordered to pay a fine and to publish a retraction.[31] Although no reference to the French court proceedings was made at the Moscow trial, no one outside the Soviet Union could doubt that Vyshinsky and Chernov had not merely overreached themselves in seeking to sully Dan's reputation; they had succeeded in reducing the rest of Chernov's confessions to absurdity.

11. The charges: Disruption at home

Wrecking

The charge of 'wrecking' held a special place in the trial. Accusations of espionage, of terrorism, of plotting the dismemberment of the union—all these might have damaged the defendants' reputation in Communist circles, but they might also have roused the sympathy of a considerable section of the population. (We now know that there were many defeatists in Russia at the outbreak of the Second World War, and since the war have learned of the strength of separatist feeling among national minorities in many regions.)[1] But when it came to fifty truckloads of eggs rotting in railway sidings near Moscow, glass and nails in the butter, mouldering seed, sick and dying herds— these were things that roused people to fury: the chaos brought by forced collectivisation and industrialisation had made this sort of gratuitous waste and destruction an everyday experience for millions. Now the scandalous blunders of the first Five-Year Plan could be put down to the machinations of the enemies of the people in the dock.*

During 1931 and 1932 the opposition had certainly encouraged the widespread resistance to Stalin's policy which had sprung up in the countryside and even in the administration, thus aggravating the mounting disorder. Bukharin saw no reason to deny this; he therefore met the prosecution halfway by assuming 'responsibility' (whatever that meant) for all acts of wrecking or sabotage committed by persons whose negative

---

*The charges of wrecking provided, during the trial, a special theme for a press campaign to place the responsibility for current shortages on the wreckers. In *Pravda* (7 March 1938) a correspondent wrote of Zelensky: 'It is he and his henchmen who stripped the shops of all their goods in order to provoke dissatisfaction among the people.'

attitude to the Party line in any way approximated to his own.[2] Faced, however, with the charge of issuing specific directives for acts of wrecking, he resisted. Both Ikramov and Khodjayev were rebuffed when they claimed to have received such directives from him.[3] In his last plea Bukharin recalled that he once told Radek he 'considered this method [wrecking] . . . as not very expedient'.

Four people bore witness at some length to their own wrecking exploits—Grinko, Chernov, Zelensky and Zubarev. The last two had both cooperated with the Tsarist police before the revolution, Zelensky with the *Okhrana* and Zubarev with the ordinary police. The prosecution made much of this, and even introduced a note of comedy by calling as a witness a former Tsarist police officer said to have recruited Zubarev.[4] The courtroom audience was highly amused by his testimony.[5]

Zubarev had held office in the Commissariat of Agriculture; a less important civil servant than the other three, he proved a cooperative witness. He said that during Rykov's visit to the Urals in 1930 he had received instructions from him to organise the Right opposition. (On this visit Rykov made a speech which was widely criticised.)* Rykov confirmed that he had recommended the sabotage of Party policy in respect to collectivisation and support of individual farming in the rural districts. What this admission implied was a 'go-slow' campaign with regard to collectivisation, and clandestine support of the individual peasant household. The 'sabotage' in no way implied the deliberate creation of shortages or destruction of agricultural produce. Far from it—it was precisely in order to maintain production and the flow of supplies that Rykov and other rightists wanted to 'sabotage' the collectivisation campaign. What Zubarev confessed to was something quite different from this form of political sabotage. It was actual damage to production brought about by means of the intentionally faulty planning of vegetable sowing schedules, the incorrect distribution of seeds

*See above, p. 72, and n. 4 (Chapter 5), p. 236.

and so on. Vyshinsky managed in this instance to amalgamate these two meanings of the word 'sabotage' and to treat them as though they were the same thing.[6]

Zelensky had since 1931 been chairman of *Tsentrosoyuz,* which controlled the bulk of the nation's retail trade. His was a more awkward case for Vyshinsky to handle. At the beginning of his interrogation, he said his 'gravest crime' was having been in the employ of the *Okhrana* in Samara from 1911 to 1913.[7] He described his relations with the Tsarist security police in some detail. However, it soon became clear from his evidence that the Party had known about his *Okhrana* connections since at least 1924. In that year, while Zelensky was Secretary of the Moscow Party Committee, his brother was shot as a former Tsarist *agent provocateur.* Soon after the execution Yagoda talked to Zelensky, showed him his brother's dossier, and left with him the dossier of his own case, which included Tsarist secret police documents on the 1911-13 phase of his career. Zelensky now maintained at the trial that he had broken off all connections with the *Okhrana* after 1913, and that his subsequent revolutionary career had been entirely honourable. In an article in the *Bulletin of Opposition*[8] Trotsky explained that under the Tsarist régime many young revolutionaries did not show sufficient stoicism when arrested. They customarily cleared their consciences by 'confessing' to their Party organisations, whereupon they would be punished by temporary or permanent exclusion from the Party. The *Okhrana* archives were minutely studied immediately after the 1917 revolution, and Stalin, who collected this kind of information systematically, must have been aware of Zelensky's and Zubarev's transgressions at least fifteen years before the trial. He permitted Zelensky to remain in high office until 1937, and then resuscitated this sin of his youth in order to extract a confession from him.

Zelensky partially resisted, at his trial, the charge of sabotaging the work of retail distribution whilst admitting that he had recruited into *Tsentrosoyuz* right-wing sympathisers who had slowed down the flow of supplies in order to create discontent. But he merely *presumed* that much of the waste, theft, embezzlement and general dislocation in the cooperative organisation was deliberate. Thus when Vyshinsky asked him whether the fifty truckloads of eggs had been purposely left to spoil he would only reply, 'I presume so',[9] and when it came to the matter of sabotaging butter supplies he said: 'There were cases where glass was thrown into the butter.'[10] Towards the end of his interrogation he was asked about his 'anti-Soviet connections abroad', and after some prompting volunteered the amazing information that while on a visit to the Soviet Union the leader of the British Cooperative Party, Alexander, had pledged his party's support for a prospective government of the rightists.[11] The matter was allowed to rest there—just as well, no doubt.

The two remaining witnesses tried to implicate Rykov in their wrecking activities. The former People's Commissar for Finance, Grinko, stated:

> This task [financial wrecking] ... was conveyed to me by Rykov, and in doing so he emphasised that the leadership of the centre, he and Bukharin, attached great importance to the development of undermining activities in the People's Commissariat of Finance ... he gave me Bukharin's formula: strike at the Soviet government with the Soviet ruble. This was conveyed to me by Rykov, and I also discussed it with Bukharin. ... Rykov came to see me about it at the People's Commissariat of Finance and we jointly drew up a programme of measures for it [i.e. wrecking].[12]

Rykov denied that he and Grinko had ever drawn up a plan for financial wrecking: 'I don't accept that. I deny it, but not because I want to minimise my guilt. I have done much worse things than this.' There had been a general discussion about wrecking, he admitted, at the beginning of 1936, but he felt certain Grinko was describing it incorrectly, as 'he enumerated a number of things which, if they had taken place, would have taken place much earlier'. Rykov denied ever having discussed Bukharin's formula. It could have existed, however, for the closest Bukharin ever came to a confession of wrecking was in his last plea, when in the midst of generalised refutations he said: 'I once spoke positively on this subject to Grinko.'[13]

Rykov found himself in a parallel situation during the interrogation of M. A. Chernov, the former People's Commissar for Agriculture. Chernov described a long series of acts of wrecking, and claimed to have discussed them with Rykov some time in 1935 or at the beginning of 1936. Rykov said he could not remember this conversation. He treated the whole case lightly, and remarked that Chernov was not a very important accomplice in his criminal activities. The infuriated Chernov began to accuse him of not wanting to confess, and demanded that he reconsider his denial.

> You know that I am a member of your organisation. How could you, having a member of your organisation occupying the post of People's Commissar of Agriculture, not invite him to discuss the utilisation of his position in the interests of the Right organisation?
>   Please forgive me for my rudeness, but either you were a bad leader of the Right organisation, which I do not think, or you do not want to confess. I cannot conceive that you could have forgotten, I do not want to say that I was a big personage and so on, but how you could have forgotten a meeting with the People's Commissar of Agriculture on the subject of wrecking work is hard to understand.[14]

When the President of the Court asked Rykov whether he wanted to reply to Chernov's question, Rykov ironically rejoined, 'He has replied too well; perhaps I should have done as he says [i.e. he should have confessed]. It was a mistake on my part.' In his final plea Rykov came back to this point. 'Of course,' he said, 'any man's memory may deceive him in some cases, but in this case I cannot admit that I could have forgotten that I directed in a practical way Chernov's counter-revolutionary wrecking work in the People's Commissariat of Agriculture. That could not be forgotten. I do not recall it.'[15]

Popular uprising and palace coup

The charge of having plotted to seize power by force was one of the principal counts in the indictment. Not only did it reinforce Vyshinsky's and Stalin's allegations against the accused at the trial; it also justified resorting to the reign of terror in the midst of which the pageant of the show trials was staged. One after another, in their several ways, the accused were made to confess that they had plotted the violent overthrow of the government. Significantly, this time none of them demurred; some even appeared eager to embrace the charge. Their testimony is somewhat confused, perhaps because the overthrow of Stalin had been a real preoccupation of many defendants in the years preceding the trial, and the prosecution did not want their evidence to approximate too closely to the facts.

This is why the most straightforward and detailed evidence is also the least plausible. Krestinsky and Rosengoltz claimed to have been privy to a military plot led by Tukhachevsky, Yakir, Uborevich, Kork and Eidemann.* Krestinsky and Bessonov helped to link the plot with Trotsky by alleging that its existence was revealed to the former during his alleged interview with Trotsky in Meran in 1933. The conspirators' decision to strike was said to have been made at the beginning of 1937 soon after the Pyatakov trial. At a meeting between Rosengoltz, Krestinsky and Tukhachevsky, the latter, it was said, had put

---

*All these were shot after the presumed trial *in camera* of Tukhachevsky. All have now been fully rehabilitated, and all references to their plotting must be regarded as without foundation.

forward various plans for a *coup d'état*. 'One of them . . .' said Rosengoltz, 'was the possibility for a group of military men, his adherents, gathering in his apartment on some pretext or other, making their way into the Kremlin, seizing the Kremlin telephone exchange, and killing the leaders of the Party and the government'.[16] Krestinsky said Tukhachevsky had insisted in spite of all the risks that before a *coup* was carried out, terrorist action should be taken, 'primarily against Molotov and Voroshilov'.[17] The 'plot' was broken up by the arrest of the participating generals in the spring of 1937.

It would be satisfying to believe that the Trotskyites and the generals really did devise some sensible plan to save their skins. But Krestinsky and Rosengoltz did not add credibility to their story with their details of a foolhardy plot to murder Molotov and Voroshilov beforehand. Moreover, if Tukhachevsky really had planned a *coup*, it seems unlikely that he would have looked for assistance to men like them. The story of the plot was probably introduced in order to provide some justification for the execution of the generals the previous summer. It could not affect most of the defendants at the trial, since by the time the conspiracy was allegedly hatched (in March or April 1937), Bukharin, Rykov, Yagoda and many of the rest were already in jail. The interesting point, though, is that the disgrace of Tukhachevsky followed immediately on Krestinsky's arrest in May 1937. We already know that after his arrest Krestinsky started to plead guilty to all manner of charges in order to gain a public hearing. Only the publication of the record of the preliminary investigation could answer the question of how far Krestinsky's tactics *vis-à-vis* his interrogators assisted the purge of the generals.

When Bukharin was summoned to testify to his complicity in the plot to seize power, Vyshinsky was extremely anxious to prevent him from speaking freely. Again and again he would let him utter a few words—enough to twist into an admission of guilt—and then cut him short. We are thus obliged to reconstruct what Bukharin might have said from scattered statements he made, remembering that the story he wanted to put across might have been just as fanciful and far from the truth as Vyshinsky's own version.

Bukharin began: 'The inception of the idea of the *coup d'état* among us Right conspirators relates approximately to the years 1929-30, and at that time this *coup d'état* in its embryo form was conceived, or rather was spoken of, as a *coup d'état* on a relatively very narrow basis . . . or . . . a "palace *coup*".' Yenukidze and Tomsky, he said, were working out the plot together.[18] Here he seemed to be describing a plot to seize power closely connected with the suppression of the right-wing opposition in 1929. Bukharin was not allowed to say why the palace *coup*—by which he obviously meant the forcible removal from power of Stalin—was later abandoned in favour of a plan for mass uprisings. 'In 1931-32,' he declared, 'in connection with the changed political situation, the main stress was laid on the development of the insurrectionary movement.'[19] He described a meeting in the summer of 1932 at which the Right centre adopted the 'Ryutin Platform'. The same summer, he said, a gathering of young supporters led by Slepkov met to discuss similar matters. 'The essential points of the Ryutin Platform,' he explained, 'were : a palace *coup*, terrorism, steering a course for a direct alliance with the Trotskyites.'[20] The explosive discontent of a large part of the population in 1932 can be clearly sensed in the background of his account of rightist activities of the time. His description of these conspiratorial meetings is paralleled in the memoirs of Margarethe Buber-Neumann, who describes a similar group to which Lominadze belonged.[21]

Bukharin and Rykov readily acknowledged that they had posted their followers to various points in the Soviet Union with orders to stiffen peasant resistance to collectivisation and organise local insurrections. Bukharin said that in 1931-32 he had sent Slepkov to the Northern Caucasus and Yakovenko to Siberia, whilst Rykov said he had sent Eismond to the Northern Caucasus. But the prosecution did not want the inference drawn that an uprising against the Soviet power could take place in the absence of foreign intervention. Vyshinsky therefore tried to get Bukharin to admit that in organising such an uprising, Slepkov had had the backing of White Guards, and through them of foreign (and more especially of Fascist) powers. Bukharin disclaimed all knowledge of Slepkov's methods, but as usual shouldered responsibility for the results of his actions.[22]

These admissions were hardly more damaging to Bukharin than his previous self-criticisms at the 17th Congress. On that occasion, as we have seen, he was re-elected a candidate member of the Central Committee, and his speech was applauded. He said then: 'After the former leaders of the Rights had admitted their mistakes [presumably in the declaration of November 1929] underground currents and open resistance on the part of the enemies of the Party found their outlet in the formation of various groups, which as time went on degenerated into counter-revolution at an increased rate, and these were the tail-pieces of the anti-Party currents; among them were a number of my former pupils, who have received the punishment they deserved.'[23]

At the trial Bukharin continued his version of the Rights' seditious plans by describing a third type of conspiracy.

In 1933-34 the kulaks were already smashed, an insurrectionary movement ceased to be a real possibility, and therefore in the centre of the Right organisation a period again set in when ... the central idea became that of a *coup d'état* which was to be accomplished by means of an armed conspiracy.

The forces of the conspiracy were: the forces of Yenukidze plus Yagoda, their organisations in the Kremlin and in the People's Commissariat of Internal Affairs; Yenukidze also succeeded around that time in enlisting, as far as I can remember, the former commandant of the Kremlin, Peterson, who, apropos, was in his time the commandant of Trotsky's train.

Then there was the military organisation of the conspirators: Tukhachevsky, Kork and others.[24]

Thus Bukharin's schedule of plans for the seizure of power
escalated from a palace *coup* to a popular uprising and thence
to a *coup d'état*. The palace *coup* postulated the elimination
of Stalin, perhaps by a mere handful of men; the popular
uprising was to exploit the spontaneous discontent of the masses.
The third conspiracy, the *coup d'état,* would have required
the cooperation of certain state forces (viz. the army and the
police) in order to overthrow Stalin's dictatorship. Little was
said during the trial to prove the existence of this last plot.
Neither the prosecution nor the accused, although they all
claimed such a plot existed, talked as if there had been any
real coordination between the Right centre (Bukharin, Rykov
and Tomsky) and the other groups of plotters—the officers
grouped round Marshal Tukhachevsky, and the Kremlin guard,
grouped round Yenukidze, Yegorov, Yagoda and other leaders
of the security forces. The prosecution was not anxious to
make the story of the *coup d'état* more concrete, and was
particularly vague on the subject of the role in the conspiracy
of the Kremlin guard. Bukharin and Rykov got no
encouragement from Vyshinsky when they mentioned
Yenukidze's and Yagoda's preparations for action in the
Kremlin.[25] Whenever they showed signs of dwelling on the
coup d'état Vyshinsky steered the interrogation into other
channels, demanding to know how the plotters had intended to resort to foreign assistance to bring their plan to
fruition. His theory was that the conspirators were defeatists,
who thought that the enemy's victory in the forthcoming war
would pave their way to power. Rykov, as we have seen,
accepted this proposition to some extent. Bukharin firmly
rejected it. He conceded that the centre had acknowledged a
Soviet defeat to be a possibility. The generals might be forced
to open the front. In that event the plotters should try to get
rid of Stalin, undo what he had done and make a fresh start,

recognising that in wartime they could not succeed without securing the goodwill of foreign powers, even at the cost of some sacrifice.

No one at the trial implied that Bukharin or Rykov had negotiated directly with the generals or the Kremlin guard. That had supposedly been done by Tomsky and Yenukidze, and they were the ones directly in touch with foreign powers. Nor was Yagoda asked to explain his part in the plans for a *coup d'état* or a palace *coup*. He conceded that he had favoured the seizure of power by a small group of conspirators, but contemptuously dismissed both the plans for a popular uprising and the theory that power could only be seized successfully in time of war. When Vyshinsky tried to get him to say that as a conspirator he would have preferred to time a *coup* for the outbreak of war, he replied: 'There was one plan, namely to seize the Kremlin. The time was of no importance.'[26] Again, Vyshinsky steered the interrogation towards questions of espionage, showing no inclination to hear the details of Yagoda's plan.

If we look at the defendants' testimony on plans for the seizure of power, we get the impression that for the first time they were talking about something approximating to actual happenings. It was typical of the prosecution's methods that no sooner did the proceedings take on some slight semblance of reality than Vyshinsky broke off the debate to revert to wholly implausible accusations. However, Bukharin and Rykov left their confessions of conspiracy a little too vague to be convincing. The idea of a plot would have been consistent with the implacable hatred of Stalin we may well suppose they nurtured. But if they really had taken concrete steps to reach agreement with the army or the Kremlin guard, they could have acknowledged the fact now without burdening themselves or their accomplices with much extra guilt. One wonders whether Yagoda's reference to their talk of the *coup d'état* (he described them as 'babblers')[27] was not partially correct, and whether at the trial they mistook for reality all the daydreams and aspirations they had cherished during the years of enforced inactivity and political ostracism.

Terrorism

The charge of terrorism formed an almost inevitable part of any indictment in a Soviet political trial of the thirties. It justified the enforcement of the special laws enacted on 1 December 1934, following Kirov's murder, furnished a pretext for the death sentence, and made it clear generally that the real point at issue was '*kto kovo?*' (who will get whom?).

In the Bukharin trial Vyshinsky was faced with a difficulty —the dearth of spectacular assassinations which could be laid at the defendants' door. He was therefore obliged to resurrect the Kirov case, this time accusing the Bloc of having sentenced Kirov to death. Not the slightest attempt was made to prove this allegation, unless, that is, one can regard Yagoda's testimony as proof. When Bukharin and Rykov formally and solemnly denied all knowledge of the circumstances of Kirov's murder Vyshinsky turned to Yagoda, who declared, 'Both Rykov and Bukharin are telling lies. Rykov and Yenukidze were present at the meeting of the centre where the question of assassinating S. M. Kirov was discussed . . . when Yenukidze told me that they, that is the "Bloc of Rights and Trotskyites", had decided at a joint meeting to commit a terrorist act against Kirov, I categorically objected.'[28]

Quite apart from the fact that it postulated a meeting of a non-existent organisation, Yagoda's statement contained a number of improbable details. He said that at first Yenukidze and Rykov had also objected to the plan for Kirov's murder, but had been overruled by the Trotskyite section of the 'Bloc'. Who were these Trotskyites? Kamenev and Zinoviev? As Rykov pointedly remarked in his final plea, if the Bloc was guilty why had this version of the murder not come to light at previous trials?[29] Bukharin's assertion that he had nothing to do with Kirov's murder was made more convincing if anything by the fact that he did not deny that under certain circumstances he approved the idea of terrorism. 'Strictly speaking,' he admitted, 'an orientation on terrorism was contained in the Ryutin Platform.'[30]

Yagoda and Bulanov described the circumstances of Kirov's murder somewhat differently from defendants at previous trials, giving a number of details not known before their own trial but later confirmed by other sources. They implied, for instance, that the GPU had played a deliberate role in preparing the assassination, saying Nikolayev had been arrested by the GPU some time before 1 December 1934, and deliberately allowed to go free although carrying in his briefcase a pistol and an incriminating diary. (Elizabeth Lermolo, in her book *Face of a Victim*, also mentions a diary belonging to Nikolayev.)* Bulanov disclosed the name of Kirov's special bodyguard Borisov, and said that he was murdered by Yagoda's deputy in Leningrad, Zaporozhets, while on his way to be interrogated. Both Lermolo and Khrushchev in his secret speech give substantially the same account of this event.

Yagoda's attitude towards the Kirov murder was however somewhat ambiguous and hard to assess. When asked whether he actually instructed Zaporozhets not to place any obstacles in the way of the murder Yagoda answered, 'Yes, I did ... [dots in text]. It was not like that.' Vyshinsky, trying to help him, asked whether the instructions were 'in a somewhat different form', and Yagoda replied in a tired and bored way: 'It was not like that, but it is not important.'[31]

Vyshinsky did not give Bukharin and Rykov a second chance in court to repeat their flat denials of complicity in the murder. In his speech for the prosecution he tried to establish their guilt by means of a cynical subterfuge: 'What are my proofs?' he asked, and answered:

*See above, pp. 88–90, and note 4 on p. 237.

If we assume that Rykov and Bukharin had no part in this assassination then it must be admitted that for some reason or other two of the principal leaders of the 'Bloc of Rights and Trotskyites' that adopted the decision to assassinate Kirov held aloof from this dastardly act. Why? Why did people who had organised espionage ... insurrectionary movements and terrorist acts ... suddenly, in 1934, stand aloof from the assassination of one of the greatest comrades-in-arms of Stalin? ... Rykov and Bukharin could not but know about this important terrorist act. It would have been anomalous if they had not known of it, it would have been entirely illogical.[32]

Bukharin did not allow such rhetoric to go unchallenged, and in his own final plea he sardonically turned all his dialectical power against Vyshinsky.

According to Yagoda's testimony, Kirov was assassinated in accordance with a decision of the 'Bloc of Rights and Trotskyites'. I knew nothing about it. But what Citizen the Procurator calls logic comes here to the aid of the factual content. He asked whether Bukharin and Rykov could have stood aside from these assassinations; and he answered that they could not have stood aside because they knew about them. But not standing aside and knowing are one and the same thing. This is what in elementary logic is called tautology, that is, the acceptance of what is yet to be proved as already proven.[33]

Kirov's murder was the only *real* political assassination discussed at the trial. Since nothing was proved against Bukharin or Rykov, we must revert to Yagoda's claim that he facilitated the murder on orders from Yenukidze, who in 1934 was still much in favour with Stalin. Yagoda said Yenukidze's orders were issued on behalf of a conspiratorial organisation to which

Rykov belonged. If we accept Rykov's denial as valid, we are still left with the question whether Yenukidze issued such orders to Yagoda. If he did, was it at the instance of some higher authority? At the instance of the Right centre, of the 'Bloc'—the very existence of which is unproven—or of his immediate superior, Stalin? Or was Yagoda simply lying, saddling the dead Yenukidze with responsibility for an order he had either issued on his own initiative or received direct from Stalin? An analysis of the trial yields no clue to such questions, but any answer, no matter how fanciful, would be at least as believable as Vyshinsky's chimera.

As for the other acts of terrorism attributed to the 'Bloc'—the alleged murders of Maxim Gorky and his son Peshkov, of Kuibyshev and Menzhinsky—these were said to have been committed by the Kremlin doctors on Yagoda's orders. The story of Yagoda's attempt to poison Yezhov, as recounted by Bulanov, was probably included in the proceedings chiefly to give Yezhov the same status of 'victim' of counter-revolutionary plotting as that already conferred on Molotov, Kaganovich, Voroshilov and other favoured Party leaders. Here again, the only evidence of a direct link between the Right leaders and the medical assassinations was provided by Yagoda when he claimed to have received orders from the Bloc through Yenukidze. As before Bukharin and Rykov rejected the claim.

The charges of murder brought against well-known respectable medical practitioners were the first of their kind, and they set a precedent for the later and even more famous 'doctors' plot' affair of 1952-53. The idea that Kremlin physicians were used for this kind of job was, however, not new. Joffe's* last letter to Trotsky contained the allegation that medical men were using their professional skills to discriminate against opponents of the régime. The Kremlin pharmacy refused to give him drugs, he said, and the medical commission of the Central Committee would not arrange for his treatment abroad, though the doctors had said it was urgently needed.

*An old Bolshevik in high office who died in 1927.

'Professors Davidenko and Dr Levin [sic], who were called to my bedside, prescribed a few small things which obviously could not help, and then "nothing could be done".'[34] When Frunze died after an operation in 1925 the writer Pilnyak published a story in which a military commander died as a result of surgical intervention.[35] He denied, however, that it had any bearing on Frunze's demise. In this kind of atmosphere the allegations made against the doctors and their own confessions would have seemed less fantastic to Russians than they did to foreigners, or than they might appear to a future, and happier, generation. We have seen the methods Vyshinsky used to elicit from Professor Pletnev the testimony he wanted, and may legitimately assume that the medical experts who acted as witnesses for the prosecution were likewise not immune from pressure. Two of them, N. A. Vinogradov and N. A. Shereshevsky, were accused in the abortive 'doctors' plot' case of 1952-53.[36]

To expose the doctors' extraordinary confessions would require an investigation by medical experts, and even that might prove inconclusive, at least in the case of Dr Kazakov. The medicaments he gave his patients, and allegedly killed Menzhinsky with, were secret drugs, mostly hormones, which he prepared himself, and their effects if any were never properly determined by any independent scientific body. Even without expert medical analysis it is clear that with the exception of Gorky's son Peshkov all the patients whose deaths the doctors said they had expedited were already sick men unlikely to live much longer, even under the best treatment.

The most puzzling aspect of the charges is that, if Stalin really did use doctors in the capacity of assassins, he would scarcely have wished to advertise the role of the GPU in the medical treatment of prominent Soviet citizens. A probable explanation of these charges is that Stalin was obsessed with the idea of being poisoned himself, or having his supporters poisoned, and that in drawing up the indictment Vyshinsky was infected with his master's *idée fixe*.

1918

Towards the end of the trial Vyshinsky levelled at Bukharin the most monstrous accusation he could have brought, namely that he had planned the assassination of Lenin in 1918, and incidentally that of Stalin and Sverdlov as well.[37] There was not the slightest chance of his pleading guilty, nor had any of the other accused been involved in the occurrences on which Vyshinsky based his charges.

In 1918 Bukharin had been one of the leaders of a faction within the Communist Party known as the Left Communists (not to be confused with the later Left opposition) which opposed the signing of the treaty of Brest-Litovsk, and later insisted that the Soviet government should refuse to comply with its terms. Only with extreme difficulty did Lenin succeed in rallying the majority in the cc that would enable him to sign the treaty. The Left Communists published their own paper, *Kommunist,* under Bukharin's editorship, and were backed by a majority of the important Moscow Party Committee.

The intra-Party struggle over Brest-Litovsk was complicated by the fact that the only other socialist party to join the Bolsheviks in forming a government after the October Revolution, the Left Socialist Revolutionaries, were also strongly opposed to the Brest peace terms. So long as they remained in the government their sympathies and tactics put the Left Communists in a delicate position vis-à-vis the Party leadership, for the Left SRs seem to have believed for a short time (in February 1918) that a coalition between themselves and the Left Communists headed by Pyatakov and Bukharin might provide the basis for an alternative Soviet government which would wage a revolutionary war. The Bolshevik leadership could of course not tolerate a legal opposition of the type of the Left SRs. Lenin took advantage of and might even have instigated a Left SR *coup* against Bolshevik Party rule, on 6 July 1918, closely connected with the still unclarified circumstances surrounding the assassination of the German ambassador in Moscow, Count Mirbach. The so-called Left SR rising was crushed and the party dissolved, thus losing all opportunity for future political action.[38]

When, in 1923-24, intra-Party strife again reached a crisis, and Bukharin found himself supporting the Stalin-Zinoviev-Kamenev triumvirate in its struggle against Trotsky, he was rash enough to remind a workers' meeting in the Krasnaya Presnya district of Moscow of the events of 1918. Speaking of the danger of intra-Party factionalism, he stressed how it had been eagerly exploited by the Left SRs. He went on to disclose that in 1918 the latter had had the temerity to approach the Left Communists with a plan to arrest Lenin and effect a change of government. Stalin and Zinoviev both pounced on this information to attack those oppositionists of 1923 who had been Left Communists in 1918, Zinoviev writing that the affair was of 'gigantic historical significance'.[39] Bukharin could have little inkling what significance his revelations would have for him fifteen years later.

The oppositionists rushed to their own defence. On 3 January 1924 *Pravda* published a letter from a group of former Left Communists, including Pyatakov, Radek, Yakovleva, Preobrazhensky, and others, protesting that the episode Bukharin had mentioned was being given undue weight. In March 1918, they recalled, those who opposed Brest-Litovsk had gained a majority in the CC. Lenin was furious, and threatened to resign if the vote went against him: the treaty was saved only because some of its opponents, including Trotsky, abstained from voting. At this point Pyatakov and Bukharin were approached in the lobby of the Smolny in Petrograd by a Left SR leader, Kamkov, who asked them half-jokingly: 'What would the majority do if Lenin went? Shouldn't it form a government with the participation of the SRs under Pyatakov?' Pyatakov and his associates said in their *Pravda* letter that

Bukharin had neither reproved Kamkov for this question nor manifested any indignation; he had merely taken it in the spirit intended—as a bit of a joke, but perhaps as a sounding, too. That was one occasion when the Left SRs made a remark concerning Lenin. On a later occasion (the letter continued) Radek visited the Left SR Commissar of Posts, Proshyan, to discuss one of those resolutions against the Brest treaty with which the Left Communists were then inundating their leaders. Proshyan remarked, again only half-seriously, that sooner than pass resolutions it would be better to arrest Lenin for twenty-four hours, declare war on the Germans and then put Lenin back in office to carry on the war. Radek, it was said, had reported this remark to Lenin, who had merely had a good laugh over it.

Bukharin's reply to the oppositionists' letter was published in the same issue of *Pravda*. He did not dispute their facts, but rebuked them for glossing over the circumstances leading up to the conclusion of the Brest treaty. 'I know perfectly well,' he said, 'that this was a period when the Party was a hair's breadth from a split, and the whole country was on the verge of catastrophe.' The fact that Lenin had laughed proved nothing, he continued. Lenin laughed about even more serious matters. Bukharin said the Smolny conversation between himself, Pyatakov and Kamkov had indeed taken place, 'if I am not mistaken', but denied that their aim had been to bring about a *modus vivendi* between the Left SRs and the Left Communists. The important part of the whole affair, he repeated, was the fact that even in this period of Party instability the Left SRs felt secure enough and bold enough to broach such impertinences to the Left Communists.

After 1924 the episode Bukharin had recalled was included in several Party histories. Yaroslavsky in his two volumes of essays on Communist Party history published in 1926 and 1928 confined himself to recording that the Left SRs had tried in 1918 to exploit the split in the Party; Bubnov on the other hand, in a history of the Party published in 1931, spoke of a 'political bloc between the two groups'. Both men were Left Communists in 1918.[40]

Vyshinsky tried to demonstrate that in 1918 the talks between the Left Communists and the Left srs had resulted in complete agreement on the need to overthrow Lenin's government—that is, he said, the Soviet régime. From the jocular suggestion that Lenin be arrested he deduced evidence of a plot to arrest and kill those Bolshevik leaders who favoured the Brest peace—Lenin, Stalin and Sverdlov. He called five witnesses to testify to the existence of such a plot. They were as much co-defendants as the twenty-one already arraigned before the court, but their cases were being 'made the subject of separate proceedings'.[41] Three had belonged to the Left Communist faction, and the other two were formerly prominent in the Left sr party. They had in all probability been arrested some time before the trial and subjected to the usual preliminary investigation.

Among the former Left Communists was V. N. Yakovleva, a member of the Party since 1904. In 1917 she had been a member of the Moscow military revolutionary committee, and later worked successively in the Cheka and the People's Commissariat of Internal Affairs (nkvd). In 1937 she still held the post of People's Commissar for Finance of the rsfsr. V. V. Osinsky, whose real name was Obolensky, had been a member of the Communist Party before the revolution, was betrayed by the *agent provocateur* Malinovsky in 1913, spent a few years in exile and actively participated in the events of 1917.* He headed the Supreme National Economic Council for some time in 1917-18, and became leader of the Left Communists during the period of the Brest treaty. Various government appointments followed; at one time he was Soviet envoy to Stockholm. He was elected a candidate member of the cc in 1934. The third former Left Communist witness, V. N. Mantsev, was a less prominent member of the group.

*On Bukharin's earlier contacts with V. Yakovleva and V. Osinsky, see above, pp. 16 ff.

The Left SRS were more colourful. B. D. Kamkov (whose real name was B. D. Katz) had been joint leader of the Left SRS, together with Maria Spiridonova, in 1917. At the Fourth Congress of Soviets in February 1918 he crossed swords with Lenin over the Brest peace terms. He must have escaped arrest after the murder of Mirbach and the Left SR revolt, for he spent the latter half of 1918 organising partisan activity against the Germans, first in Vitebsk and later in Kiev. He continued to resist the Bolsheviks after the Red Army occupation of Kiev, was arrested, and tried before the Supreme Revolutionary Tribunal for 'counter-revolutionary activities'. After serving his sentence he worked as a statistician, and emigrated some time during the late twenties. In 1935 he was reported to be living in Berlin and contributing to the Left SR magazine *Znamya*. The trial proceedings yield no clue as to how he and the other Left SR witness, Karelin, were induced to return to the Soviet Union to act as witnesses. Karelin represented the Left SRS on the All-Russian Central Executive Committee of Soviets (TSIK) in 1917-18, and for a short time during the period of Bolshevik-Left SR collaboration (25 December 1917-15 March 1918) was People's Commissar for State Property of the RSFSR. He was on the second Russian delegation to Brest-Litovsk, played an active part in the SR uprising of July 1918, and was sentenced to three years' imprisonment by the Supreme Revolutionary Tribunal. He subsequently emigrated, and in 1936 was stated to be living in Berlin and writing in *Znamya*.[42]

The witnesses had been well schooled, although Kamkov refused to follow Vyshinsky in every particular. This is how Leonard Schapiro describes the impression their testimony makes on the historian:[43]

> The three Left Communists told a grotesque story in which the open opposition of 1918 was now portrayed as a secret conspiracy. The resolution of the Moscow *Oblast* Bureau of 24 February in opposition to Lenin's peace policy became a secret resolution, the destruction of which had been ordered

by Bukharin—although everyone who had access to the current edition of the works of Lenin could find it quoted *in extenso* in his article 'The Strange and the Monstrous'. (This article had been published by Lenin soon after he had received the offending resolution from the Moscow *Oblast* Bureau.) The open conferences of Left Communists after the signing of the peace now became conspiratorial meetings. Obolensky's evidence even went to the length of implicating Bukharin in the rising of the Left Socialist Revolutionaries which followed the assassination of von Mirbach.

When Bukharin began to put questions to the witnesses, both Vyshinsky and the president of the court ruled them out as irrelevant. Several times Vyshinsky simply interrupted Bukharin's questioning to waste time on repetitive dialogues with the witness.[44] Nevertheless, outside observers say Bukharin never put up a more effective defence than he did that day.[45]

Yakovleva alleged that in February 1918, at a meeting of the Moscow regional Party Bureau, the Left Communist Stukov, in moving a resolution against the Brest treaty, suggested that they should 'arrest the leading, most resolute part of the government, as represented by Lenin, Stalin and Sverdlov. And if the struggle were to become more acute we must not shrink even from their physical extermination.'[46] Stukov told Yakovleva he had made his speech on Bukharin's instructions. The minutes of this meeting of the Party Bureau were later expunged from the record.[47] When she questioned him about this speech, Bukharin had told her himself that both he and Trotsky favoured the overthrow of the government and 'the physical extermination of the leading people in the government and the Party'.[48] Yakovleva said he had thereupon mentioned Lenin, Stalin and Sverdlov. At a conference of Left Communists held at the end of April or the beginning of May 1918, she continued, Bukharin had reported progress in the negotiations with the Left srs, who advocated the formation of a joint government if the Left Communists would agree

M

to assist in preparations for a seizure of power. 'There undoubtedly was a conspiracy with the "Left" Socialist-Revolutionaries inasmuch as quite definite negotiations were conducted with them.'[49]

Faced with these accusations Bukharin pointed out that the period preceding the conclusion of the Brest peace treaty should be differentiated from that which succeeded it. Before the treaty was signed, Kamkov and Karelin had once suggested to him and Pyatakov in conversation that Lenin should be arrested for twenty-four hours, and they had both indignantly rejected the idea. At that juncture, he said, 'we [the Left Communists] and the Trotskyites had the majority in the Central Committee and we hoped to win the majority in the Party, so that to speak of conspiratorial activities at that time is nonsense'.[50] He tried to get Yakovleva to confirm that such irreproachable Party leaders as Kuibyshev, Yaroslavsky and Menzhinsky had also been Left Communists in 1918,* but the president of the court would not let him ask the relevant questions. It was not until his final plea that he was able to explain his intentions on this point, and at last had the satisfaction of presenting his argument without interruption.

Most of the evidence on the Left Communist-Left SR negotiations after the signing of the Brest treaty came from Karelin, who claimed to have heard Proshyan say at a Left SR meeting that Bukharin favoured the forcible overthrow of the Soviet government and would not shrink from exterminating its leaders. After some suggestive questioning from Vyshinsky, he volunteered the information that Lenin, Stalin and Sverdlov had been mentioned by name.[51] Kamkov's corroboration of this was at best indirect. He testified that his information about an agreement between the two groups came only from Karelin, and gave no date.

Bukharin was quite ready to admit that negotiations had

---

*See quotation from the Stenographic Report of the *Proceedings* in Appendix I on pp. 210 ff.

taken place after the signing of the treaty. They were conducted chiefly through Pyatakov, he said, and there had been talk of the arrest of government leaders although it was never suggested that any of them should be physically harmed. 'This,' Bukharin explained in his last plea, 'may be considered, as Citizen the Procurator, if I am not mistaken, formulated it, an attempt to overthrow the Soviet power by forcible means.'[52]

With the help of Osinsky, Mantsev and Karelin the prosecution also tried to prove that the Left SRs and the Left Communists had reached agreement on an uprising, and that the latter were well aware of the preparations for the July *coup* and the assassination of Count Mirbach. Bukharin effectively quashed these accusations by pointing out that he and many other Left Communists had actively helped to suppress the Left SR rising. But his defence was most telling when he recalled the fluid political atmosphere of 1917 and 1918. In those days even the sharpest conflicts among revolutionaries were visible to all and sundry; they could never have led to plans for mutual extermination. And he showed, by implication, how great was the change that had taken place between those years and 1938, the year of the *Yezhovshchina* and of his own trial. In his last plea he made his point with the utmost clarity :

As to the plan of physical extermination, I categorically deny it, and here the logic to which Citizen the State Prosecutor referred, namely, that forcible arrest implied physical extermination, will not help in the least. The Constituent Assembly was arrested, but nobody suffered physically. We arrested the faction of the 'Left' Socialist-Revolutionaries, yet not a single man of them suffered physically. The Left Socialist-Revolutionaries arrested Dzerzhinsky, yet he did not suffer physically. And I say— and this was omitted from the speech of the State Prosecutor —that in these criminal and dastardly conversations, it was specifically stipulated that not one hair of the persons concerned should be injured.* You may think what you like, but it is a real fact.⁵³

---

*Without wanting to weaken Bukharin's argument on this occasion, we feel bound to recall that the relative restraint shown in the political struggles of 1918 was much more characteristic of the behaviour of Lenin's opponents than of his supporters. While it is quite true that Dzerzhinsky, who was arrested by the Left srs on 6 July 1918 as well as the People's Commissar for Posts and Telegraph, Podbelsky, and the Cheka official, Latsis, were not harmed by their gaolers, the Left sr Alexandrovich and others were shot without trial the day after, and Muravyev, who commanded the Red Army troops on the Volga, died in circumstances suggesting that he also had been killed.

12. Bukharin's last stand

The end of the defendants' interrogation and their last pleas can be regarded as the end of the trial. Nothing that happened afterwards altered its character. Vyshinsky's speech, full of gross abuse and dishonest manipulation of the material obtained in cross-examination, was merely an elaboration of the indictment. He spoke for the whole of the morning session on 11 March, and concluded by saying that 'there exist no words with which one could depict the monstrousness of the crimes committed by the accused'. No more words are necessary to persuade the entire people what these monsters are, said Vyshinsky.

> Our people and all honest people throughout the world are waiting for . . . [a] just verdict. . . . Our whole country, from young to old, is awaiting and demanding one thing: the traitors and spies who were selling our country to the enemy must be shot like dirty dogs!
>
> Our people are demanding one thing: crush the accursed reptile!
>
> Time will pass. The graves of the hateful traitors will grow over with weeds and thistles, they will be covered with the eternal contempt of honest Soviet citizens, of the entire Soviet people. But over us, over our happy country, our sun will shine with its luminous rays as bright and joyous as before. Over the road cleared of the last scum and filth of the past, we, our people, with our beloved leader and teacher, the great Stalin, at our head, will march as before onwards and onwards, towards Communism![1]

The speeches of defending counsel were equally superfluous.

Kommodov and Braude entered a plea for mercy only on behalf of the doctors, which sounded like an indictment of their supposed blackmailer, Yagoda. With the exception of the doctors the accused had all undertaken their own defence, and agreed to combine their defending speeches with their final pleas. But very few of them grasped this opportunity to shed fresh light on the events which had brought them into the dock, or indeed on the trial as a whole. They all spoke in much the same way as they had already given evidence: some were mechanical and subservient, others persisted in denying the charges they had already refuted in cross-examination or tried to salve their honour by reminding the court of their revolutionary exploits in the past. Yagoda pleaded for mercy, which occasioned some surprise. Rykov and Bukharin made it plain that they believed themselves to be speaking for the last time. Bukharin, striking a personal note, tried to explain why after three months of stubborn resistance in prison he had at last decided to give evidence. He had done so

because while in prison I made a revaluation of my entire past. For when you ask yourself, 'If you must die, what are you dying for?' an absolutely black vacuity suddenly rises before you with startling vividness. There was nothing to die for, if one wanted to die unrepented. And, on the contrary, everything positive that glistens in the Soviet Union acquires new dimensions in a man's mind. . . . And when you ask yourself: 'Very well, suppose you do not die; suppose by some miracle you remain alive, again what for? Isolated from everybody, an enemy of the people, in an inhuman position, completely isolated from everything that constitutes the essence of life. . . .' And at once the same reply arises. And at such moments, Citizens Judges, everything personal, all the personal incrustation, all the rancour, pride, and a number of other things, fall away, disappear. And, in addition, when the reverberations of the broad international struggle reach your ear, all this in its entirety does its work, and the result is the complete internal moral victory of the USSR over its kneeling opponents.[2]

The trial ended in the early hours of 13 March, in an atmosphere of anti-climax, with a death sentence for all the accused with the exception of Pletnev, Rakovsky and Bessonov. Stalin's work was done. He may even have watched it draw to a close, for Fitzroy Maclean reported that 'at one stage of the trial a clumsily-directed arc-light dramatically revealed to attentive members of the audience the familiar features and heavy, drooping moustache peering out from behind the black glass of a small window, high under the ceiling of the court-room'.[3]

Unlike those that preceded it the Bukharin trial had relatively little impact on world opinion. Its conclusion coincided with an international event of extreme gravity—the Austrian *Anschluss*. The socialists of the Second International were torn between disgust at the bloodthirstiness and mendacity of Stalin's régime and the wish to have Soviet military might on their side when the Fascist onslaught began. Too much publicity for the trial, too many protests, might jeopardise the chances of an anti-Nazi alliance. Even émigré Russian social democrats like Dan, directly implicated in the proceedings, declared that in spite of the infamous Stalin régime the socialist workers of the world must stand shoulder to shoulder with the Russian workers against the common enemy. Trotsky in his *Bulletin of Opposition* adopted a similar stand.

Such an attitude towards the international crisis may well have been the motive force behind the 'capitulation' of Bukharin and Rykov. Bukharin spoke movingly in his final plea of the abyss facing any Communist leader who cut himself off from the Soviet Union. He was told, and he believed, that the Fascists were threatening to destroy the Soviet state. Was he to throw in his lot with them on the very eve of his death? Dan openly proclaimed from the security of the West that the defence of the Soviet Union in the coming war was more

important than any other political consideration. Could
Bukharin identify himself with a surrender to Fascism? He must
have known that thousands of his followers and millions of the
wretched peasants for whose sake he had risked and finally
forfeited his political career would take a defeatist line in the
coming war. Bukharin firmly believed that the bondage of
Fascism was in no way preferable to that of Stalinism; but
he also knew that his own followers and the rank and file,
especially of the peasantry, would begin by welcoming any
change, no matter whence it came. The conduct of millions of
Soviet citizens, many of them Party members, under German
occupation showed that he was not mistaken. It is perhaps
relevant that one of the most brilliant propagandists of the
Vlasov movement in the Second World War, Zykov,[4] was
widely thought to have been a close editorial collaborator of
Bukharin.

The behaviour of a man like Zykov, of the millions of Red
Army men who surrendered in 1941 and of the millions more
Soviet citizens who greeted the German invaders with bread
and salt as their liberators may help to explain the otherwise
unaccountable and indeed repugnant attitudes of Bukharin and
his co-defendants, and especially to explain Bukharin's final
plea. He must have known that his utter disillusionment with
the attempt to introduce socialism in Russia was shared by
millions. Had he remained free, and thus able to keep in contact
with the people who thought as he did, he might well have
wanted to lead them in every eventuality, even in those of
war and defeat. He might then have had an opportunity to
wrest power from Stalin (discredited by the inadequacy of his
military preparations) and to become a national leader. As it was
now, granted only a last chance to give advice to those who
shared his profound aversion for Stalin's régime, he had only
two courses of action open to him. He could either tell them he
was going to die in a state of unrepentant hostility to Stalin,
thus encouraging them to seize the first opportunity to topple
the régime; or he could advise them—at that particular

juncture in international politics, with a German attack imminent—to rally round Stalin in spite of all their bitterness. The factor that must have decided him to choose the latter course was his conviction that there was no one except him who could, or would, do anything better than collaborate with a future invader.

In his final plea he said:

> I refute the accusation of having plotted against the life of Vladimir Ilyich, but my counter-revolutionary confederates, and I at their head, endeavoured to murder Lenin's cause, which is being carried on with such tremendous success by Stalin. The logic of this struggle led us step by step into the blackest quagmire. And it has once more been proved that departure from the position of Bolshevism means siding with political counter-revolutionary banditry. Counter-revolutionary banditry has now been smashed, we have been smashed, and we repent our frightful crimes.[5]

As on so many other occasions, these last words of Bukharin's conceal a whole system of secret connotations. He was admitting that he had lost faith in the teachings of Lenin, or at least in Stalin's interpretation of them in both theory and practice. In accordance with the unspoken agreement between the prosecutor and the accused which alone made a public trial possible, Bukharin refrained from making the claim that he had worked out a programme of his own, which presented an alternative to that of Stalin and opened up the way to something in the nature of 'humanised Communism'—although such a claim could easily have been substantiated. Instead he chose to admit that in departing from Leninist-Stalinist doctrine, the oppositionists had headed straight for the path of conspiratorial and subversive activities which, in the agreed parlance, he described as 'counter-revolutionary banditry'. He thereby conceded his failure to impose his own political ideas on the existing system, but did not explain why he now chose to repent of siding with the 'banditry'. 'The reverberations of the broad international struggles' that reached him in prison could well have determined his stand. For he did not believe that his followers, and other anti-Stalinists inside Russia, would prove equal to organising national resistance in the event of world war, and feared they could only pave the way to national surrender, this time to a foreign tyranny. Using the limited opportunities afforded him by his last plea, he made strenuous efforts to ward off such a disaster.

In judging Bukharin's behaviour at the trial, his admissions of guilt and protestations of penitence, we must never lose sight of the extremely difficult position in which he was placed. The freedom of the courtroom was restricted by the agreements and promises already extracted from the accused, subjected to all kinds of brainwashing and coercion during their preliminary investigation. At the slightest attempt on their part to deviate from their agreed stand, the Public Prosecutor adopted a threatening tone, and even declared that he might cut short the interrogation. It was therefore no minor personal achievement of Bukharin's to have insisted that his motive in assuming a 'counter-revolutionary' attitude was his political disagreement with Stalin's line and, in the last resort, with Lenin's own programme. He never expressed regret at holding ideas divergent from Leninist-Stalinist teaching, but only at trying to implement these ideas against the will of the Party, whose decision-making mechanism was, he knew, manipulated by Stalin.

One is at first surprised by the fact that Vyshinsky did not make better use of Bukharin's admission of disillusionment with Communism and of his subsequent ideological and political degeneration. A closer analysis of the Prosecutor's tortuous methods in conducting the trial helps to clarify his tactics. We realise that he refrained even from mentioning in court certain compromising circumstances of Bukharin's life which could have provided a far more realistic basis for the prosecution's case than the purely imaginary subversive activities with which he—as principal defendant—was charged. Thus, nothing was said at the trial about a 'document' which had circulated outside the Soviet Union during the twenties and was widely believed to have been written or inspired by Bukharin. This was a letter purporting to have been written by him to an old left-wing friend living in emigration. It appeared under the title 'Brothers in Lenin' in the American magazine *Living Age,* on 18 April 1925. The magazine did not guarantee the authenticity of the letter. It is in fact spurious in a sense, being a slightly modified translation of a pamphlet published in Berlin in 1924 under the title *Ibo ya bolshevik* (For I Am a Bolshevik). An émigré Menshevik writer and poet, Ilya Britan, later confessed that he had written the Russian pamphlet, and claimed that it was based on certain information he had collected from hearsay while still living in the Soviet Union.[6]

'Brothers in Lenin' is written in an intimate, semi-jocular epistolary style that reflects the profound disillusionment with their cause of its supposed author, and other leading Bolsheviks, after the death of Lenin. Although not uncritical of some of Lenin's theoretical views, the letter is full of admiration for his political and tactical acumen. Lenin refused to surrender to the Kerensky government for trial in 1917 despite pressure from his party because he foresaw that the Bolsheviks would come to power in October. In 1918 Lenin insisted against Trotsky's advice on signing the 'obscene peace' of Brest-Litovsk because he foresaw the inevitable downfall of Wilhelm II. And in 1921 Lenin forced the New Economic Policy on the Party. He was right in his decision, but his followers were much too weak and insignificant to make the complicated mechanism of the NEP work. In fact Lenin's successors, according to the letter, were all 'nullities'. 'Stalin,' it says, is 'a zero who sees the [sic] salvation in one million more—how many will that make?—one million more dead bodies.'

One by one Kamenev, Krupskaya, Zinoviev, Rykov and even Dzerzhinsky are similarly dismissed, and the Party rank and file charged with bureaucratism and corruption. The writer does not except himself from this condemnation. 'My dear friend, I too am a zero if you take me off the platform or away from the writing desk and put me to real work. I know it and therefore never accept any "business posts"—the more so as I happen to have Spartan tastes and no liking for embezzlement.'

This indictment of the cynicism and bloodthirstiness of the Soviet leaders could not have appeared very credible to many observers of the Soviet scene in 1925. Yet we must certainly admit that the author's foreknowledge of the main characteristic of Stalin's rule—Stalin's callous indifference to the sufferings and deaths of millions of people—is remarkable. When in 1928 Stalin's policies began to take shape a number of periodicals outside Russia, such as *La Revue Universelle* and *L'Avenir,* reprinted the letter and argued from internal evidence in favour of its authenticity. A year earlier Volume 8 of the *Large Soviet Encyclopaedia,* of which Bukharin was one of the editors, had carried a long article on Bukharin himself written by his pupil, D. Maretsky. In the bibliography attached to it 'Brothers in Lenin', as published in *Living Age,* is cited as one of the sources for the study of Bukharin's views. In 1928, however, when Bukharin's position was becoming precarious, he published in *Pravda* on 7 March a letter entitled : 'A denial, which would have been superfluous had there been fewer fools in the world.' Here he claimed that the *Living Age* letter was stuffed with 'nonsense, idle conjecture and provincial gossip', and said he had heard its author was a certain Britan, whom he had never met in his life. 'For a long time I paid no heed to the publication of this "document". But when it began to appear again and again, and was greeted with enthusiastic applause by bourgeois pressmen and overfed shopkeepers, I came to the firm conclusion that more people are charlatans and fools than I originally believed, and decided to communicate this conclusion to my readers.' It is curious that Bukharin did not explain how such a bogus letter came to be listed in the article

about him in the *Large Soviet Encyclopaedia*—all the more as
he must have read and 'vetted' the article himself.[7]

But whatever reasons Bukharin may have had for playing
down the incident of the *Living Age* letter, they could scarcely
have been the same as those which caused Vyshinsky to omit it
completely from his indictment. Vyshinsky must have known of
the *Encyclopaedia* article, particularly after its author Maretsky
had been purged and severely punished. The *Living Age* letter
and its use in the *Encyclopaedia* could have provided him
with excellent material to mock Bukharin and other victims
of the trial. We know from many instances of his behaviour
during the macabre pageant of the show trials that he took
special pleasure in this ceremonial of derision of the defendants
before their execution.* In fact, however, Vyshinsky was only
acting in consistency with the principles he had set himself
when undertaking the prosecution. He could naturally have
referred to many of Bukharin's anti-Stalinist writings, and produced them in court as incriminating evidence. But he did not
do so. Nor did he reveal the contents of Bukharin's allegedly
seditious conversations with Kamenev in 1928, although these
conversations were one of the main props of the indictment.
It was Bukharin, not Vyshinsky, who quoted the Ryutin Platform,† which had circulated among the oppositionists in 1932;
even so he was not permitted to disclose what it actually said
but only to observe that it advocated the use of terrorism and
violence.

There is one more instance of Vyshinsky's deliberately
omitting to make use of incriminating material against the
accused. Early in 1936 with Stalin's express permission
Bukharin had been sent to Western Europe to purchase some
Marx archive material for the Institute of Marxism-Leninism.‡
To have despatched him at such a time on a journey abroad
involving contacts with Western socialists looked very much

*Cf. Vyshinsky's treatment of Rosengoltz. See Appendix I, 5.
†See above, p. 163.
‡See above, pp. 93 ff.

like an encouragement to him to compromise himself, for it was to be assumed that he would be none too discreet in discussing the Stalin régime with the people he was supposed to meet. At the trial, in fact, Bukharin himself referred to his journey in the following terms: 'I had to meet with this Nicolaevsky by virtue of my official business. Thus I had a quite legitimate cover behind which I could carry on counter-revolutionary conversations and make agreements of one kind or another.'[8] One would have expected Vyshinsky to seize on this confession to try to elicit what the 'counter-revolutionary conversations' were about, and what 'agreements' had been concluded. But instead he simply shrugged the whole matter off, urging Bukharin yet again to admit that he was an agent of the Austrian, German, Polish, English and Japanese intelligence services. And all through the trial we find Vyshinsky consistently ignoring every verifiable fact capable of reinforcing the charge of seditious activities levelled against Bukharin and his associates. At the same time, we find him making allegations that stretched the credulity of the world to the very limit, and demanding confessions of the accused which even after months of brainwashing they could only regard as ridiculous. Viewing the trial as a whole, therefore, we are driven to the conclusion that it was staged, not in order to reveal the *real* transgressions of the defendants—those for which they were to be executed—but to conceal them, from both the Soviet people and the world at large. This is why entirely fictitious offences had to be substituted for the real ones which brought the accused to their doom.

Stalin viewed it as an intolerable threat to his régime that former prominent Party members, including his closest collaborators, should have turned away from him and wanted to abandon his programme. The mere fact that an alternative programme to his own had ever existed and been suppressed had to be blotted out and never referred to in any public utterance. Those who had dared to oppose his policy had to be destroyed, but let none dare to say they were being destroyed on account of their political opposition. Vyshinsky deployed all his skill to achieve Stalin's destructive purpose, using the special rules for fabricating evidence he so cynically advertised in his writings just before he turned from the practice of the law to that of diplomacy.

In resisting Vyshinsky's onslaught in court, Bukharin scored only a partial success. He was the only one of the defendants who systematically refused to play the villain's part devised for him by the Public Prosecutor, and his protestations seemed convincing even at that time. After Stalin's death and the period of 'de-Stalinisation', the allegations of treason and espionage were quietly dropped from all references to Bukharin and his co-defendants, and now he is no longer described as an enemy of the people. This might not have been the case had he not shown the courage and presence of mind to refute Vyshinsky's accusations. But in another respect he suffered total defeat. All the attempts he made to confess to his 'real crimes', i.e. his heretical views, and to explain the danger they represented to Stalin's régime, were cut short and suppressed by Vyshinsky, backed by the President of the court. In his last plea, Bukharin abandoned these attempts, and accepted the inevitable sentence with resignation as just retribution for his defection from Lenin's cause. For reasons on which we can only speculate, he did not repeat his endeavour to expound the tenets of his political deviation, or the ideas he proposed as alternatives to those of Stalin: considerations of Soviet patriotism, or the fear of a slow and painful death, may have determined his behaviour on the last occasion when he spoke in public.

It would be inhuman to judge him too harshly for it, but we should not forget that this failure to reveal the political character of the trial meant the loss of a unique opportunity to thrust his political ideas on future generations. It is possibly the reason why even now, thirty years after the trial, no public rehabilitation of the accused has yet been officially declared in the Soviet Union. Those who were put to death without trial at about the same time have since been rehabilitated almost to a man. The defendants of the show trials were not, because in the process of such a rehabilitation the ideological struggles which were the reason for their prosecution would have had to be resuscitated, particularly those relating to Stalin's collectivisation programme and his agrarian policy in general. Neither Khrushchev nor his successors were ready to countenance this. One may even doubt whether Bukharin himself would have approved of such a rehabilitation. For he knew too well how important it was for the maintenance of the régime and the security of the state to suppress all deviations. He agreed to play a role in the abject drama staged by Vyshinsky even though he deviated from the producer's instructions. He did so in order to be able to make a last public appearance before his death, and present his defence to the world at large. But in the process he found himself ensnared in a net of equivocation and ambiguous phrases, so that instead of defending what he believed to be the truth, he upheld that most powerful weapon of the very tyranny to which he had fallen victim—institutionalised mendacity.

APPENDIX I
Trial proceedings

APPENDIX I

Trial proceedings

In this appendix we reproduce five extensive quotations from the stenographic report of the trial *Proceedings*. The first shows the technique Bukharin employed in order to limit the accusations brought against him of having hatched a plot against the Soviet government in 1928. The second is an exchange between Bukharin and Vyshinsky on the subject of espionage. The third shows Rykov trying to disengage himself from the net of admissions and confessions he made at the preliminary investigation. The fourth vividly illustrates the manner in which Vyshinsky and the President of the Court tried to muzzle Bukharin when he wanted to elicit from the witness Yakovleva a statement to the effect that many Bolsheviks belonged in 1918 to the so-called Left Communist opposition who were never charged, on that account, with plotting against the Soviet régime. The fifth is an example of the *Galgenhumor* of Vyshinsky mocking his victim Rosengoltz. Some cuts in the quotations are indicated by a line of dots. It should be borne in mind that many of the admissions Bukharin made at the trial while under interrogation he later repudiated either explicitly or implicitly in his last plea. I refer the reader to my comments on the last plea in Chapter 12 of the present work.

1. Opposition or insurrection?

Vyshinsky: You consider that the accused Ivanov quite rightly stated that in 1927-28, when he was leaving for the North Caucasus, you gave him instructions?

Bukharin: It is perfectly true that when he was leaving for the North Caucasus, I, on behalf of the Right centre, gave him instructions regarding the recruitment of people and the formation of an organisation there. Moreover, he had certain persons in mind, like Stepanov, Pivovarov, Tomachev and others.

And it is perfectly true that in 1931-32, to use his jargon, I passed him over to Lobov, who was to direct him.

Perfectly true is the assertion made by the accused Ivanov to the effect that I kept him informed of the stand of the Right centre, from the Ryutin Platform to the latest stands, of which the Court is fairly well informed.

It is quite true that I also met him later, in 1931-32, but I cannot recall the dates just now.

Vyshinsky: That we shall ask later. I once more repeat that what interests me is 1928. Consequently, do you confirm this part of the testimony of the accused Ivanov?

Bukharin: I confirm that I had meetings with him at that time.

Vyshinsky: And that you carried on those conversations with him, as he informed the Court, about anti-Party and anti-Soviet activities.

Bukharin: We did.

Vyshinsky: The accused Ivanov testified that you proposed that he should form an organisation of Rights in the North Caucasus with certain definite aims. Do you confirm that too?

Bukharin: He has got the dates mixed up.

Vyshinsky: First of all, do you confirm the fact itself?

Bukharin: I confirm the fact itself that I instructed him to form an organisation.

Vyshinsky: A secret one?

Bukharin: A secret, illegal, counter-revolutionary one. But at that period the acute struggle against the Party and the Soviet government had not taken the forms . . .

Vyshinsky: I am just now interested in the testimony of the accused Ivanov, which the Court has heard. He says that Bukharin gave me, i.e., Ivanov, instructions to proceed to form a secret organisation of Rights in the North Caucasus. Do you confirm this?

Bukharin: That part I do confirm.

Vyshinsky: Consequently, in 1928 you had adopted the method of illegal, underground activities?

Bukharin: That was a moment of such transition ...

Vyshinsky: I am not asking you when it was. Is this a fact, or not a fact?

Bukharin: That I confirm.

Vyshinsky: Did you also tell Ivanov at the time that a centre of the Right organisation was already functioning?

Bukharin: I did.

Vyshinsky: Consisting of whom?

Bukharin: Consisting of three persons: Tomsky, Rykov, and myself, Bukharin.

Vyshinsky: Did you tell him that this centre was preparing for the overthrow of the Soviet power?

Bukharin: I did, but this refers to a later period.

Vyshinsky: To which exactly?

Bukharin: I think it refers roughly to 1932-33.

Vyshinsky: That is, somewhat later. But the fact that you had such a conversation with Ivanov you do confirm?

Bukharin: I do. I do not remember the date, nor the month, but that was the general orientation of the Right centre.

Vyshinsky: And do you confirm that you said that you were preparing for open battles?

Bukharin: There could have been no open battles in 1926. When Ivanov says that we were preparing for open battles, he is mixing the dates.

Vyshinsky: But during the preliminary investigation you said that it relates to 1926.

Bukharin: Yes, but not in the sense in which it is understood here, Citizen the State Prosecutor....................................

Vyshinsky: Let us turn to your volume, p. 120. Just look for your testimony there.

Bukharin: I was arranging for this with Ivanov: 'In 1926-27, when we were preparing for open battles against the Party, I advised Ivanov not to take part in the open battles, but to remain in reserve.' I do not deny that.

Vyshinsky: Then in 1927 Ivanov went to the North Caucasus, and you gave him instructions. Do you confirm that? I ask the question to check this. You gave him instructions to organise an illegal Right group. Is that true?

Bukharin: It is.

Vyshinsky: An illegal group?

Bukharin: An illegal one.

Vyshinsky: This you confirm. You also instructed him to carry out a number of tasks you gave him with regard to this organisation in the period of 1928. It was not only a question of recruiting, but also of the organisation of insurrectionary bands?

Bukharin: I did not go into the technical side of this business.

Vyshinsky: I am not referring to the technical side of the organisation of insurrectionary bands, but to the platform of the Rights, in which the line of insurrection was adopted. When you instructed Ivanov to form an illegal organisation, did you say anything about insurrectionary bands?

Bukharin: I did not, and could not at that time.

Vyshinsky: But what were the illegal organisations to do?

Bukharin: The illegal organisations were to muster forces for the fight against the Party, which was growing acute.

Vyshinsky: Only preparations for a fight?

Bukharin: It was such a stage in the general development of the Right deviation.

Vyshinsky: And when did you raise the question of insurrectionary bands?

Bukharin: The adoption of violence roughly relates to 1932.

Vyshinsky: Where was Ivanov at that time?

Bukharin: This I do not remember.

Vyshinsky: Accused Ivanov, where were you in 1932?

Ivanov: In 1932 I was in the Northern Territory.

Vyshinsky: Was the question of organising and forming insurrectionary bands discussed by you, and if so, in what form?

Ivanov: It was discussed. Bukharin bluntly put the question of establishing connections with the discontented kulak elements of the Cossacks.

Vyshinsky: This was not in the Northern Territory, but in the North Caucasus?

Ivanov: Yes, in the North Caucasus.

Vyshinsky: This refers not to 1932. Were you in the Northern Territory in 1932?

Ivanov: Yes, in 1932 I was in the Northern Territory.

Vyshinsky: And was the question of preparing insurrectionary bands raised then?

Ivanov: The question of preparing insurrectionary bands was also put before me by Bukharin in 1932, when the question was raised of creating Right organisations in the Northern Territory.

Vyshinsky: In 1932 did not Bukharin speak about the necessity of strengthening insurrectionary bands?

Ivanov: He did.

Vyshinsky: Hence you remember that you had two such talks —in 1928 and in 1932?

Ivanov: Yes.

Vyshinsky: In connection with your work in the North Caucasus and in the Northern Territory?

Ivanov: Yes.

Bukharin (to the Court): I assert that in 1928 there was no talk at all about an insurrectionary orientation, as is evidenced by numerous documents and facts, including ...

Vyshinsky: But in 1929?

Bukharin: The fixation of the question about insurrectionary organisations that was approved by the Right centre was first indicated in what is called the Ryutin Platform.

Vyshinsky: The Ryutin Platform, its first variant, in what period was that?

Bukharin: There was no variant at all. There was a preliminary conference, if I am not mistaken, in the spring of

1932 at which the theses were outlined. But in the platform which you mention—the platform of 1928-29—there was no reference to insurrection. . . .

Vyshinsky: Hence, you assert that the question of insurrectionary bands was raised only in 1932?

Bukharin: The question of an insurrectionary orientation arose in 1932.

Vyshinsky: The question of an 'insurrectionary orientation'. What is an 'insurrectionary orientation'?

Bukharin: It means that every line has its strategy, tactics, organisation, etc. An insurrectionary band is a category of organisation, but not a category of strategy, and not even a category of tactics. In my terminology I usually distinguish between them because it seems to me that they can be distinguished. . . .

Vyshinsky: Of course; they can. But I ask: in your activities there was a line of insurrectionary movement. Is this what you call an 'insurrectionary orientation'?

Bukharin: Yes, tactics.

Vyshinsky: And the organisation of insurrectionary bands followed from these tactics?

Bukharin: Yes, it did.

Vyshinsky: And what did you do in this matter? What instructions did you give?

Bukharin: I did not give Ivanov any instructions in this sense.

Vyshinsky: But Ivanov says that instructions were given . . . Accused Ivanov, did you understand it in that way?

Ivanov: The instructions were conveyed to me in sufficiently clear terms to enable me to understand their simple meaning. The point was raised that the kulaks were in an angry mood. These were the social forces on which we were to rely. Our task was to head the insurrection. And even in regard to the North Caucasus it was said, although in a somewhat different version, that the North Caucasus could provide considerable kulak cadres, that there the peasant and Cossack movement might start earlier than in any other place, and therefore we should take our place at the head of this movement.

Vyshinsky: Bukharin, do you corroborate this?

Bukharin: This is correct, but not in relation to Ivanov. I said this to another person.

Vyshinsky: The other person we shall discuss separately. What is important just now is whether the explanation given here coincides with the orientation towards insurrection, about which you have spoken.

Bukharin: I could not have said this to Ivanov because he was not in the North Caucasus in 1932.

Vyshinsky: Ivanov, what year were you referring to?

Ivanov: I was speaking of the Northern Territory, but at the same time I said that in a somewhat different version this also applied to the North Caucasus.

Vyshinsky: When did you leave the North Caucasus?

Ivanov: I left the North Caucasus on April 2 or 1, 1931.

Vyshinsky: While you were in the North Caucasus when did you speak with Bukharin?

Ivanov: In 1928.

Vyshinsky: And in 1929-30?

Ivanov: I was meeting him, but I do not think we talked about these things. ....
Permit me to put a question to Bukharin. Perhaps Bukharin will exert his memory and recall whether we had a conversation in 1928 about the growing discontent among the upper stratum of the rural population, and about a tendency towards a sharp expression of this discontent with the Soviet power. Let him answer this question.

Bukharin: Of course, in 1928 a conversation about the growing discontent did take place; I cannot deny it, because we were meeting in 1928. But I categorically deny that I spoke about insurrection in 1928.

Ivanov: Another question. Did Bukharin put it to me that in the carrying out of the line that was adopted by the Rights,

the North Caucasus was of exceptionally great importance,
and why it was of great importance?

Bukharin: It is quite true, Citizen Procurator and Citizens
Judges, that when I spoke about the North Caucasus I said
that the North Caucasus was one of the places where discontent among the peasantry was manifesting itself and will
manifest itself most vividly, without, however, drawing any
insurrectionary conclusions, because these arose at a much
later period.

Ivanov: Bukharin said that an acute manifestation of discontent among the peasantry in the North Caucasus was possible.
This comes very close to what I said about this conversation.
In conformity with your conceptions did you not instruct me
and the Right organisation to clutch at this discontent and
to do everything to work up the peasants against the Soviet
power?

Bukharin: First you spoke about insurrection, but I spoke about
the suitable social base for the Right organisation, about
recruiting members for this Right counter-revolutionary
organisation.

Vyshinsky: With what object?

Bukharin: With the object of creating mass bases for the
struggle against the Party line.

Vyshinsky: Cossack, kulak circles for the struggle against the
Party line?

Bukharin: Well, what of it?

Vyshinsky: For the struggle against the Soviet power?

Bukharin: The struggle against the Party line is a struggle
against the Soviet power.

Vyshinsky: But the struggle against the Party line finds expression in other forms.

Bukharin: I think that the Citizen Procurator, the Citizens
Judges and the whole country are interested in seeing how
out of certain deviations monstrous conclusions are formed
by the logic of the struggle. That is why I want to preserve a
certain time-proportion in this respect. In 1928 the anti-

Party platform was formulated. At the end of 1928 and the transition of 1929 the slogan was issued to form an illegal organisation. In the course of the further intensification of the struggle all this led to what you know.

Vyshinsky: The question is, did you not orientate Ivanov on the grounds that in your opinion there was favourable soil in the North Caucasus for insurrection against the Soviet power?

Bukharin: There was no talk about such an orientation at that time. The orientation was that there was soil there for growing discontent with the Soviet power.

Vyshinsky: On whose part?

Bukharin: On the part of the kulak well-to-do strata of the peasantry, and partly also of the middle strata of the peasantry, as the middle peasantry there was very strong.[1]

2. '*Opening the front*', *and espionage*

Bukharin: When the Fascists came to power in Germany, exchanges of opinion commenced among the leaders of the counter-revolutionary organisation concerning the possibility of utilising foreign states in connection with a war situation. Here I must say frankly, and I tell the Court what I precisely remember, that in this major question, which is a very important subject for the Court's consideration and for the determination of the legal sanction, the Trotskyites were outright for territorial concessions, while on the whole the leading circles of the Right counter-revolutionary organisation were primarily concerned with concessions, trade agreements, duties, prices, supplies of raw material, fuel, etc.—in short, various concessions of an economic nature. When I began my testimony I told the Court that I, as one of the leaders of the counter-revolutionary bloc, am not just as a cog in the wheel, bear responsibility for absolutely everything done by this organisation. But in so far as concrete things are concerned, I think that it can be said of this case that the guiding principle in the bloc, the most active political principle in the sense of the acuteness of the struggle, in the sense of far-reaching criminal connections, etc., was after all the Trotskyite section. I repeat, I say this not in order to disclaim the responsibility of the Right section, since in this case from the point of view of criminology it is not important who first said 'a', who repeated this 'a', who exposed and reported it; but from the point of view of the internal mechanics of this case and from the point of view of elucidating the personal role of Trotsky, who, unfortunately is beyond the reach of the Court, I think this question has a certain importance, and that is why I make bold to emphasise it here.

In the summer of 1934 Radek told me that directions had been received from Trotsky, that Trotsky was conducting negotiations with the Germans, that Trotsky had already promised the Germans a number of territorial concessions, including the Ukraine. If my memory does not fail me, territorial concessions to Japan were also mentioned. In general, in these negotiations Trotsky already behaved not only as a conspirator who hopes to get power by means of an armed *coup* at some future date, but already felt himself the master of Soviet land, which he wants to convert from Soviet to non-Soviet.

I must say that then, at that time, I remonstrated with Radek. Radek confirms this in his testimony, just as he confirmed at a confrontation with me that I objected to this, that I considered it essential that he, Radek, should write and tell Trotsky that he was going too far in these negotiations, that he might compromise not only himself, but all his allies, us Right conspirators in particular, and that this meant certain disaster for us. It seemed to me that with the growth of mass patriotism, which is beyond all doubt, this point of view of Trotsky's was politically and tactically inexpedient from the standpoint of the plan of the conspiracy itself, and that much greater caution was needed...............................

Tomsky considered it permissible to take advantage of war and preliminary agreements with Germany. This I opposed by the following arguments. I said that in the first place if Germany were to intervene in one way or another during the war to help the counter-revolutionary *coup,* then, as it always happens, Germany, being rather a strong military and technical factor, would inevitably put her feet on the table and tear up any preliminary agreement which had been concluded. Secondly, I advanced the argument that since this was to be a military *coup,* then by virtue of the very logic of things the military group of the conspirators would have extraordinary influence, and, as always happens in these cases, it would be just that section of the joint upper group of the counter-revolutionary circles that would command great material forces, and consequently political forces, and that hence a peculiar Bonapartist danger might arise. And Bonapartists—I was thinking particularly of Tukhachevsky—would start out by making short shrift of their allies and so-called inspirers in Napoleon style. In my conversations I always called Tukhachevsky a 'potential little Napoleon', and you know how Napoleon dealt with the so-called ideologists.

Vyshinsky: And you considered yourself an ideologist?

Bukharin: Both an ideologist of a counter-revolutionary *coup* and a practical man. You, of course, would prefer to hear that I consider myself a spy, but I never considered myself a spy, nor do I now.

Vyshinsky: It would be more correct if you did.

Bukharin: That is your opinion, but my opinion is different.

Vyshinsky: We shall see what the opinion of the court is. Tell us how you conducted this 'ideological' conversation with Tomsky then or at any other time; did Tomsky propose two variants for the seizure of power?................................

Bukharin: There I wanted to say that after these premlinary conversations in 1935—I do not know what other factors played a part before the adoption of any decision on the part of the Right centre and on the part of the contact centre: whether Tomsky was being pressed by Yenukidze or the military circles, or jointly by Yenukidze, the Trotskyites and the Zinovievites—but the fact is that Karakhan left without a preliminary conversation with the members of the leading centre, with the exception of Tomsky.

Now I want to tell the Court what I remember concerning the three conversations that took place after Karakhan's arrival. The first conversation was with Tomsky, the second with Yenukidze and the third with Karakhan, who introduced certain details and an added coefficient into the conversation.

As I remember, Tomsky told me that Karakhan had arrived at an agreement with Germany on more advantageous terms than Trotsky.

Vyshinsky: First of all, tell us about Tomsky. I am interested in your talk with Tomsky concerning your plan of a *coup d'état,* as you call it, the seizure of power. When did you have a conversation about opening the front to the Germans? ....

Bukharin: When I asked Tomsky how he conceived the mechanics of the *coup* he said this was the business of the military organisation, which was to open the front.

Vyshinsky: So Tomsky was preparing to open the front? ......
....

Bukharin: He said he 'was to' (*dolzhna*); but the meaning of these words is *müssen* and not *sollen.*

Vyshinsky: Leave your philology aside. In Russian 'was to' means 'was to'...

Bukharin: That is what you would like, but I am entitled not to agree with you. It is well known that in German *sollen* and *müssen* have two meanings . . .

Vyshinsky: You are accustomed to speak in German, but we are speaking in the Soviet language.

Bukharin: The German language in itself is not odious.

Vyshinsky: You are continuing to speak in German, you are already accustomed to negotiate with the Germans in their language. But here we speak in Russian. When Tomsky told you that it was necessary to open the front to the Germans, then, if you objected, you should have said as follows: 'I objected, I said that I would not consent to such a betrayal, to such treason.' Did you say that?

Bukharin: No, I did not. But if I said that it was necessary . . .

Vyshinsky: To play on patriotic slogans, that is, to speculate on them, to pretend that somebody committed treason, but that you were patriots. . . .

Bukharin: That is not quite so, because in other parts of my testimony, including the confrontation with Radek, and during all the conversations with Radek, I objected to what Radek said and declared that Tomsky did not understand . . .

Vyshinsky: Accused Bukharin, that you have here employed a jesuitical method, a perfidious method, is borne out by the following. Permit me to read further: 'I had in mind that by this, that is, by the conviction of those guilty of the defeat, we would be able at the same time to rid ourselves of the Bonapartist danger that alarmed me.'[2]

3. Did Bukharin know about espionage?

The matter arose out of a quotation from the minutes of the preliminary investigation of Rykov, during which Rykov admitted under interrogation that he had known of the treasonable activities in Byelorussia of certain persons not present in court. The interrogator asked Rykov whether his accomplices knew about them. Vyshinsky quoted Rykov's alleged reply: 'The other members of the centre, Bukharin and Tomsky, knew of it too.' At this point Rykov, interrupting Vyshinsky, claimed he had said that Bukharin and Tomsky 'obviously' knew of it too; by 'obviously' he meant that this was an assumption of his not based on direct fact. Vyshinsky insisted that elsewhere in his deposition Rykov had repeated the same phrase without the word 'obviously'. Here Bukharin broke into the dialogue, and the following nightmarish debate took place:

Bukharin: I was not asked a single word about this during the preliminary investigation, and you, Citizen Procurator, did not question me for three months, not a single word.

Vyshinsky: I am questioning you now. This is my right.

Bukharin: But at the preliminary investigation...

Vyshinsky: Be so kind as not to instruct me how to conduct a preliminary investigation, the more so since you do not understand a thing about it. You understand more about the affairs for which you find yourself in the dock.

Bukharin: Possibly.

Vyshinsky: Was the accused Rykov, by your decision, put in charge of the connections with the counter-revolutionary organisations?

Bukharin: In a general way, he was put in charge.

Vyshinsky: And your status was that of a secret member?

Bukharin: Inside there was no status of secrecy.

Vyshinsky: With regard to connections with the Byelorussian group?

Bukharin: Generally everything was done with secrecy.

Vyshinsky: But your status was that of particular secrecy?

Bukharin: This term cannot be applied here, it does not fit.

Vyshinsky: Do you want to argue about the term?

Bukharin: No, I do not want to argue, on the contrary, I keep silent.

Vyshinsky: I ask the Court to authenticate this. What I have cited here is fully identical with what was written in the original record signed by Rykov. And I request that this be presented to Rykov so that he may identify his signature.

Rykov: I do not deny it.

Vyshinsky: The word 'obviously' refers to the previous sentence, but with regard to Bukharin there is no 'obviously'. 'Bukharin and Tomsky knew, Schmidt was partly initiated'.

The President: I corroborate that these quotations correspond to the original record which has Rykov's signature on each page.

Rykov: I affirm that the word 'obviously' refers to what has been read.

Vyshinsky: The word 'obviously' is not there.

Rykov: My deposition—'Bukharin and Tomsky knew, Schmidt was partly initiated'—should be understood with the word 'obviously'. I am not a very good stylist. If I said the word 'obviously' in the first sentence, and the second sentence represents a paraphrase of the first sentence, the word 'obviously' is implied.

Vyshinsky: According to your supposition, did Bukharin know of these espionage connections, or did he not?

Rykov: He should have known, but in less detail and fewer particulars than I knew. But which details, which particulars, which facts out of those I related and knew in greater detail than he, that I cannot tell.

Vyshinsky: If by the decision of the centre you were entrusted with maintaining the connections with the Byelorussian group, that means that you knew all the details of the connections.

Rykov: No.

Vyshinsky: Through the connections which you maintained you should have known everything you were doing.

Rykov: I should have known what I was doing? I don't understand what you are driving at.

Vyshinsky: I am asking you, were you supposed to know what you were doing?

Rykov: What I was doing?

Vyshinsky: Of course.

Rykov: That is to say, you are asking me whether I was in a state of consciousness or unconsciousness? Always in a state of consciousness.

Vyshinsky: And did Bukharin know everything?

o

Rykov: I did not speak to Bukharin about details.

Vyshinsky: I am not asking you about details but about the substance. Did Bukharin know the substance?

Rykov: Bukharin was informed about the substance of the connection and knew about it.

Vyshinsky: That is what I wanted to establish. Permit me to consider it established that Rykov and Bukharin knew the substance of the treasonable connection which included espionage. Is that correct, Rykov?

Rykov: That is, espionage followed.

Bukharin: So it appears that I knew something from which something followed.

Vyshinsky: You will argue it out at leisure.

Rykov: I am afraid that there will be no leisure.

Vyshinsky: That is for the court to decide. I have no more questions.[3]

4. *Bukharin's abortive attempt to interrogate Yakovleva*

Commandant of the court: The Court is coming, please rise.

The President: Please be seated. The session is resumed. Comrade Commandant, call witness Yakovleva. (*Witness Yakovleva enters the Court.*) Accused Bukharin, have you any questions to put to witness Yakovleva?

Bukharin: Yes, I have several, if you will allow me.

The President: Please.

Bukharin: Firstly, I wish to ask witness Yakovleva whether she is aware that I was the first during the struggle against Trotsky to give publicity to the conversation with Kamkov and Karelin?

Yakovleva: I am aware of that, but I am also aware of the point that when Bukharin, in the heat of the Party's struggle against Trotsky, reported on this fact, he did not tell the whole story, far from it.

Bukharin: That's another question ...

The President: Accused Bukharin, let her finish.

Yakovleva: He did not have the courage to pull the whole curtain aside, and only raised a tiny corner of it. I am aware of that too.

The President: What other questions are there?

Bukharin: I have another question ...

Vyshinsky: Excuse me. I have a question to put to witness Yakovleva. What in your opinion did Bukharin conceal, what did he suppress?

Yakovleva: He suppressed all that I have told the Court today.

Vyshinsky: That is to say?

Yakovleva: That is to say, the fact that there was a plot between the 'Left Communists' and the 'Left' Socialist-Revolutionaries.

Vyshinsky: It was organised with the direct, active, leading ...

Yakovleva: ... part being played by Bukharin himself.

Vyshinsky (to Bukharin): Is that true?

Bukharin: What I testified is true.

Vyshinsky: Is that true?

Bukharin: What Yakovleva says regarding the period prior to the Brest-Litovsk Peace is untrue.

Vyshinsky (to Bukharin): I am not talking of that. Is it true that you were one of the organisers of the plot against the Soviet power, that is to say, of the plot of the 'Left Communists' and the 'Left' Socialist-Revolutionaries?

Bukharin: I testified to that effect. Now I wish to ask whether the witness Yakovleva was aware that Kuibyshev, Menzhinsky and Yaroslavsky belonged to the 'Left Communists'?

Vyshinsky: I ask this question to be ruled out as having no bearing on the case.

The President: You need not answer this question, as it has no bearing on the case.

Bukharin: Then I ask Citizen the President to explain to me whether I have the right to put such questions as I wish, or whether my questions are determined by Citizen the Procurator.

The President: Accused Bukharin, Yakovleva was called here to give testimony as to your anti-Soviet activity, the activity of Nikolai Ivanovich Bukharin. In connection with her testimony you wished to put several questions to her in relation to matters concerning you, and not any other persons.

Bukharin: Quite so, but I ask for an explanation from Citizen the President as to whether I have the right to put such questions as I consider necessary to put, or whether their character is determined by someone else, particularly by Citizen the Procurator. In that case, of course, I cannot put questions.

The President: You put one question and received a reply to it. Do you still wish to put questions?

Bukharin: Yes, very much so.

Vyshinsky: Allow me to make the following remark: I consider it necessary to explain Article 257 of the Code of Criminal Procedure, which defines, firstly, that the President guides the Court investigation, and, secondly, that at the Court investigation the President rules out of the Court investigation and the speeches for the prosecution and the defence all points that have no bearing on the case under trial.

Bukharin: Then, Citizen Procurator, I ask for an explanation . . .

The President: Citizen the Procurator will give you no explanation.

Bukharin: Then I ask Citizen the President of the Court to explain to me whether the question of the composition of the central group of the 'Left Communists' has any bearing on the case or not?

The President: I completely rule out your question. Have you any questions to witness Yakovleva as far as you are concerned, or not?

Bukharin: I still have a number of questions.

Vyshinsky: I ask permission to explain the contents of Article

257 of the Code of Criminal Procedure to Bukharin, in order to avoid further misunderstanding, and to ensure that the accused Bukharin does not put such questions in the future.

The President: I quote Article 257 of the Code of Criminal Procedure of the RSFSR:

The president at a Court trial shall direct the course of the trial, endeavour to keep the Court investigation and the speeches for the prosecution and the defence free of everything extraneous to the case under examination, and direct the Court investigation in the way best calculated to elicit the truth.

Bukharin: Am I to understand this as meaning that you bar this question as having no relation to the point at issue?

The President: Accused Bukharin, if you have questions to witness Yakovleva, put specific questions to her.

Bukharin: Yes, I have questions. I ask witness Yakovleva to say whether she denies that in the Central Committee prior to the Brest-Litovsk Peace the majority of the votes was held by the 'Left Communists' plus the Trotskyites.

The President: What bearing has this question on your criminal role?

Bukharin: It has this much bearing, that I wish thereby to motivate and explain the point that it was absolutely senseless to strive for a plot . . .

The President: The Court is interested in your role in the plot against the leaders of the Soviet government, and this is now the subject of the testimony.

Bukharin: Good, then allow me to put the following question. Does witness Yakovleva deny that the 'Left Communists' prior to the Party Congress strove to receive a majority in the Party by legal means?

The President: The question has nothing whatever to do with the charge preferred against you of organising a plot against the Soviet power, and therefore I rule it irrelevant.

Bukharin: Does Yakovleva deny that I was one of the members of the Presidium of the Congress in Moscow, one of the members of the Presidium which at the time of the murder of Mirbach arrested the faction of 'Left' Socialist-Revolutionaries?

The President: This question has no bearing whatsoever on your criminal activity. I rule it irrelevant.

Bukharin: Does witness Yakovleva deny that in 1919 I was wounded at a meeting of the Moscow Committee by a 'Left' Socialist-Revolutionary bomb?

The President: This question has nothing whatever to do with the charge against you of being concerned in a plot. I rule this question irrelevant also.

Bukharin: I have no more questions.[4]

5. *Vyshinsky's mocking of Rosengoltz*

Vyshinsky: Accused Rosengoltz, as is evident from the record —in Vol. VI, p. 17—when Rosengoltz was arrested, a small piece of dry bread wrapped up in a bit of newspaper and sewed into a piece of cloth was found in his hip pocket, and in this bit of bread was a prayer written out on a piece of paper. I would like the Court's permission to read some passages from the text of this so-called prayer and to ask the accused Rosengoltz to give his explanation of this. (*To Rosengoltz.*) Do you deny this fact? Here is the text:

Let God arise, let his enemies be scattered: let them also that hate him flee before him. As smoke is driven away, so drive them away: as wax melteth before the fire, so let the wicked perish at the presence of God. . . .

He that dwelleth in the secret place of the most High shall abide under the shadow of the Almighty. I will say of the

Lord, He is my refuge and my fortress: my God, in him
will I trust. Surely he shall deliver thee from the snare of
the fowler, and from the noisome pestilence. He shall cover
thee with his feathers, and under his wings shalt thou trust:
his truth shall be thy shield and buckler. Thou shalt not be
afraid nor for the pestilence that walketh in darkness, nor
for the destruction that wasteth at noonday. . . .

How did this get into your pocket?

Rosengoltz: My wife put it in my pocket one day before I
went to work. She said it was for good luck.

Vyshinsky: And when was this?

Rosengoltz: Several months before my arrest.

Vyshinsky: And you carried this 'good luck' in your hip pocket
for several months?

Rosengoltz: I did not even pay attention . . .

Vyshinsky: Nevertheless, you saw what your wife was doing?

Rosengoltz: I was in a hurry.

Vyshinsky: But you were told that this was a family talisman
for good luck?

Rosengoltz: Something of the sort.

Vyshinsky: And you agreed to become the keeper of a talisman?
I have no more questions.[5]

APPENDIX II
Biographies

Biographies

S. A. BESSONOV was born in 1892 in the town of Kirzhach, Vladimir Guberniya. Before the revolution he was a Socialist Revolutionary, was expelled for his political activities from the Vladimir divinity school, travelled abroad, and was finally exiled to Vologda Guberniya. In 1918 he opposed the Brest peace, but fought with the Red Army in the Civil War and became a member of the Communist Party in 1920. His career in the Soviet government was in the field of foreign trade. In 1931 he was sent to Berlin as director of the commercial policy department of the Berlin Trade Representation. He also held the position of Counsellor of the Soviet Embassy there. He left these posts in February 1937, when he was called home and almost immediately arrested in connection with the Bukharin trial. His pre-trial was held *in camera*.[1]

The biographical material on N. I. BUKHARIN has been included in the main body of the memoir.

Nothing is known of P. P. BULANOV (1895-1938) except that he was Yagoda's private secretary from 1929 until his employer's demotion in September 1936. He remained working in the Commissariat of Internal Affairs until his arrest in March 1937.

M. A. CHERNOV (1891-1938) began his political career as a Menshevik in 1916, and became leader of the Menshevik party organisation in Ivanovo-Voznesensk. He was arrested for his political activity once but not imprisoned. During the Civil War in 1920 he joined the Bolshevik Party, and after the armistice went to the Ukraine, where he served as People's

Commissar for Trade (1928). He was sympathetic towards NEP, and confessed at the trial that his duties as a supervisor of forced grain collections in 1927 were what first alienated him from the Party. When the drive for collectivisation went into high gear, he was transferred to Moscow, where he worked in the Commissariat for Agriculture and as a member of the Collegium of the Commissariat for Trade. Having served as Deputy People's Commissar for Trade (1930) and become a member of the CC he was appointed in 1933 People's Commissar for Agriculture.

G. F. GRINKO (1889 (90)-1938) was a native Ukrainian and a leader of the *Borotba* party until after the revolution, when his group merged with the Bolshevik Party. During the twenties he held a number of important posts in the Ukraine, among them those of People's Commissar for Education of the Ukraine and head of the State Planning Commission. His reputation as an economist and industrial planner caused him to be transferred to Moscow where, as Vice-Chairman of *Gosplan,* he took a leading part in the preparation of the First Five-Year Plan. His book, *The Five Year Plan,* was published in 1930 simultaneously in Russian, French and English. He showed little sympathy in it for the economic programme of the Right opposition : 'In face of the unchallenged facts of the successful socialist construction, the Right opportunist opposition has been broken up and its leaders have capitulated.'[2] In 1934 Grinko was elected to the CC, a sign of grace in a year when many of his former Ukrainian nationalist colleagues were being arrested. In the last six years before his own arrest he was People's Commissar for Finance of the USSR.

One of the youngest of the defendants at the Bukharin trial, A. IKRAMOV, was only nineteen when the revolution broke out. He joined a legal nationalist youth organisation in his native Uzbekistan, and through it the Bolshevik Party. He became Secretary of the CC of the Uzbekistan CP and in 1923 joined the Trotskyite opposition. In the mid-twenties he was the passionate advocate of a programme for radical land and irrigation reform in Uzbekistan, which he pushed through the Uzbek Party Congress despite the strong opposition of F. Khodjayev, President of the Republic and his future co-defendant at the Bukharin trial. Their disagreement developed into a protracted factional struggle which was still smouldering at the show trial, where both men, though mutually hostile and suspicious, were forced to declare that they had been secret collaborators in counter-revolution for years. In the years before the trial, however, Ikramov gained the ascendancy in Uzbek Party affairs. He became a member of the CC and in 1930 succeeded another future co-defendant, Zelensky, as Secretary of the Central Asiatic Bureau of the Party. He was Secretary-General of the Uzbek CP in 1937, when he was arrested by a delegation from Moscow which arrived in Tashkent and presented him with a telegram expressing Stalin's lack of confidence in his leadership.

V. I. IVANOV was born in Tula in 1893. In 1912 he entered Moscow University as a medical student but was expelled the following year for taking part in a strike. He joined the Bolsheviks in 1915. In 1918 he was a Left Communist. In 1928 he was sent to the North Caucasus to be Second Secretary of the Party there, and in 1931 he was transferred to the Northern Territory, where he was First Regional Party Secretary. He left the Northern Territory in October 1936, and worked in the Commissariat of the Timber Industry in Moscow for the last few months before his arrest.

The most colourful of the three physicians in the trial, DR I. N. KAZAKOV, was a controversial figure in the medical world. He considered that there was no such thing as an incurable disease, and had developed a series of chemical remedies known as lysates, for which he alone knew the formulae. In the early thirties he treated a number of important Bolsheviks, including

Menzhinsky and Rakovsky, with these lysates, and acquired not only a good deal of notoriety but also an Institute for his patients and a laboratory for his experiments. The majority of the physicians in the medical service opposed him, and at the trial Kazakov complained that he had been unable to get his work published and had been discriminated against at medical congresses. The other medical defendants regarded him as a charlatan.

F. KHODJAYEV was born in 1896 in Bokhara and grew up to become famous as the 'Lenin of the Uzbeks'. His father was a merchant trader in Persian lamb who died when his son was fourteen, leaving him a substantial property. The young Khodjayev joined a nationalist underground organisation which attempted to overthrow the Emir in 1916. Outlawed and sentenced to death, he fled to Tsarist Russia and in 1917 founded the Young Bokhara Party, which declared its loyalty to the Russian revolution and in 1920 succeeded with the help of a Red Army detachment in destroying the Emirate. Bokhara became the Bokhara People's Republic, with Khodjayev at its head. Khodjayev was one of the few leaders of this still-feudal Asiatic state who wanted to plan its future on the Soviet model. He helped the Soviet government to reorganise Bokhara and the surrounding region into the Republic of Uzbekistan, and became President of the new federal state. In 1925 he was appointed Chairman of the Council of People's Commissars of Uzbekistan. He was a right-wing sympathiser, and his later career was somewhat clouded by the long factional dispute with Ikramov already mentioned.

P. P. KRYUCHKOV was Maxim Gorky's private secretary and a member of his household.

N. M. KRESTINSKY was born in 1883 in Mogilev of Ukrainian parents. He became a social democrat in 1901 and from 1903 was a member of the Vilna social democratic organisation.

Between 1907 and 1917 he combined revolutionary work with a career as a barrister. He wrote for *Zvezda* and *Pravda* in Petrograd, was a Bolshevik candidate to the Fourth Duma, and was several times arrested and exiled. In 1917 he was in charge of Party work in the Urals; in 1918 he became People's Commissar of Finance; and after Sverdlov's death he was made Secretary of the cc and was Lenin's organisational assistant. Between 1921 and 1930 he served as Russian ambassador to Berlin, and thereafter as Vice-Commissar for Foreign Affairs in Moscow. During the twenties his political sympathies lay with Trotsky, but he broke with him after the November fiasco of 1927. In January 1937 he lost his Foreign Office position and was given a minor post in the Department of Justice for the few months remaining before his arrest and disgrace.

DR L. G. LEVIN appeared at the Bukharin trial at the end of an eminently respectable medical career. Born of a poor middle-class family, he had worked his way through medical school and from 1896 onwards practised his profession at the Moscow Workers' Hospital, in factories and industrial plants. During the revolution he was put in charge of several hospitals run by the Commissariat of Health, and later served as a doctor in the Red Army. He was assigned to the Kremlin hospital in 1920 and remained there until his arrest, treating top Communists like Dzerzhinsky, Menzhinsky and Lenin himself. One of his distinguished patients, Joffe, complained in his suicide note to Trotsky that Levin was one of the doctors whose indifference—dictated by the Kremlin—had hopelessly undermined his health; but other patients described him as sympathetic and kindly.[3] He was Gorky's physician and travelled with him to Italy several times. At his trial the prosecution made much of the fact that Levin had never belonged to any political party, and labelled him one of those 'non-party specialists' whose political ignorance made them so vulnerable to degenerate bourgeois influences.

V. A. MAXIMOV-DIKOVSKY (MAXIMOV) was born in 1900 and was the youngest defendant at the Bukharin trial. He became a Party member in 1918, fought with the Red Army and was for a time a prisoner of the Whites. After the end of the war he spent several years as a Party organiser in a factory before moving into the Soviet bureaucracy; he was eventually made secretary to Kuibyshev.

The third medical defendant, PROFESSOR D. D. PLETNEV, was described by Louis Fischer as 'Russia's best-known heart specialist'.[4] Before the revolution he had been a Kadet, but served as a Kremlin physician from 1917 on. He edited a leading Russian medical journal, and was the author of a number of research papers well known inside and outside the USSR. In mid-1937, as a prelude to the show trial, he was accused of having assaulted a woman patient, tried *in camera* and bound over for two years. The available evidence indicates that the charge was probably false. Pletnev spent his time in prison writing a medical monograph. He was one of the three defendants not sentenced to death.

K. G. RAKOVSKY was born in 1873 in Kotel, Bulgaria, the son of a well-educated landowner and merchant. His nationality was somewhat complicated by the fact that in 1878, as a result of a Russian invasion, his home became part of Rumanian territory. His revolutionary apprenticeship began when he was expelled from his gymnasium for political activity, and continued in Geneva, where as a medical student he came under the influence of Plekhanov, Zasulich and Axelrod. He obtained his doctorate in medicine at Montpellier, France, and combined work as a physician with a career in the front line of the Bulgarian and Rumanian social democratic movements. He translated Deville's *The Evolution of Capitalism* into Bulgarian, wrote one book on the Dreyfus case and another, *Russia and the East,* which inspired the Bulgarian social democratic party. From 1904 to 1907 and from 1912 to 1917 he was an active revolutionary leader in Rumania. Early in 1917 he was released from a Rumanian jail by a Russian garrison. He claimed to have been, at one time or another, under arrest in Rumania, Bulgaria, Russia, Germany and Sweden. After the October revolution he worked in the Ukraine as an organising commissar, was appointed chairman of the Ukrainian provisional government and later chairman of the Council of People's Commissars of the Ukraine. From 1918 on, he was a member of the CC. At the end of the Civil War he entered the Soviet Russian foreign service, first as Vice-Commissar for Foreign Affairs and then as ambassador to London and Paris. He conducted the negotiations for the recognition of the USSR by the British and French governments. An old personal and political friend of Trotsky—whom he had known since 1903—he was expelled from the Party in 1927 and sent into exile, first in Astrakhan and later in Barnaul. In 1934 he finally capitulated to the government, one of the last Trotskyites to do so, and was brought back to Moscow and given a post in charge of the scientific research institutes of the Commissariat of Health. In connection with this work he was sent to Japan as a delegate to an international Red Cross conference in 1935, a trip which was used against him at the trial as evidence for his connections with Japanese intelligence. It is said that after his arrest in early 1937 he did not confess for eight months. He was one of the three defendants at the trial who received only a prison sentence.

A. P. ROSENGOLTZ was brought up as a revolutionary. An orphan, he was raised by a woman who was a social democrat, joined the Bolsheviks at fifteen or sixteen, and was a delegate to the Unification Congress at seventeen. During the October revolution he fought in Moscow, was a member of the Military Revolutionary Committee, and during the Civil War served as a trouble-shooter for the CC on the more difficult sectors of the front. During the twenties he worked for a time in the Soviet Embassy in London, and was sympathetic to Trotsky.

P

However, when the opposition was defeated in 1929, he transferred his allegiance to Stalin without a murmur, and became Commissar of Foreign Trade during the difficult period of the first Five-Year Plan. His former subordinate at the Commissariat of Trade, Alexander Barmine, has described him as 'an iron administrator', and 'the perfect bureaucrat'.

A. I. RYKOV (1881-1938) was born in Saratov, one of six children of a peasant family, and endured a childhood of deprivation followed by a manhood as a revolutionary outlaw. He managed to support himself by giving lessons, in order to study law at Kazan, where he became a social democrat. During a May Day demonstration in 1902 he was arrested, but escaped to avoid being sent to Archangel. From that time until 1917 he never spent more than two months at any one address. From 1905 he was a member of the Bolshevik CC and a close associate of Lenin, helping to organise the Fourth (Unification) Congress in Stockholm. Lenin frequently sent him as an emergency representative to regional Party cadres in which rivalries with the Mensheviks had become acute. Rykov could boast a total of seven escapes from Siberia. After February 1917 he became a member of the Presidium of the Moscow Soviet, and in August of the same year organised the transport strike against the Moscow state conference. A leader of the October uprising, he became the first People's Commissar for Internal Affairs and chairman of the Supreme Council of the National Economy. During the Civil War he was in charge of supplies to the Red Army. He became Lenin's personal deputy in 1921, and in 1923 succeeded him as Chairman of the Council of People's Commissars—a post with the titular dignity of a Premier. When the Right opposition collapsed in 1929 he was expelled from the Politburo along with Bukharin and Tomsky, and in 1930 he was dismissed from the premiership and put in charge of the uninfluential Commissariat of Posts and Telegraphs. Although he was allowed to return to the CC together with the other Right leaders in 1934, his reputation was ruined. On 27 September 1936, he was again dismissed from office, and five months later he was arrested. Rykov's fondness for liquor—which was famous during the twenties, and caused a brand of vodka to be named after him—became more compulsive as his fortunes declined, and many have attributed his breakdown at the Bukharin trial to the degenerative effects of alcoholism.

V. F. SHARANGOVICH (1897-1938), was born in Byelorussia. He fought in the Red Army in the Polish war and for a time was a prisoner of the Poles. In the course of his Party career he worked as assistant to the Procurator of the Republic of Byelorussia, in the regional trade unions, and as a member of the Central Committee of the Byelorussian Communist party. At the time of his arrest in 1937 he was First Secretary of the Byelorussian Central Committee.

The third leader of the Right opposition, M. P. TOMSKY (1880-1936), was born in Petrograd to a working-class family. He joined a social democratic circle in 1904, and in 1905 was president of the first Soviet ever founded, at Reval (Tallinn). The first of his many arrests occurred in 1906. On that occasion he succeeded in escaping to Petrograd, where he worked in the City Party Committee. Between sojourns in prison and in exile he managed to travel to Paris and to write for a number of left-wing papers, including the *Proletariy* in Paris and the Moscow *Krasnoe Znamya*. In 1917 he played a leading role in consolidating labour unions behind the revolution, and at the end of that year became chairman of the All-Russian Association of Trade Unions. Throughout the twenties he was President of the Central Council of Trade Unions. Beginning in 1919 he was a member of the CC, and after 1922 he also had a seat on the Politburo. After 1929 his influence waned along with that of the other Right opposition leaders; and he was dismissed from the Politburo in 1929 and from the chairmanship of the Council of Trade Unions soon afterwards. In 1932 he became chairman of the board of OGIZ, the State Publishing House. He was referred to by name at the first show trial (in August 1936), and it is believed that he knew he was about to be arrested when he committed suicide on 20 August 1936.

G. G. YAGODA was born in 1891 and became a Party member at the age of sixteen or seventeen, while he was working as a compositor in an underground printing press. In 1911 he was arrested and exiled for two years. After he returned from exile, he worked at the Putilov works, Leningrad, in the sick benefit society on insurance. It was during this period that he probably qualified as a pharmacist, for by 1917 he was working as a pharmacist in Nizhny Novgorod. It is said that at the beginning of the Civil War Dzerzhinsky suffered a heart attack while passing through Nizhny Novgorod and was carried into Yagoda's shop for treatment. As a result of this meeting Yagoda was appointed head of a military Cheka unit, and was soon one of the coming men in the office of Internal Security. During the years when Menzhinsky was chairman of the OGPU, Yagoda was his first assistant, and owing to Menzhinsky's physical and mental incapacity exercised effective control over this powerful organisation. In 1929 he was suspected of having rightist sympathies, and there are indications that as early as 1931 Stalin was anxious to diminish his dangerous influence as state security chief. In June 1931 Yagoda was replaced by Akulov, and demoted to the post of second assistant to Menzhinsky. However, the apparatus refused to function under its new leader, and within four months Yagoda was back in control. In 1934, when Menzhinsky finally died, and the OGPU was reorganised as the People's Commissariat of Internal Affairs, Yagoda was unreservedly placed in charge. In 1935 he was made General Commissar—a title created especially for him. However, his supremacy did not last. In the autumn of 1936 he was removed as People's Commissar of Internal Affairs and shifted to the ill-omened Commissariat of Posts and Telegraphs as a short-lived successor to Rykov. Early in April

1937 he was arrested. People who met this hated and feared man describe him as rather colourless on the surface, and curiously uneasy and diffident in manner.

A. S. YENUKIDZE was born in 1877 in the Kutais Guberniya. After a rural childhood, he went in 1893 to Tiflis, where he joined the social democratic party and probably first formed the lifelong ties with Stalin which made him the object of a good deal of attention in later years. During the early days of their friendship Stalin is said to have relied on Yenukidze for much of his education in Marxism. Most of Yenukidze's own revolutionary work was carried on in Baku, where he first went as an engine-driver in 1898. He soon abandoned engines for the career of a professional revolutionary, took part in the Baku group of *Iskra,* and worked in the local underground printing press. From 1902 onward his life was broken up by repeated arrests and exiles. He refused the Party's offer to send him abroad and let him work as an expatriate. In 1914 he was banished to the Turukhansk region of Siberia. In 1916 he was drafted into the army, and when the revolution broke out was despatched to Petrograd, where he worked in the city garrison. After the October revolution he became a member of the Presidium and Secretary of the Central Executive Committee of the Soviets (later the Central Executive Committee of the USSR). Thanks to his friendship with Stalin, his unofficial influence was enormous, and it was a mark of the trust in which he was held that for a long time he was the state executive in charge of the Kremlin, with control over its armed guard. A robust and pleasure-loving man, he was nicknamed 'lionhead' because of his large head covered with bushy red hair, and yellow eyes. He was a patron of the theatre and a powerful protector of the Moscow ballet. Although throughout the years of oppositionist crisis he was never suspected of disloyalty to Stalin, it was announced on 19 December 1937 that he had been shot after being convicted at a secret trial held a few days earlier.

I. A. ZELENSKY (1890-1938) joined the revolutionary movement in 1906. He carried on Party work in Samara, in the sick benefit societies of Tsaritsyn, and in the power transmission plants at Bogorodsk and Sormovo. Several times he was arrested and temporarily sent into exile. After the February revolution he became a district Party organiser in Moscow, and between 1918 and 1920 worked in the Moscow supply service. Between 1921 and 1924, he was a secretary of the Moscow Party Committee and was elected to the CC at the 11th Party Congress. In 1924 he was sent to Tashkent as Secretary of the Central Asiatic Bureau of the Party. He said at the trial that the problems of forced grain collections in Central Asia were what first turned his sympathies towards the Right opposition. In 1931 he was brought back to Moscow and made chairman of the Cooperative Organisation of the USSR (*Tsentrosoyuz*). He held this position until shortly before his arrest.

P. T. ZUBAREV (1886-1938) occupied a number of minor posts in the agricultural bureaucracy, first in his native Urals, then in the seed cultivation department of the Commissariat of Agriculture in Moscow, and finally in the Commissariat of Agriculture of the RSFSR.

References

REFERENCES

Preface (Pages 9-11)
1 'Who cares for you?' said Alice. . . .
'You are nothing but a pack of cards.'

Chapter 1 (pages 15-31)
1 N. Gumilev (1886–1921), outstanding poet and leader of the Acmeist school; shot by the OGPU in the autumn of 1921 for alleged counter-revolutionary activity. The quotation is from the poem 'Memory' (*Pamyat*) in the book 'Pillar of Fire' (*Ognenny Stolp*), Petrograd, 1921.

2 Article on Bukharin in the *Large Soviet Encyclopaedia*, first edition, 1927, Vol. 8.

3 See L. Haas (ed.) *Lenin. Unbekannte Briefe*, Zürich/Köln, 1967, pp. 60, 83. The Malinovsky incident has been described in some detail many times. We refer the reader to Bertram Wolfe, *Three Who Made a Revolution*, New York, 1948, p. 550.

4 See Olga Hess Gankin and H. H. Fisher, *The Bolsheviks and the World War. The Origin of the Third International*, Stanford/London, 1940, p. 215.

5 *Ibid.*, p. 216.

6 On Bukharin's tribulations on this journey and during his stay in Stockholm, see Michael Futrell, *Northern Underground. Episodes of Russian Revolutionary Transport and Communications through Scandinavia and Finland, 1863–1917*, London, 1963.

7 Gankin and Fisher, *op. cit.*, p. 241.

8 *Ibid.*, p. 217.

9 On Lenin's attitude to the German *Revolutionierungspolitik* see G. Katkov, *Russia 1917. The February Revolution*, London, 1967, pp. 72–115, and G. Katkov, 'German Political Intervention in Russia during World War I' in *Revolutionary Russia*, ed. R. Pipes, Harvard UP, Cambridge, Mass., 1968, pp. 63–88.

10 For the intricate details of this incident see M. Futrell, *op. cit.*, Chapter VI, where the primary sources are quoted.

11 L. Trotsky, *Moya Zhizn*, Berlin, 1930, pp. 310 ff.

12 Lenin, *Works*, 5th edn, Vol. 49, p. 390.

13 L. Trotsky, *op. cit.*, p. 311.

14 Recorded by Lydia Dan in *Novy Zhurnal* No. 75, New York, 1964, p. 181. See also pp. 93ff. above.

15 We base our conjectural apologia of Stalin on Krivitsky's report, quoted in n. 15, p. 238. See also W. G. Krivitsky, *I Was Stalin's Agent*, London, 1940, p. 209.

Chapter 2 (pages 32-53)

1 L. Schapiro, *The Origins of the Communist Autocracy*, London, 1955.

2 *Ibid.*, pp. 59 ff., 91 ff.

3 See G. Katkov, 'The Kronstadt Rising', in *St Antony's Papers* No. 6, *Soviet Affairs* No. 2, London, 1959.

4 Resolution of the Xth Congress on 'The Unity of the Party', in *VKP(b) v rezolyutsiyakh*, 1936, 5th edn, pp. 374 ff.

5 'Resolution on the Anarchist-Syndicalist Deviation', in *VKP(b) v rezolyutsiyakh*, 1936, 5th edn, p. 375.

6 Paragraph Seven of the resolution was kept secret until its existence was disclosed by Stalin at the 13th Party Congress.

7 *Proceedings of the XVth Congress,* 1st edn, 1928, p. 254.

8 *Ibid.*, p. 255.

9 *Ibid.*, p. 258.

10 See L. Schapiro, *The Communist Party of the Soviet Union*, London, 1960, pp. 198 ff.

11 *Proceedings of the XVth Congress,* 1st edn, Leningrad 1928, p. 373

12 *Ibid.*, p. 378.

13 *Ibid.*, p. 687.

14 Cf. e.g. *Izvestiya*, 23 August 1936.

15 Stalin, *Works,* Vol. 12, p. 1.

16 *Proceedings of the XVth Conference*, p. 601.

17 *Proceedings of the XVth Congress.*

18 The text of the notes dictated by Lenin on his deathbed and commonly known as the Lenin Testament was first published in the Soviet Union after the 20th Congress. See *Kommunist* No. 9, 1956.

19 When questioned on this point by the Dewey Investigation Commission, Trotsky was at pains to explain why he had yielded to pressure and virtually denounced Eastman as a forger. He later published on his own authority the very text he had denounced as a 'malicious invention'—Dewey Commission Report, *The Case of Leon Trotsky*, New York, 1937, pp. 429, 431.

20 Stalin, *Works*, Vol. 10, pp. 172–205.

21 *Proceedings of the XVth Congress,* p. 550

22 *Ibid.,* pp. 561 ff.

23 Stalin, *Works,* Vol. 12, p. 63.

24 'Letter of an Old Bolshevik', Allen & Unwin, 1938, reprinted in Boris Nicolaevsky, *Power and the Soviet Elite,* with introduction by George Kennan, New York, 1965, p. 54. In this work Nicolaevsky owns to having composed the 'Letter of an Old Bolshevik' himself but explains that it is based on many conversations he had with Bukharin during the latter's visit abroad in February/April 1936. Nicolaevsky's claim that he had these contacts with Bukharin is beyond doubt, even if we disregard Bukharin's own confession at his trial (Trial *Proceedings,* p. 426). It is corroborated in a memoir by Martov's sister, Lydia Dan, which appeared in *Novy Zhurnal,* No. 75, New York, 1964. See above, p. 29.

Chapter 3 (*pages 54-64*)

1 I. Bukharin, *The Way to Socialism and the Union of Workers and Peasants,* 1925, p. 52, reprinted in *Put' k Sotsializmu v Rossii* by Sidney Heitman, New York, 1967, pp. 317–353.

2 On Bukharin's agrarian policy, put forward as an alternative to Stalin's, see Alexander Erlich, *The Soviet Industrialisation Debate 1924–1928,* Harvard UP, 1960, p. 23, and Moshe Lewin, *Russian Peasants and Soviet Power.* See also n. 16, p. 236

3 See Erlich, *op. cit.,* p. 125.

4 See Stalin, *Works,* Vol. 12, pp. 28 ff., in particular p. 30.

5 A course adopted some thirty years later by Khrushchev.

6 See the masterly exposition of the grain crisis debate in Alexander Erlich, *The Soviet Industrialisation Debate 1924–1928,* Harvard UP, 1960, pp. 170 ff.

7 Ruth Fischer, *Stalin and German Communism,* Cambridge, Mass., 1948, pp. 543–544.

8 'On the Right Deviation in our Party'. Full text published in Stalin, *Works,* Vol. 12, pp. 39 ff.

9 For a partial translation see B. Wolfe, *Khrushchev and Stalin's Ghost,* New York, 1957. The full Russian text is reproduced in S. Heitman, *Put' k Sotsializmu v Rossii,* pp. 375–397. See also Valentinov, *Doktrina pravogo kommunizma,* Munich, 1960.

10 *Pravda,* October 1928. As quoted in Bukharin, ed. Heitman, *op. cit.,* p. 385.

11 Stalin, *Works,* Vol. 12, p. 213.

12 *Ibid.,* Vol. 11, pp. 222–238, and in particular p. 236.

13 *Ibid.*, pp. 318 ff., and in particular p. 321.

14 *Pravda*, 20 January 1929.

15 Stalin, *Works*, Vol. 12, p. 90

16 On the whole political debate of 1928–30 concerning the peasantry and collectivisation, see the excellent study of Moshe Lewin, *La Paysannerie et le Pouvoir Soviétique, 1928–1930*, Mouton, Paris/La Haye, 1966. Translated into English as *Russian Peasants and Soviet Power*, London, 1968. Like other authors, Moshe Lewin (*op. cit.*, p. 470) uses the Russian word *peregib* (which we translate as 'overbending') coined by the Right oppositionists to describe an over-zealous observance of the established Party line with regard to pressure on the kulaks and middle peasants. Stalin mocked at the Bukharinites' concern at the excesses of the anti-peasant measures he had instituted, and dismissed the expression *peregibi* as a dishonest criticism of the way the Party line was being implemented.

Chapter 4 (*pages 65-69*)

1 This was stated by Bertram Wolfe in a private conversation with the author.

2 B. Gitlow, *I Confess*, New York, 1940, p. 507.

3 *Ibid.*, p. 503.

4 Ruth Fischer, *Stalin and German Communism*, Cambridge, Mass., 1948, p. 568.

5 M. Buber-Neumann, *Von Potsdam nach Moskau*, Stuttgart, 1957, pp. 127 ff.

6 Stalin, *Works*, Vol. 12, p. 24. See also Babette Gross, *Willi Münzenberg*, Stuttgart, 1967, pp. 216 ff.

7 *Pravda*, 26 November 1929.

Chapter 5 (*pages 70-85*)

1 Stenographic report of the *Proceedings of the XVIth Congress*, p. 130.

2 *Ibid.*, pp. 142–148.

3 *Ibid.*, pp. 147 ff.

4 See *ibid.*, p. 263, for quotations from this speech of Rykov's, which were read out by Mirzoyan. They do not bear out Stalin's accusation that Rykov tried to 'wriggle and manœuvre' at the Urals Conference. When attacked by hecklers Rykov replied with dignity that he and his friends had renounced their oppositionist views, and that he refused to discuss political ideas he had abandoned.

5 *Proceedings of the XVIth Congress*, pp. 134 ff.

6 *Ibid.,* pp. 336 ff.

7 *Ibid.,* pp. 291 ff.

8 2 November 1930.

9 See, e.g., Fainsod, *Smolensk Under Soviet Rule,* London, 1959, pp. 237–264 and *passim.*

10 M. Buber-Neumann, *Von Potsdam nach Moskau,* Stuttgart, 1957, p. 233. See also Kravchenko's appraisal of Ordzhonikidze in *I Chose Freedom,* London, 1947, pp. 238 ff. and *passim.*

11 N. Jasny, *Soviet Industrialisation 1928–1952,* Chicago/Toronto, 1961.

12 These papers still await publication. Professor Fainsod in his *Smolensk Under Soviet Rule* gave us an ample but not an exhaustive analysis of this unique collection.

13 Pp. 350 ff.

14 Report of the *Proceedings of the XVIIth Congress,* p. 518

15 *Ibid.,* p. 518.

16 *Ibid.,* p. 209.

17 *Ibid.,* p. 129.

18 *Ibid.,* p. 253.

Chapter 6 (*pages 86-97*)

1 See B. Nicolaevsky, *Power and the Soviet Elite* (with an introduction by George Kennan), New York/Washington/London, 1965, p. 92.

2 See A. Ouralov, *Staline au Pouvoir,* Paris, 1951, p. 164.

3 B. Wolfe, *Khrushchev and Stalin's Ghost,* New York, 1957, pp. 130 ff.

4 E. Lermolo, *Face of a Victim,* New York, 1955. 'Elizabeth Lermolo' is certainly a pseudonym, and her memoirs have been affected by camouflage technique (used to protect certain persons who might still suffer in consequence of being described) and by literary embellishment. However, the late Boris Nicolaevsky told the author that he had investigated the origins of the book and saw no reason to doubt the veracity of the substance of it. He himself developed his own theory of what took place in an article reprinted in his *Power and the Soviet Elite,* New York, 1965, pp. 69–102.

5 Trial *Proceedings,* pp. 558 ff.

6 *Trial of the Bloc of Rights and Trotskyites,* pp. 572 ff.

7 See *Stenographic Report of the XXIInd Congress,* Vol. II, p. 584. Since then not only the men Khrushchev denounced as guilty of the abuse of power, but Khrushchev himself, have ceased to belong to the supreme Party organ. However, no progress in the investigation of the Kirov case has yet been announced.

8 Bukharin at the XVIIth Congress. *Proceedings,* p. 125.

9 '*Marshruty istorii—mysli vslukh.*' The article has inexplicably been left out of existing bibliographies of Bukharin's writings.

10 The notice actually appeared in *Pravda* on 10 September 1936 (see above, p. 106). We have found no independent confirmation of Ouralov's account (see *Staline au Pouvoir,* pp. 37 ff.) of the cc meeting, or even of the fact that it took place. The controversy over the alleged plenum of the cc of September 1936 flared up in 1967. We refer the reader to the *Slavic Review,* Vol. XXVI, December 1967, where A. Avtorkhanov (i.e. Ouralov) repeats his contention that there was such a meeting, while Professors Armstrong, Slusser and Kennan remain unconvinced.

Chapter 7 (*pages 101-118*)

1 A. Ya. Vyshinsky, *Teoriya sudebnykh dokazatelstv v sovetskom prave,* 3rd edn, Moscow, 1950 (the first edition appeared in 1946), pp. 215 ff.

2 *Ibid.,* p. 258.

3 *Izvestiya,* 23 May 1936.

4 *Report of Court Proceedings in the Case of the Anti-Soviet Trotskyite Centre,* Pyatakov Trial, Moscow, 1937, pp. 512–13.

5 *Pravda,* 15 July 1936.

6 B. Wolfe, *Khrushchev and Stalin's Ghost,* p. 130.

7 *Pravda,* 10 September 1936. See above, p. 106.

8 See *The Case of Leon Trotsky,* ed. Dewey *et al.,* New York, 1937, pp. 519 ff.

9 *Proceedings in the Case of the Anti-Soviet Trotskyite Centre* (Pyatakov Trial, January 1937), p. 549.

10 *Ibid.,* p. 55.

11 *Ibid.,* p. 100.

12 I. V. Stalin, *Works,* in Russian, ed. Robert H. McNeal, Stanford, California, 1967, Vol. 1 (XIV), pp. 199–201.

13 Stalin, *Works,* ed. McNeal, Vol. 1 (XIV), pp. 227 ff.

14 *Proceedings,* pp. 297–298.

15 W. Krivitsky in *Sotsialistichesky Vestnik* No. 6, 1938, p. 5.

16 *Master i Margarita,* in *Moskva* No. 11, 1966, No. 1, 1967. English translation, including parts omitted in the Soviet version, by Michael Glenny, London/New York, 1967.

Chapter 8 (*pages 119-133*)

1 *Proceedings, Case of the Bloc of Rights and Trotskyites*—henceforth referred to as *Proceedings*—Moscow, 1938, pp. 58–59.

2 See F. Maclean, *Eastern Approaches*, London, 1949, p. 88. See also *Sotsialistichesky Vestnik* No. 5, 1938.

3 *Proceedings,* p. 716.

4 *Ibid.,* p. 55.

5 *Ibid.,* p. 155.

6 *Ibid.,* p. 157.

7 *Ibid.,* pp. 596 ff.

8 As confirmed in Khrushchev's secret speech and in the memoirs of General Gorbatov (see *Novy Mir* No. 4, 1964, p. 120).

9 *Proceedings,* pp. 313–314.

10 The book in question is L. Feuchtwanger's *Moscow 1937*, New York, 1937.

11 *Proceedings,* p. 778.

12 See the remarks of an unnamed 'informer' in Leites and Bernaut's *Ritual of Liquidation: The Case of the Moscow Trials*, Santa Monica, California, 1954, p. 405.

13 *Moscow 1937*, p. 148.

14 *Ibid.,* p. 144.

15 *Sovietskaya Iustitsiya* No. 5, 1937, p. 32.

16 *Proceedings,* p. 383.

17 *Ibid.,* p. 136.

18 *Ibid.,* p. 390.

19 For its probable content see L. Schapiro, *The Communist Party of the Soviet Union*, New York, 1960, p. 392, and B. Nicolaevsky, *Power and the Soviet Elite*, pp. 11, 17 ff.

20 *Proceedings,* pp. 166–168, 377, 389.

21 F. Maclean, *Eastern Approaches*, p. 105.

22 *Proceedings,* p. 375.

23 *Ibid.,* p. 530.

24 *Ibid.,* p. 572.

25 *Ibid.,* p. 624.

Chapter 9 (pages 134-141)

1 *Proceedings,* p. 184.

2 *Ibid.,* p. 183.

3 *Ibid.,* p. 396.

4 *Ibid.,* p. 370.

5 *Ibid.,* p. 379.

6 *Ibid.,* pp. 380–381.

7 *Ibid.,* p. 387.

8 *Ibid.,* p. 387.

9 *Ibid.,* pp. 769–770.

10 *Ibid.*, pp. 274 ff.
11 *Bulletin of Opposition* No. 64, March 1938.
12 *Ibid.*
13 *Proceedings*, p. 65.
14 *Ibid.*, p. 282.
15 *Ibid.*, pp. 249–250.
16 *Ibid.*, pp. 21, 42.
17 *Ibid.*, p. 404.
18 *Ibid.*, p. 430.

Chapter 10 (*pages 142-155*)

1 *Proceedings*, pp. 178, 402.
2 *Ibid.*, pp. 186 ff.
3 *Ibid.*, p. 189.
4 *Ibid.*, pp. 191 ff.
5 *Ibid.*, pp. 431 ff.
6 *Ibid.*, p. 403.
7 *Ibid.*, p. 438.
8 *Ibid.*, pp. 203–204.
9 *Ibid.*, pp. 383–384.
10 *Ibid.*, pp. 417–419.
11 *Ibid.*, p. 121.
12 *Ibid.*, p. 122.
13 *Ibid.*, p. 383.
14 *Ibid.*, p. 769.
15 *Ibib.*, p. 137.
16 *Ibid.*, pp. 229–230.
17 *Ibid.*, pp. 419–420.
18 *Ibid.*, p. 422.
19 *Ibid.*, p. 423.
20 *Ibid.*, pp. 423–424.
21 *Idid.*, p. 360.
22 *Pravda Vostoka*, 28 December 1957.
23 *Proceedings*, p. 295.
24 Nos. 3–4, August–September, 1930.
25 *Proceedings*, p. 299.
26 *Ibid.*, p. 304.
27 *Ibid.*, p. 301.
28 On 16 November 1917, the Under-Secretary of State at the German Foreign Office, von dem Bussche, wired to the liaison officer at GHQ asking for permission for Rakovsky's wife to travel from Bucharest to Stockholm. Bussche, who had been German

minister in Bucharest in 1915, stated plainly that 'Rakovsky was connected with us and was working for us in Rumania'. Indeed on 13 January 1915, while still serving in Bucharest, Bussche had asked the German Foreign Office to approve the expenditure of 100,000 *lei*, which would be conveyed in an inconspicuous manner to Rumanian socialists working to prevent Rumania's entry into the war. The following day Bussche reported having met Rakovsky, 'whose energetic stand for peace is well known'. See Z. A. B. Zeman, *Germany and the Revolution in Russia*, London, 1958, pp. 85 ff.

29 See Gerald Freund, *Unholy Alliance*, with an introduction by J. W. Wheeler-Bennett, London, 1957.

30 See an article by Léon Blum in *Le Populaire*, March 1938.

31 *Sotsialistichesky Vestnik* No. 5, 1938.

Chapter 11 (*pages 156-180*)

1 See G. Fischer, *Soviet Opposition to Stalin*, Cambridge, Mass., 1952.

2 *Proceedings*, p. 769.

3 *Ibid.*, pp. 348, 372.

4 *Ibid.*, pp. 148–150.

5 See F. Maclean, *op. cit.*, p. 92.

6 *Proceedings*, pp. 140–141.

7 *Ibid.*, p. 314.

8 No. 65, April 1938.

9 *Proceedings*, p. 332.

10 *Ibid.*, p. 330.

11 *Ibid.*, p. 338.

12 *Ibid.*, p. 78.

13 *Ibid.*, p. 769.

14 *Ibid.*, p. 109.

15 *Ibid.*, p. 739.

16 *Ibid.*, p. 253.

17 *Ibid.*, p. 285.

18 *Ibid.*, p. 394.

19 *Ibid.*, p. 396.

20 *Ibid.*, p. 390.

21 M. Buber-Neumann, *Von Potsdam nach Moskau*, Stuttgart, 1957, pp. 232 ff.

22 *Proceedings*, pp. 398–399.

23 *Proceedings, XVIIth Party Congress*, p. 125. See also above, p. 83.

24 *Proceedings*, p. 419.

Q

25 *Ibid.,* pp. 177, 419.
26 *Ibid.,* p. 575.
27 *Ibid.,* p. 575.
28 *Ibid.,* p. 375.
29 *Ibid.,* p. 738.
30 *Ibid.,* p. 377.
31 *Ibid.,* p. 376.
32 *Ibid.,* p. 679.
33 *Ibid.,* p. 771.
34 L. Trotsky, *The Real Situation in Russia,* p. 328.
35 B. Pilnyak, *Povest nepogashennoy luny,* in *Novy Mir* No. 5, 1926.
36 See *Pravda,* 13 January 1953.
37 *Proceedings,* p. 499.
38 Cf. L. Schapiro, *The Origins of the Communist Autocracy,* London, 1955, pp. 133–146 and G. Katkov, 'The Assassination of Count Mirbach', in *St Antony's Papers* No. 12, *Soviet Affairs* No. 3, London, 1962, pp. 53–93.
39 *Pravda,* 16 December 1923. See also Stalin's article in *Pravda* of 15 December 1923.
40 L. Schapiro, *The Origins of the Communist Autocracy.*
41 *Proceedings,* p. 35.
42 For Kamkov and Karelin, see Lenin, *Works,* 2nd/3rd edn, Vol. XXII, p. 638.
43 L. Schapiro, *The Origins of the Communist Autocracy,* p. 144.
44 *Proceedings,* pp. 481, 492 ff.
45 F. Maclean, *op. cit.,* p. 99.
46 *Proceedings,* p. 440.
47 *Ibid.,* p. 441.
48 *Ibid.,* p. 442.
49 *Ibid.,* p. 446.
50 *Ibid.,* p. 447.
51 *Ibid.,* p. 499.
52 *Ibid.,* p. 774.
53 *Ibid.,* p. 774.

Chapter 12 (*pages 181-192*)

1 *Proceedings,* p. 697.
2 *Ibid.,* pp. 777–778.
3 F. Maclean, *op. cit.,* pp. 119–120.
4 cf. e.g. George Fischer, *Soviet Opposition to Stalin,* pp. 39ff. and *passim.*

5 *Proceedings,* p. 778.

6 Bukharin was not a reserved man, in the habit of keeping his views to himself. Whilst in his public utterances he submitted himself to Party discipline and tried as far as possible to abide by official conventions, in private conversations he would certainly have vented his real feelings to a great many people. It was therefore no mere coincidence that some of his more extreme ideas and expressions should have reached us via such spurious writings as that of Ilya Britan or the far more serious 'Letter of an Old Bolshevik' which the late Boris Nicolaevsky admitted he had composed on the basis of his conversations with Bukharin. (See B. Nicolaevsky, *Power and the Soviet Elite,* pp. 8 ff.) Ilya Britan was shot by the Gestapo in 1943 in Fresnes Prison in France.

7 These circumstances are pointed out in an unpublished Ph.D. thesis of Columbia University by R. Flaherty.

8 *Proceedings,* p. 427.

Appendix I (*pages 193-215*)

1 *Proceedings,* pp. 128-136.
2 *Ibid.,* pp. 429-436.
3 *Ibid.,* pp. 417-419.
4 *Ibid.,* pp. 453-456.
5 *Ibid.,* pp. 622-623.

Appendix II (*pages 217-230*)

1 *Proceedings,* p. 604.
2 G. Grinko, *The Five Year Plan,* New York, 1930, p. 335.
3 A. Barmine, *One Who Survived,* New York, 1945, p. 207.
4 L. Fischer, *Men and Politics,* New York, 1941, p. 500.

Index

INDEX

The numerals in **bold** type refer to the figure numbers
of the illustrations